The Seagull

This book is an insiders' account of the groundbreaking Moscow production of Chekhov's *The Seagull* directed by Anatoly Efros in 1966, which heralded a paradigm shift in the interpretation and staging of Chekhov's plays. It is a unique glimpse behind the curtain of the laboratory of the new Russian theatre in the late twentieth century. Efros's articles about Chekhov and *The Seagull*, his diaries, interviews and conversations, and most importantly the original rehearsal records combine to form an in-depth account of the director and his working process. This is an essential book for anyone with an interest in Chekhov and the history of modern Russian theatre.

James Thomas is Professor of Theatre at Wayne State University.

The Seagull

An Insiders' Account of the
Groundbreaking Moscow Production

Translated and edited by
James Thomas
With a Foreword by
Anatoly Smeliansky

LONDON AND NEW YORK

First published 2019
by Routledge
2 Park Square, Milton Park, Abingdon, Oxon OX14 4RN

and by Routledge
711 Third Avenue, New York, NY 10017

Routledge is an imprint of the Taylor & Francis Group, an informa business

© 2019 selection, translation and editorial matter, James Thomas; *The Seagull* and associated material, Anatoly Efros; Foreword, Anatoly Smeliansky.

The right of James Thomas to be identified as the author of the editorial material has been asserted in accordance with sections 77 and 78 of the Copyright, Designs and Patents Act 1988.

All rights reserved. No part of this book may be reprinted or reproduced or utilised in any form or by any electronic, mechanical, or other means, now known or hereafter invented, including photocopying and recording, or in any information storage or retrieval system, without permission in writing from the publishers.

Trademark notice: Product or corporate names may be trademarks or registered trademarks, and are used only for identification and explanation without intent to infringe.

British Library Cataloguing in Publication Data
A catalogue record for this book is available from the British Library

Library of Congress Cataloging in Publication Data
Names: Efros, Anatoly author. | Thomas, James, 1943- translator editor.
Title: The seagull : an insiders' account of the groundbreaking Moscow
    production / translated and edited by James Thomas ; with a foreword by
    Anatoly Smeliansky.
Description: London ; New York, NY : Routledge, 2018. | Consists of director
    Efros' articles about Chekhov and The Seagull, his diaries, interviews and
    conversations, and the original rehearsal records. | Includes bibliographical
    references and index.
Identifiers: LCCN 2017060236| ISBN 9780815374510 (hardback : alk. paper) |
    ISBN 9780815374527 (pbk. : alk. paper) | ISBN 9781351242011 (ebook)
Subjects: LCSH: Chekhov, Anton Pavlovich, 1860-1904. Chaæika. | Chekhov,
    Anton Pavlovich, 1860-1904—Stage history—Russia (Federation)—
    Moscow. | Chekhov, Anton Pavlovich, 1860-1904—Dramatic production. |
    Theatre—Production and direction—Russia (Federation)—
    Moscow. | Theatre—Production and direction—History—20th century.
Classification: LCC PG3455.C52 E37 2018 | DDC 891.72/3—dc23
LC record available at https://lccn.loc.gov/2017060236

ISBN: 978-0-815-37451-0 (hbk)
ISBN: 978-0-815-37452-7 (pbk)
ISBN: 978-1-351-24201-1 (ebk)

Typeset in Bembo
by Swales & Willis Ltd, Exeter, Devon, UK

Printed and bound in Great Britain by
TJ International Ltd, Padstow, Cornwall

Contents

Translator's preface	vii
Acknowledgements	xvi
Foreword: how the New Chekhov began	xvii

1 Anton Chekhov's *The Seagull* on the Russian stage   1

Introduction: "Slaughtering Sacred Seagulls: Anatoly Efros's Production of The Seagull *at the Lenkom in 1966"* 1
"What kind of play is The Seagull*?"* 16
*"*The Seagull *is very difficult to produce"* 25

2 Efros's preliminary thoughts on *The Seagull*   29

3 Rehearsal records of Anatoly Efros's production of *The Seagull* at the Lenkom Theatre, 1965–1966   33

About the transcripts 33
Cast list 33
13 December 1965^P 34
14 December 1965^P 38
14 December 1965^S 41
16 December 1965^P 44
16 December 1965^S 49
20 December 1965^P 52
21 December 1965^P 55
25 December 1965^P 58
28 December 1965^P 60
28 December 1965^S 66
30 December 1965^P 72
2 January 1966^P 76

3 January 1966^P 77
4 January 1966^P 82
4 January 1966^S 86
5 January 1966^P 93
6 January 1966^P 95
6 January 1966^S 100
7 January 1966^P 103
7 January 1966^S 106
8 January 1966^P 109
9 January 1966^P 113
9 January 1966^S 117
10 January 1966^P 119
11 January 1966^P 121
15 January 1966^S 124
20 January 1966^S 129
21 January 1966^S 131
24 January 1966^S 134
27 January 1966^S 140
29 January 1966^S 143
1 February 1966^S 145
12 February 1966^S 150
14 February 1966^S 151
17 February 1966^P 151
17 February 1966^S 156
18 February 1966^P 159
19 February 1966^P 160
19 February 1966^S 162
20 February 1966^P 162
21 February 1966^P 164

Epilogue   167

"How quickly time passes!" 167

Images   175
Glossary   193
Bibliography   203
Index   206

Translator's preface

Anatoly Efros: *The Seagull*

Efros' surprising and unconventional production of *The Seagull* opened on March 17, 1966 at the Lenin Komsomol Theatre on Malaya Dimitrovka Street in the heart of Moscow. This book is an insiders' account of that groundbreaking production; it is conceived as a volume for anyone seeking to know more about the birth of modern Chekhovian dramatic production (i.e. "the New Chekhov") in Russia during the Soviet era, and the development and central directorial methods of Anatoly Efros.

This translation makes the rehearsal records of this production available for the first time to English-speaking readers. The records were originally published in Nonna Mikhailovna Skegina's *"Chaĭka": Kinostsenarii, stat'i, zapisi repetitsii, dokumenty, iz dnevnikov i knig* ("The Seagull": screenplay, articles, rehearsal records, official documents, diaries, and notebooks, 2010), a larger documentary work originally published for a Russian readership already familiar with Efros's life and work, and, as one would expect, with the play itself, if not Efros's production. Anatoly Smeliansky's original Foreword goes a long way toward explaining the book's basic impetus, and Ros Dixon's Introduction situates the production within the longer history of Chekhov on the Russian stage before and during the Soviet era. In this preface, then, I will first provide general biographical information about Anatoly Efros that includes supplementary cultural and political contextualization of the development of his aesthetic. Second, I will address some key issues that presented special challenges for this translation.

Anatoly Efros: a brief biography

Anatoly Efros (1925–1987) belongs to that special group of Russian artists and intellectuals who contributed to the era between the early 1950s and early 1960s known as the "Thaw." The name came from Ilya Ehrenberg's eponymous novel of 1954, comparing the atmosphere of the era to climatic change. Prompted by the succession of moderate leader Nikita Khrushchev after the death of Joseph Stalin in 1953, the Thaw era witnessed a recovery of cultural freedom after a prolonged period of chilling censorship. It awakened a desire to rediscover authentic Russian imagination instead of its Sovietized surrogate, to escape from Stalin's wearisome ideas and stereotypes in art and literature, and to feel confident that original creative work was possible once again. Anatoly Efros was one of the leading creative figures of the Thaw era. His life and work not only contributed to the hopes of that era but also left an important theatrical legacy.

Anatoly Vasilyevich Efros (née Natan Isayevich) was born on July 3, 1925, in Kharkov, a large city located in northeast Ukraine and an important center of Jewish life. His parents worked at an aviation factory founded by family patriarch Isaac Vasilievich Efros, his father an aviation designer and his mother a translator of technical literature. Efros said he always loved the theatre and enjoyed stories and books about Stanislavsky and the Moscow Art Theatre; conceivably that is why, after the end of the war in 1945, he ventured to Moscow to study acting. He auditioned for and was accepted at the acting studio of the Mossoviet Theatre, which was established in 1923 and located a short distance northeast of Red Square. This was a signal moment for Efros. The Mossoviet was led by Yuri Zavadsky, and here was where Efros's personal contact with the Moscow Art Theatre (MAT) legacy began. Artistic "family trees" have always been a crucial factor in Russian theatre, and it was well known that Zavadsky had studied directly with Stanislavsky and Yevgeny Vakhtangov.

By way of Zavadsky's prescient sponsorship, Efros reconsidered his original plans for an acting career and in 1947 transferred to the Directing Program of the Lunacharsky State Institute for Theatre Arts (GITIS). It was another signal moment for Efros. GITIS was Moscow's leading theatre training institute at the time, and Nikolai Petrov, who studied directly under Vladimir Nemirovich-Danchenko, was head of the directing faculty. Furthermore, Maria Knebel, Alexei Popov and Mikhail Tarkhanov—also direct students of MAT celebrities—were members of the same faculty. Maria Knebel's artistic influence on Efros turned out to be particularly significant. Efros graduated from this extraordinary faculty in 1950.

By this time, 33 years after the October Revolution, the Communist Party had consolidated its authority over all the arts through a doctrine called "Socialist Realism." In the service of this doctrine, furthermore, the Soviet government empowered itself to expropriate Stanislavsky and his principles because of their perceived affinity with Realism in general. The government even established a committee to make sure Stanislavsky's writings conformed with Marxist–Leninist dialectical materialism. Soviet versions of Stanislavsky's teachings were then declared the official communist theatre aesthetic, while unpolitical and unsuspecting Stanislavsky was canonized by the Soviets in the process. Drained of their original inspiration, Stanislavsky's principles were turned into covert means of Soviet indoctrination and thus no longer an actor's personal work. Consequently, from 1934 until the death of Stalin in 1953, many if not most Russian actors and directors lost respect for Stanislavsky and his (albeit misappropriated) teachings—except Efros. He always remained committed to Stanislavsky and what he learned from Stanislavsky's direct students.

Upon graduating from GITIS, Efros honed his skills at a succession of short engagements. In 1950, he directed plays with a touring theatre Knebel organized, travelling to provincial cities and sharing quarters in a railway carriage. In 1951, he directed a Socialist Realism play at the Ostrovsky Drama Theatre in Mikhailov about 130 miles south of Moscow. In 1952, he obtained a position on the directing staff of the State Dramatic Theatre in Ryazan, an industrial city about 125 miles southeast of Moscow. He remained there for the next two years, directing *The Ardent Heart* by Alexander Ostrovsky and *Dog in the Manger* by Lope de Vega (dutifully adhering to Stanislavsky's directing notes in each case), as well as a Russian Civil War history play, an anti-fascist play, an Estonian folk play, a comedy about modern Soviet life, and a Byelorussian folk comedy— a repertory typical of that time. These three years at Moscow provincial theatres formed a gestation period for the aesthetic for which Efros was later celebrated.

After honing his craft in the provinces, in 1954 Efros became a staff director, then the leading director at Moscow's Central Children's Theatre, where he met up again with Maria Knebel, his mentor from GITIS. The Central Children's Theatre (CCT) was established in 1936 from the remainders of

MAT II and Stanislavsky's First and Second Studios. It was located close to the legendary Bolshoi (Big) and Maly (Small) Theatres in an area called Theatre Square, a short walk northeast of Red Square and the Kremlin. In 1950, Maria Knebel became Artistic Director there after her dismissal from MAT in an anti-Semitic purge of the company she had been a member of since 1921. For the previous two decades, Soviet ideology prohibited talk about spirit, subconscious, or soul, thus forcing Knebel to talk about Stanislavsky's original principles only in ways that avoided too much notice. With the emergence of the Thaw era in 1954, Stanislavsky's "life of the human spirit" no longer needed to be secreted, and Knebel could realize her lifelong mission of promoting Stanislavsky's original principles—most importantly, his groundbreaking, improvisation-based rehearsal method, Active Analysis. With Knebel's proactive support at CCT, Efros was empowered to shun the outcomes of Socialist Realism in the theatre (static compositions, clichéd characters, unimaginative scenery and oppressive propaganda), and develop an aesthetic of his own, namely, psychologically truthful acting, "psychophysics" (psychology made visible through expressive movement), modernist scenery, and a feeling of genuine contemporaneity. These features were to become the basis of Efros's creative principles, empowering CCT to become one of the most popular theatres in Moscow, even, as Anatoly Smeliansky declared, the center of modern theatre life in Russia.

In 1963, Efros was appointed Artistic Director at the Lenin Komsomol Theatre as an acknowledgement of his decade of success at CCT. The Lenkom, as it was nicknamed, had a checkered history. Komsomol is an acronym for Communist Youth League, and the official mission of this theatre was to produce plays supportive of Soviet ideology for audiences of young workers. Located close to Pushkin Square, one Metro stop north of Theatre Square and CCT, the building began life as a merchants' club for light entertainments, then a political club, a Communist university and a movie theatre. From 1938 to 1951, the Lenkom was led by MAT II alumnus Ivan Bersenev and became one of the most important theatres in Moscow. Since that time, however, artistic directors had come and gone while leaving few traces in memory.

At the Lenkom, Efros found a company dispirited from years of neglect and the absence of any unifying aesthetic. He revived their spirits by introducing the aesthetic with which he had previously energized CCT: Stanislavsky-based psychological acting, a keen contemporary sensibility, animated staging and modernist production values. He started with new plays by Thaw-era writers Viktor Rozov, Edward Radzinsky, Alexei Arbuzov and Samuel Alyoshin. The stories and themes were just as current as before at CCT (namely, the desire to lead a good life in a ruthless social environment), but now the implications were sharper because the characters were no longer adolescents but adults newly in charge of things, like Efros himself. Moscow's theatrical center of gravity began to shift towards the Lenkom, which was thriving under Efros's progressive leadership. Unfortunately, the artistic and socio-political pressures of leading the Lenkom into uncharted territory took their toll on his health, and in 1965 he suffered his first heart attack.

A significant moment in this cultural shift—and the justification for this book—occurred in 1966 when Efros directed *The Seagull*, his first play by Anton Chekhov and the first historical play ever to be produced at the Lenkom. In the Introduction below, Ros Dixon speaks eloquently of this production in the context of the play's production history in Russia in addition to the other successes and commotions Efros went through during his time at the Lenkom.

Upon leaving the Lenkom in 1967, Efros joined the directing staff of the Moscow Drama Theatre on Malaya Bronnaya Street (aka Malaya Bronnaya Theatre), a 20-minute walk east of MAT. The choice of venue was significant. Originally, this was the Moscow State Jewish Theatre (GOSET) under the direction of the great Yiddish actor Solomon Mikhoels. GOSET closed in 1949 owing to anti-Semitic oppression, and professional operation had resumed only a few years before Efros arrived there. At the Malaya Bronnaya, Efros began with *Three Sisters* (1967), another modernist interpretation of Chekhov, which, like *The Seagull*, offended traditionalists and was promptly removed from the repertory. After this, Efros tried not to "tweak the tiger's tail" any further, as the saying goes. From then on, he turned his attention largely to plays drawn from the established classical repertory. Released from leadership responsibilities, he could focus on pursuing his own aesthetic. His productions of *Romeo and Juliet* (1970), *Don Juan* (1973) by Molière, *Marriage* (1975) by Nikolai Gogol, *Othello* (1976) and Turgenev's *A Month in the Country* (1977) instantly became classics of modern Russian theatre. He also began to publish his directorial explications and professional reflections: *Repetitsiya-lyubov moia* (Rehearsal is My Love, 1975), *Professia: Rezhisser* (Occupation: Director, 1979) and *Prodolzheniye teatralnovo romana* (Theatre Novel Continued, 1985).

Efros's standing with the authorities improved correspondingly and he was invited to direct at other theatres as well: the Mossoviet Theatre (1969, 1974), Taganka Theatre (1975), Moscow Art Theatre (1981, 1982), and even theatres outside the USSR (a rare privilege at the time), such as the Guthrie Theatre in Minneapolis (1978, 1979) and Toen Theatre in Tokyo (1981–1982). His productions of *Marriage* and *A Month in the Country* received the Grand Prize at the Duisburg Theatre Festival. He also directed nine productions for Central Television, seven for All-Union Radio, and four movies for Mosfilm. In 1975, at the age of 50, he suffered a second heart attack, but recovered quickly and continued to work as actively as before. An official sign of his political "rehabilitation" took place in 1976, when he was awarded the title of People's Artist of the USSR.

Then things reversed direction again. In 1978, a communist party factotum was added to the Malaya Bronnaya's management staff, and the working atmosphere there began to change for the worse. A full account of the theatrical, political, and anti-Semitic maneuverings that followed would require an entire monograph. It is enough to say Efros found it more and more difficult to work at the Malaya Bronnaya and in 1984 he resigned. As fate would have it, this happened to be the same year Yuri Lyubimov was deprived of his Soviet citizenship and dismissed from his position as Artistic Director of the Taganka Theatre for publicly criticizing the Soviet Union while working abroad. Several well-known directors declined the open Taganka position because it was too risky. At that point Efros was offered the position and, despite the doubts of family and colleagues, he accepted the offer.

Founded in 1946, the Taganka Theatre is located southwest of Moscow center in an Art Nouveau building on Taganka Square, across the street from the busy Taganka Metro station. It was one of the least attended theatres in Moscow until 1964, when Yuri Lyubimov, its new artistic director, brought his students from the Shchukin School of the Vakhtangov Theatre to reprise their graduation performance of Brecht's play, *The Good Person of Setzuan*. Devoted to the principles of Brecht and Vakhtangov, Lyubimov never used a front curtain and seldom used conventional scenery, rather preferring dynamic stage installations. In 1975, when Lyubimov was working abroad, Efros directed a remarkable production of *The Cherry Orchard* there. But when he accepted the leadership of the newly leaderless Taganka in 1984, he was censured by members of the Moscow theatre community for what they considered an attempt to undermine Lyubimov's reputation. Several Taganka actors rebelled by departing from the company; others showed their displeasure more underhandedly, through anti-Semitic behaviors, for example. Convinced the Taganka actors would forget the past after a few successful productions, Efros began to work right away. He started with *The Lower Depths* (1984) by Maxim Gorky and Tennessee Williams's *A Lovely Sunday for a Picnic* (1985). In 1985, he led the company to the Belgrade International Theatre Festival, where *The Lower Depths* and a revival of *The Cherry Orchard* won the Grand Prize. In 1986, he directed a successful production of *The Misanthrope*. Efros seemed on his way to transforming the Taganka just as he had done with CCT, Lenkom, and Malaya Bronnaya. Then, on January 13, 1987, he suffered a third and fatal heart attack. His body was laid to rest in Novokuznetsk Cemetery on the eastern edge of Moscow. A pending production of Ibsen's *Hedda Gabler* was aborted.

Two years after Efros's death, the Berlin Wall fell, communist regimes across Eastern Europe collapsed, and in 1991 the USSR disbanded. Almost immediately there commenced wide public recognition of Efros's talent, regret over the loss to Russian culture, and remorse (albeit often shamefaced) over his mistreatment. In 1992, Moscow's Bakhrushin Theatre Museum organized an exhibition of his life and work. In 1993, the Russian Theatre Agency organized a conference in St. Petersburg devoted to him. In 1994, the Russian Theatre Fund republished Efros's three books as a set, adding an assortment of his unpublished notes called *Chetvertaia Kniga* (The Fourth Book). Efros's standing continues to grow in this century. In 2000, 46 actors, writers and critics contributed to *Teatr Anatolia Efrosa: vospominania i stati* (The Theatre of Anatoly Efros: Recollections and Articles) and Vagrius Publishers re-issued selected passages from his books under the title *Anatolii Efros–Professia: Rezhisser*

(Anatoly Efros–Profession: Director). In 2005, Moscow television's Culture Channel observed the 80th anniversary of his birth with a retrospective of his filmed plays, films and teleplays and a documentary of his life and work. English translations of his books were published in 2006, 2007 and 2009. In 2016, the Bakhrushin Theatre Museum presented a brand-new exhibition devoted to Efros's life and work. In 2018, "Anatoly Efros's Principles of Acting and Directing" will appear in *Russian Theatre in Practice*.

Efros was not a fashionable or intentionally scandalous director and his brilliance was not showy or popular in the sense of him being a celebrity. Others of that era were the celebrity directors. Efros's standing was always highest among fellow professionals—actors, directors, playwrights, and critics. The general audience recognized the worth of his productions too, of course, but it was professionals who really understood the depth and innovation of his work. This is probably the highest type of recognition, to become not only a legendary director during one's lifetime but also a legend among one's peers, who generally are not inclined to enthusiastic public appraisals.

Key translation issues

This book has been edited with English-speaking readers in mind. For that reason, information has been omitted that would likely be of less interest to readers who have not had much knowledge of its Russian background. Omitted information includes Efros's film scenario for *The Seagull* along with official correspondence associated with this "film not made," various articles he wrote about his general approach to the classics, and official government documents related to his appointment and dismissal as Artistic Director of the Lenin Komsomol Theatre.

These records were transcribed from rehearsals, where speech is obviously colloquial and idiomatic, whose remarks jump from one actor to another, one character to another, often containing unannounced shifts of personal pronoun referents. In Russian, case endings can orally clarify much of this understanding, but the general absence of case endings in English does not offer the same clarification. Furthermore, rehearsal participants tend to use first names and nicknames, while formal patronymics—middles names derived from the father's first name—might be appended to first names out of respect or to make a point. Owing to these oral and written difficulties, bracketed words or phrases have occasionally been added to clarify referents, interlocutors, meaning, and actor or character identity. Punctuation follows the original transcripts, though again with occasional changes for clarity. Footnotes refer to incidental mentions, and a Glossary explains unfamiliar references and information too lengthy for footnotes. The Introduction by Ros Dixon discusses Efros's innovative approach within the framework of the play's production history in Russia.

The heart of this book is, of course, Efros's uniquely modern understanding of *The Seagull* and the rehearsal records revealing the process of communicating this understanding to the actors. At the time, most Russians were accustomed to the revered tradition of what Vsevelod Meyerhold termed "Theatre of Mood" regarding Chekhov's plays. Consequently, it was no easy task for Efros to persuade his actors—and, it must be said, audiences and critics—to see this hallowed play anew. The interpersonal dynamics of this crucial director–actor relationship are also observable in these records.

Beyond Efros's sharply modern grasp of the play, evident here as well is the unique rehearsal atmosphere he created. Surprisingly perceptive character motivations appear everywhere, but more than that is Efros's distinctive way of physicalizing his intentions with demonstrative "etudes" using improvised text. Etudes serve as stepping-stones that lead the actor to a deeply personal assimilation of the author's text. Etudes are central to the rehearsal process called Active Analysis, which Stanislavsky developed in his later years and was subsequently taught and promulgated by his personal student Maria Knebel. By the time of Efros's production, the principles of Active Analysis had been in existence for over 30 years, yet its practice was still largely unknown in Russian theatre because of Soviet ideological constraints. It was Efros, a devoted follower of Stanislavsky and a student of Knebel, who was the first to employ Active Analysis extensively in professional work. Active Analysis, which today is ubiquitous in Russian and Eastern European theatre practice—even as it is still nascent in English-speaking theatre—consequently required extra effort to communicate to his actors. This effort will be noticed in the rehearsal records.

This covers most of the key translation issues, but something more also needs to be said. [The following remarks about reading and interpreting rehearsal records are freely adapted from Vitaly Vilenkin, *Vl. I. Nemirovich-Danchenko vedet repetitsiu "Tri sestry"* (Moskva: Iskusstvo, 1965) 37–56.] General readers whose love for the theatre makes them interested in a purely professional book will encounter some difficulties reading rehearsal transcripts outside the context of the rehearsal hall. These difficulties are complicated by the publication requirement of strict chronological sequence of rehearsal, without organized selection or grouping. It is not easy for an outsider to navigate what happens in an ordinary theatrical rehearsal, much less in a kind of rehearsal book. Repetition—endless returning to the same event, pattern, or even word—is a permanent feature that cannot occur in any other kind of book, while here it becomes the structural basis of the text, its essence and meaning. It cannot be otherwise due to the nature of rehearsal as a creative endeavor. The very word rehearsal comes from the French *répéter*, which means to repeat.

Besides the transcripts themselves, readers will generally have the play's text before them. Otherwise, they will be unable to understand either the general progression of the rehearsal or the sense of one or another of its moments; unable to compare the intentions and outcomes of corresponding rehearsals or notice the gradual deepening and growth of characterizations. This parallel reading itself requires readers' closest attention and sometimes even their independent analysis, imagination, and insight.

Rehearsal transcripts cannot be converted into a stylistically consistent and smooth literary text, otherwise reality will immediately disappear from them. After all, rehearsal transcripts are fixed on the page, not spoken. And rehearsal speech is often connected with the subtlest of mental processes. It is full of incompleteness, unexpected associations and half-hints, neologisms and clumsy phrases, metaphors and comparisons that make sense only in the moment. Sometimes it is almost tongue-tied in its striving for extreme accuracy.

But mainly this book is intended for theatre practitioners and teachers, for whom it will share a common language. Nevertheless, even they will meet certain difficulties. Immediately, they will realize the unavoidable incompleteness of these transcripts, where a phrase like "They repeat the scene." conceals from view what really happens in the acting. Moreover, the voice of the director predominates, while that of the actors is heard only when they speak to the director and not when they speak to each other. It is impossible to record in a transcript all the innumerable subtleties of this joint creativity that excite the thinking, imagination, and temperament of the actor and are sometimes more important for comprehending and embodying the character than a director's lengthy utterances.

The transcript cannot convey such important elements of direction as "showing" or "hinting" at some parts of the role, cannot convey the director's "performing" of a scene or its fragments. The director's gestures and intonations in the speaking of the same phrase, hints of future staging, special imitations of what the actors have done to give them the opportunity to see themselves as in a mirror—all this remains beyond the limits of a transcript. In addition, private rehearsals, face-to-face with the actor, which usually no outsider can see, are not recorded

In short, although this unavoidably incomplete book requires a special approach and creative interpretation, nonetheless it can actively affect those who study it. It looks a lot like the theatre of today and not something from the distant past. Turning the pages of these transcripts, readers can go through Efros's work on creating a performance step by step. Not just the factual content but also the very atmosphere of his rehearsals. Here are glimpses of that true art, which rarely happens in the theatre, but which all true artists yearn for.

Acknowledgements

I wish to acknowledge the invaluable help provided for this project:

Dmitry Krymov, for his continuing support and permission to translate and publish the writings of Anatoly Efros.

The Irish Association for Russian, Central and East European Studies, for their permission to repurpose Ros Dixon's excellent article about Efros's production of *The Seagull*.

Anna Nagayko, for her expert editing of my translation.

Ben Piggott, for his unwavering support of this project.

Anatoly Smeliansky, for his generous support of all my work.

Jessica Thomas, for her expert proof reading and editing.

Sergei Zemtsov, from whom I learned so much about how to understand the work of the actor.

Margaret, for her forbearance of my prolonged passion for the work of Anatoly Efros.

All images "by permission of Anatoly Efros Archives."

Foreword
How the New Chekhov began

Anatoly Smeliansky

This book is called *Anatoly Efros: The Seagull*.[1] Readers ought to be surprised: with all due respect for the remarkable director, still, he did not write *The Seagull*. Nevertheless, the title addresses the essence of the book. Anatoly Efros did not write *The Seagull*, but in 1966 he directed a production of this play at the Lenin Komsomol Theatre. He returned to Chekhov in a heightened sense, he studied and probed the play's lines word by word, syllable by syllable, pause by pause. He checked its "legs," gestures, intonations, he repeatedly played it before the actors, trying to infect them with his vision of the story. He admitted *The Seagull* into our collective life. He interpreted Treplev's conflict with Arkadina and Trigorin personally and at the same time universally. In the contents of the play, as through a funnel, he poured the new rhythms of life and social relations of the 1960s. He invested *The Seagull* with his understanding of the theatre, an understanding that overtly resisted all the experience of the pausing and comforting, safe and empty, remote Chekhov – the latter a direct consequence of the "decontamination" of the writer, which was accomplished by the joint efforts of the Soviet school, many Soviet Chekhovites, and many Soviet theatres. Efros achieved a complete breakthrough. And if we agree the most important polemic interpretations of the classics (including those of Chekhov) eventually enter and become inseparable from the very contents of the play, enriching its semantic substance, then it is quite possible to name Efros among the coauthors of the playwright. That is how I interpret the title of this book or, more precisely, the collection prepared by Nonna Skegina, Anatoly Efros's long-time literary manager.

In the book, everything possible is collected relating to Chekhov's *The Seagull* and Efros the director. We can read Efros's scenario of the film not made on *The Seagull*. We can plunge into Efros's diaries and interviews of the time. We can familiarize ourselves with his conversations with students on the themes of *The Seagull* (at that time Efros was already teaching at GITIS). But the most important discovery of the book is the publication of rehearsal records of *The Seagull* at the Lenin Komsomol Theatre. These records are of paramount interest for anyone who wants to understand what happened in the Soviet–Russian theatre at a critical moment in its history.

Efros arrived at the Lenin Komsomol Theatre at the end of 1963. He could direct the works of emerging playwrights Viktor Rozov, Edvard Radzinsky, and Alexei Arbuzov. These productions meant a great deal for the Moscow of those days, but Efros needed to assert his directing on something more definitive. He needed a manifesto and consequently he decided it was necessary to show his *Seagull* to the world. *The Seagull* (as considered by critic Boris Zingerman at the time) was acceptable for opening or closing a season, but it was dangerous to put on *The Seagull* without having any special occasion. Efros's *Seagull* began a newer, freer theatre, threw open the thematic and emotional perspectives of Chekhov, in both the past and the present. Efros demolished the dead psychology of the academic tradition, which had become the accepted way to play Chekhov. With amazing courage, he departed from what was considered inviolable. He "discarded" Stanislavsky's great tradition of playing Chekhov as "continuous communication." He also "discarded" Nemirovich-Danchenko's equally great tradition, which in the late 1930s argued against Stanislavsky by proposing to play Chekhov through so-called "contact without communication." Efros was convinced that from infinite repetitions both MAT approaches had ceased to stir the living emotions of the public. The New Chekhov evolved from a different thesis, which was authoritatively carried out by Efros: "complete misunderstanding along with complete, stormy communication."

The director treated Chekhovian action and inaction anew, groped with the underlying themes of Chekhov's theatre anew. He rethought and reinterpreted the very concept of the "Theatre of Mood," so beloved of all MAT imitators. "No mood on stage," he said, "the mood should be in the auditorium."

Thus, in the mid-sixties the New Chekhov began.

The rehearsal records of *The Seagull* were made at the time by [graduate theatre students] Gnessa Sidorina and Nellie Plyatskovska. They were made with exemplary accuracy and subtle understanding of their central character, whose words they wrote down for themselves, but which also proved to be – for history. After all, Efros was anything but an inventor of concepts. He was an intuitivist of the purest water.[2] Focusing on the labyrinth of associations in *The Seagull*, he trusted not so much in its theses but in his mighty artistic intuition. He stopped, guided, despaired, turned back, pushed aside. I was present at Efros's rehearsals more than once and had the good fortune to see his fantastic demonstrations, when he represented the whole play from beginning to end, amazing and inspiring those for whom all this lay ahead to perform. The power of his displays cannot be described, and video did not record them at the time. To try to document such rehearsals would have been torture, because the most important things did not happen in the words.

> It is as if we do not know this is Chekhov [Efros said]. We take a deep breath, and then – what will be, will be . . . How could this possibly be boring?

I think Chekhov should feel like a puff of wind, not a solid mass. Movement, not a solid mass.

In the records of Efros's rehearsals this "puff of wind" is caught very often. As a result, we have a knowing, clear, sympathetic "peek" into the very laboratory of the new Russian theatre that was born at Efros's rehearsals. The authors of these records do not overlook any reversals in Efros's thinking; they are not frightened of any contradictions and extremes of his directorial technique, which in later years Efros will compare to a "bent wire."[3] He bent this "wire" in different directions, bent it, as I say again, intuitively. The talent of those who documented those rehearsals consisted of recording all those twists and turns wherever possible, and not straightening the fancifully bent wire into a straight line (a straight line on a cardiogram, as we know, indicates death).

This book presents Efros the director during the inspired moments of creating "his own Chekhov." *The Seagull* opened in March 1966, premiering in Vilnius [Lithuania] and then playing in Moscow. The life of the production was ended within a year. By order of the Moscow Ministry of Culture, it was declared that "Comrade Anatoly Efros, Artistic Director of the Moscow Lenin Komsomol Theatre, has not provided the correct direction in the development of the theatre's repertoire, and therefore he is relieved of his post as of March 7, 1967."[4]

Thus, they decided to "re-educate" the "Soviet Treplev" [Efros himself]. They sent him into exile, although not so very far away. They transferred him to the directing staff of the Malaya Bronnaya Theatre. Many actors from *The Seagull* followed him there. At the new theatre Efros did not provide the "correct direction" either. On the contrary, he resumed his Chekhovian studies. There, at the formerly unheralded Malaya Bronnaya Theatre, the director staged one of the most important works of his career – Chekhov's *Three Sisters*. The performance caused a scandal and was very quickly suffocated by the efforts of government officials and comrades in art (including some well-known actors from the Moscow Art Theatre). This Chekhov turned out to be dangerous for the existing regime because it happened to fall directly within the context of the "Prague Spring."[5] It remained on stage only for several months, until August 1968.

This book about *The Seagull* begins Efros's "Chekhov series." A similar book is promised for *Three Sisters*.[6] And then there is to be a collection devoted to *The Cherry Orchard*, which was developed at the Taganka Theatre in the mid-seventies.

Efros's Chekhovian cycle extended over the course of many years. It began at the onset of the "Thaw" and continued during the [subsequent] stagnant late Soviet years. The life of the director ended in January 1987. Consequently, seeing the New Chekhov inside the New Russia was not meant to be. But the most important work was already done—it is impossible to imagine a modern production of Chekhov without the "close reading" of his plays that Anatoly Efros accomplished. And this was done—forever.

Notes

1 Smeliansky is referring to the Russian title of the book.
2 Efros was not as thoroughly intuitive as he might have appeared in rehearsals. He considered himself an "emotional structuralist" (Efros, *Beyond Rehearsal* 91).
3 "When we look at a medical cardiogram and we see a straight line without any change in direction, it means there is no life. A change in direction indicates life. It is the same in our profession. I shall act, perhaps, worse or better, but all the time I should read the design. *Everything must be as clear as a bent piece of wire*" (Efros, *Joy of Rehearsal* 45).
4 Anatoly Efros, *Anatoly Efros: Chaika* (Sankt-Peterburg: Baltiiskie Sezon, 2010).
5 Brief period of liberalization in Czechoslovakia under Alexander Dubček in 1968.
6 Anatoly Efros, *Anatoly Efros: Tri sestry* (Sankt-Peterburg: Baltiiskie Sezon, 2012).

Chapter 1

Anton Chekhov's *The Seagull* on the Russian stage

Introduction: "Slaughtering Sacred Seagulls: Anatoly Efros's Production of *The Seagull* at the Lenkom in 1966"

[The following extract is taken from Ros Dixon, "Slaughtering Sacred Seagulls: Anatoly Efros's Production of *The Seagull* at the Lenkom in 1966," *Irish Slavonic Studies* 21 (2000), 49–73.]

Anatoly Efros directed *The Seagull* in 1966 at the Lenkom Theatre, where he had been Artistic Director since 1964. His interpretation of Chekhov's drama was entirely new to the Russian stage, and generated a critical uproar in the theatre world of Moscow. The production was said to have failed to express the mood of optimism demanded in Soviet interpretations of Chekhov. It also deliberately challenged the expectations of critics and audiences familiar with the approach and style of presentation used by Konstantin Stanislavsky at the Moscow Art Theatre (MAT). This [Introduction] discusses Efros's innovative approach in the context of the play's performance history in Russia, with particular reference to Stanislavsky's production of 1898, but shows too in what ways Efros's *Seagull* reflected the political situation of its time and clarifies its role in his evolution as a director.

The true beginning of MAT was a marathon, eighteen-hour meeting between its founders, Stanislavsky and Vladimir Nemirovich-Danchenko, which began at the Slaviansky Bazaar on 22 June 1897. But in both theatre mythology and authoritative histories, the origin of the new art of MAT is often seen to have been Stanislavsky's production of *The Seagull*. That production is said to have been remarkable for its stunning sharpness, unrelenting fidelity to life and innovative staging.[1] But the real success of the play in 1898, as Edward Braun has maintained, was for the theatre itself: it gave the new company a sense of identity, a corporate style which, though still tentative, held infinite promise.[2] Indeed, the theatre affirmed that identity by adopting as its emblem the seagull which to this day is emblazoned across its front curtain.

The Seagull at MAT in 1898 was the second production of the play, the first having been staged two years previously at the Alexandrinsky Theatre in

St. Petersburg. Theatre histories and biographies of Chekhov have frequently dismissed this first production as an unmitigated disaster, and at the same time have lauded Stanislavsky's interpretation as a complete success. But, as Laurence Senelick has acknowledged, this excessively simple assessment owes much to theatre legend, and like most legends is an accretion of half-truths and exaggerations around a kernel of truth.[3] It is important to note, however, that Stanislavsky's production was a significant turning point for Chekhov, who had been acclaimed as a writer of short stories and theatrical farces, but had enjoyed mixed success as a serious dramatist. He subsequently became closely associated with the theatre, working as the equivalent of an in-house playwright. As a result, the approach evolved by Stanislavsky became the definitive performance style for Chekhov's work.

The Seagull was also a triumph for Stanislavsky in the evolution of a new theatrical aesthetic and can be said to have laid the foundation of the future development of MAT.[4] The theatre, first in its production of *Tsar Fyodor* and then with *The Seagull*, explored the concept – new at the time – of designing a production from scratch.[5] In *The Seagull* Stanislavsky's aim was to create a setting which would present as great an illusion of reality as possible. At that time, his company was housed in the Hermitage Theatre, and he used all that theatre's resources in an attempt to create a complete world for the play. Every detail was incorporated into a complex visual and aural *mise-en-scene*, which was also intended to evoke atmosphere and to hint at a sub-text. The indoor scenes were crowded with authentic stage properties and loaded with realistic detail: thus, for instance, a real fire burned in the grate, and a glass held by Treplev shattered when he dropped it. In Chekhov's stage directions, the opening act is set outdoors on the estate. He specifies that there is a lake and an avenue of trees, obscured from view by a stage hastily constructed for the presentation of Treplev's play. Contrary to this instruction, the lake in Stanislavsky's production dominated the stage area, and the designer, Viktor Simov, attempted to recreate the beauties of a moonlit country estate by using a half-lit tracery of foliage.

The technical resources of the Hermitage limited the realization of some of Stanislavsky's plans, and his idea of creating a total illusion of reality appears to have been better as a concept than in its execution.[6] In fact, at one point Simov resorted to using dimmed lighting in order to draw the audience's attention away from the obvious artificiality of the set and from its crudely painted scenery.[7] Nevertheless, for spectators accustomed to stock sets and painted drops this setting created a stunning effect. As Braun has remarked, one of the great merits for a contemporary audience of Stanislavsky's production lay in the fact that everyday life was portrayed with a degree of fidelity that was entirely unprecedented.[8] Stanislavsky also augmented Chekhov's directions by adding an orchestrated score of sound effects throughout the action. The purpose of this was twofold: on the one hand, it generated a sense of a world beyond the set, on the other, it was used to create an appropriate mood for each scene.

Mood was created through sound, and through silence. Stanislavsky's production extended the pauses and silences, timing them exactly to between five and fifteen seconds. The entire pace of the play was slowed, and for the most part it was played as a mournful and lyrical elegy in which theatrical time was replaced, as it were, by real time.

Stanislavsky's production was greeted with ovations on its opening night, but it subsequently enjoyed only moderate success, playing just thirty-two times in four seasons. It was revived in 1905, but after only eleven performances was dropped from the repertoire completely.[9]

Having once found what he believed to be an appropriate style and mood for the works of Chekhov, Stanislavsky tended to repeat salient aspects of his first success in other productions. In fact, he developed something of a subgenre in the Russian theatre of the time, a form which came to be known as the "Theatre of Mood."[10] In this manner, the very features of *The Seagull* which had recently seemed so innovative became instead the norm, and were judged to be an inherent part of the style of MAT.

That style, however, was inevitably affected by political developments. From the mid-1930s onwards, under the dictates of Socialist Realism, experimentation with literary and theatrical forms was discouraged, and departures from realism using symbols or other consciously theatrical techniques were condemned as decadent formalism. Instead, it became necessary for all theatre art to conform to a particular model, and, in keeping with this idea, the supposed realism of MAT was recast as the primary example of the Socialist Realist ideal. MAT's presentational style was then actively promoted as a model to be copied in theatres throughout the Soviet Union.[11]

The theatre was encouraged to produce, often in the manner of a factory production line, monumental and ideological epics extolling revolutionary and military victories, and these dramas began to overshadow its previous works. By this time, Stanislavsky had effectively retreated from the theatre he had founded, and those of his productions which continued to run became increasingly fossilized museum pieces.[12] Others, like *The Seagull*, although no longer part of the repertoire, became theatre legends and entered a kind of collective memory.

Furthermore, Stanislavsky's productions of Chekhov in particular came to be synonymous with what were seen as "correct" interpretations and were frequently used as the 'blueprint' for subsequent productions. In terms of Chekhov's scripts, this meant a failure to recognize the complexity of his writing, and therefore the possibility – indeed necessity – of multiple interpretations. Ironically, such rigidity of thought regarding Stanislavsky's interpretations was directly contrary to his own credo and to the very essence of a theatre that had been founded on innovation and experimentation.[13]

During the Second World War, innovation in the Soviet theatre gave way to the imperatives of propaganda. In addition, many theatres were evacuated and new productions were few. The only Moscow production of *The Seagull* at this period was staged in 1944 by Aleksander Tairov in his bomb-damaged Kamerny Theatre. Tairov's set was minimalist and consisted of a platform surrounded by grey and black velvet curtains. Different locales were established using a few stage properties and with delicate drapes, which were arranged differently for each scene and through which spotlights filtered, lending an airy and dreamlike quality. The director's primary purpose was to reveal what he saw as a central theme of Chekhov's play: the need for new art forms to attain the highest truth. He reduced the drama to a discourse on the nature of art, and to this end cut the script by a third. He eliminated lines and stage directions that referred to characters which he considered secondary, and removed details intended to produce a fuller picture of everyday life. Music was an important feature of all Tairov's work, and in this case, he used the music of Tchaikovsky as an accompaniment to Treplev's play. However, the production was essentially a concert performance and not a critical success. It soon closed, and indeed the theatre itself, condemned as an example of bourgeois decadence, was forced to do the same some six years later. However, the importance of Tairov's *Seagull* should not be underestimated. Until Efros's production 22 years later, this flawed version represented the only significant attempt to find a completely new interpretative key to Chekhov's play.

Other productions tended to preserve the legend of MAT, and to copy the style of Stanislavsky.[14] In fact, MAT used his 'blueprint' when Viktor Stanitsyn and Joseph Raevsky staged *The Seagull* in 1960 to celebrate the centenary of Chekhov's birth – an event which every Soviet theatre was expected to honor. This revised production, which even reproduced Stanislavsky's pauses exactly, appears to have been a poor copy of the original. Yelena Poliakova noted that it was a lifeless rendering of the text which, played as a mournful elegy, met with a polite, but indifferent response.[15] For Konstantin Rudnitsky, it entirely failed to present the complexity of emotions that he believed was central to Chekhov's characters.[16] Maya Turovskaya, writing in *Literaturnaya gazeta*, harshly criticized the production for its want of originality and its failure to interest a modern audience.[17] The lack of innovation on the part of MAT was mirrored in the work of other theatres: most of the celebratory productions were programmatic and dutiful responses to a government edict.[18]

However, one production in 1960, Boris Babochkin's *Ivanov* at the Maly theatre, stood out in stark contrast to the rest. In fact, this production, together with Georgy Tovstonogov's *Three Sisters,* staged at [Leningrad–St. Petersburg's] Bolshoi Drama Theatre in 1965, and Efros's *Seagull* the following season, came to be identified with what was perceived as a new approach to the work of Chekhov for the Soviet theatre. For Tatiana Shakh-Azizova the central premise of all three productions was what she termed 'obyektivnost sploshnaya' ([complete] objectivity).[19] By this she meant that the sympathetic identification with Chekhov's characters that had provided the pathos of productions in the past was now to be replaced by what was intended to be objective inquiry. Furthermore, previous productions had scrutinized society in order to explain, or indeed excuse, the actions of Chekhov's characters, in these new productions the characters themselves were to be subjected to a critical analysis that revealed, but did not excuse, their frailties. The indecisiveness, failure to act and apparent indifference to the plight of others demonstrated by Chekhov's intelligentsia was to come in for particularly harsh treatment. In these productions, frequently referred to as "cruel," "Chekhov the doctor" delivered a shrewd and sometimes mercilessly severe diagnosis of his characters' ills and weaknesses.[20]

For both Tovstonogov and Efros, in order to achieve a ruthless objectivity in their approaches to character, it was necessary for the actors to distance themselves from their roles, and the key to this was to use techniques similar to Brechtian alienation.

In Tovstonogov's *Three Sisters*, however, in performance such objectivity was not fully conveyed because, as Shakh-Azizova observed, in the course of the production it was overpowered by the sympathy the director felt for the characters in their tragic plight.[21] Efros, as we shall see, was to show the characters much less mercy. In addition, while rehearsing *Three Sisters*, Tovstonogov had expressed great admiration for Nemirovich-Danchenko's production of the play at MAT in 1940, and had no quarrel with its method. Efros, by contrast, though familiar with the performance history of *The Seagull*, deliberately rejected any established approaches. His explicit intention was to look at Chekhov afresh:

> Today we must remove the layers of convention that are wrapped around the entire play, which make it tedious and invoke a predictable response: "Ah, yes . . . *The Seagull*. We've read that play! We know it."[22]

Efros chose to work on the principle that the play had just been written by a new dramatist, and perhaps more importantly as if it had been commissioned by Efros himself.[23] He urged his actors to imagine that they were reading and rehearsing this drama for the first time.

The production opened on 17 March 1966, not in Moscow, but while the Lenkom company was on tour in Vilnius. In an interview published in *Sovetskaya Litva* before the premiere, Efros revealed the weight of responsibility he felt in adopting such a radical approach:

> Chekhov's *The Seagull* is the first classic production to be performed by the present troupe of the Lenkom. We have previously produced only contemporary dramas, and in turning to Chekhov feel an extraordinary responsibility, particularly when one considers the great and glorious performance tradition of his plays. But in approaching this work we tried to forget about this and attempted to produce *The Seagull* as a contemporary drama, as if Chekhov were our dramatist and as if he had written especially for our actors, for our theatre.

Efros also directly linked his 'first classic' with his productions of contemporary dramas:

> We wanted our production of Chekhov to be a new departure and yet at the same time to be a natural continuation of the feelings and ideas that had concerned us in our most recent previous works.[24]

Indeed, as Anatoly Smeliansky recognized, this was Chekhov interpreted through Viktor Rozov and Edvard Radzinsky. Rozov provided the theme of uncompromising youth in confrontation with the adult world, and the biting, ironic tone came from Radzinsky.[25]

Efros's desire to reveal the contemporary relevance of the play was also in keeping with his assessment of the history of productions of Chekhov in Russia. He saw in the West a fundamental difference of approach to classic plays, and specifically in the attitude of English actors to Shakespeare. In an essay 'Kak bystro idet vremya' (How Quickly Time Passes), published in *Teatr* in 1967, he maintained that in England the plays of Shakespeare are performed everywhere, with an endless variety of slants and conceptions and in every conceivable style. They were perceived as familiar and in keeping with contemporary experience. In fact, in a barbed jibe he remarked:

> Sometimes it appears to me that an English actor can take on a Shakespearean role with the same degree of ease as our wonderful actor at the Vakhtangov Theatre, Nikolai Plotnikov, can play yet another collective farm boss.
>
> In England a play by Shakespeare, although viewed perhaps as greater than other dramas, is still seen as if it were a familiar and contemporary work. When English actors or directors pick up Shakespeare they know what to do with him.[26]

The Russian approach to Chekhov, he went on, was very different:

> In Russia, there are a good twenty years from one production of *The Seagull* to the next. And when at long last a young actor takes up the role of Treplev, he holds it in his hands as if it were a crystal orb which he has been asked to look after but only on the proviso that if he breaks it he will never in his whole lifetime be able to pay for the damage. You can just imagine how self-confident and courageous he feels.[27]

Efros's refusal either to accept traditional interpretations of Chekhov or to conform to an existing performance style can be seen as a legitimate expression of artistic freedom, and also as an assault on MAT as a political, or perhaps more accurately a politicized, institution. Efros maintained, however, that his work was never intended as an attack on that theatre or indeed on its director. As a youth, in his training at the State Institute for Theatre Arts [GITIS], and in his early career, his work had been dominated by the ideas of Stanislavsky. Efros made a distinction between what he saw as the "old" and "new" MAT. He idealized the "old," the theatre of Stanislavsky and Nemirovich-Danchenko, which in his view had been characterized by spontaneity and innovation, but he disparaged the "new," the theatre of his own day, in whose work these features were sadly lacking.[28] In this light, his attack was less on Stanislavsky himself and more on what he saw as the later debasement of his ideas.

Over the span of his whole career, however, Efros drew inspiration from a range of other sources, too. He remarked in an interview that Stanislavsky, Meyerhold and Vakhtangov were the "great teachers and holy men" of the Russian theatre, but he also discussed the importance for him of the work of Brecht and of Peter Brook, and of the film director Federico Fellini, for whom he had a life-long admiration.[29] Nonetheless, his early involvement with the techniques of Stanislavsky had made a deep and lasting impact upon him. Although he never knew his predecessor personally, the founder of MAT as an imagined figure was something of a mentor for him. He used Stanislavsky's methodology as a touchstone throughout his life, and never completely broke with the ideas of the "great teacher." In fact, Efros became increasingly convinced that the only real way to preserve "the legacy of Stanislavsky" was to develop it.[30] He was to forge his own unique style, combining his early training in the methods of Stanislavsky with more overtly theatrical techniques, and his production of *The Seagull* was a significant step in his evolution.

Thus, in 1966 he was throwing down a gauntlet to the Moscow theatre world and at the same time making a decisive break with his own past. Viewed in this light, for Efros *The Seagull* becomes a rite of passage. He found his own sentiments echoed in the words of Treplev: "we need new forms." For Efros, as for Treplev, if theatre was to progress it needed to break with the past and create anew.

Although he consistently maintained, as mentioned above, that his production of *The Seagull* was never intended to be willfully anti-Stanislavskian, their approaches in 1898 and 1966 could not have been more different. Whereas Stanislavsky had expanded the written text by adding vast quantities of extra detail, Efros wanted to reduce the play to something more essential, to strip it of all preconceived ideas derived from literary criticism and past performances, and to pursue a single, very clear thematic line.

Efros forced his performers (and indeed his audience) to make the familiar – that is, their preconceptions of the play – appear strange. He encouraged his actors to view their characters objectively, and to inject aggression into their performances. This sense of aggression was introduced from the very beginning, in the dialogue between Medvedenko and Masha. This scene, according to Efros, was traditionally played in a low-key, almost gentle manner. As they walk across the stage, waiting for Treplev's play to begin, the pair engage in an idle exchange of words. In Efros's understanding, Medvedenko, although he wants to talk to Masha of love, also has a more pressing purpose. Efros explained this as follows:

Medvedenko is courting Masha, but at the same time he raises a certain significant point of principle and poses the question of whether someone can be unhappy for spiritual or moral reasons. He understands that a person might be unhappy from a lack of money, entailing difficulty in buying daily necessities like tea and sugar, but to wear mourning when living in plenty he does not understand. I wanted to approach this issue almost in a Brechtian manner in order to reveal these ideas.[31]

Medvedenko was played by Lev Durov and, in his interpretation, as B. Yevseev suggested, the character lost many of his traditional traits. Durov's Medvedenko was not the poor but respectable and well-meaning school-teacher, steadfastly prepared to bear his life's cross.[32] Instead he was demonstrative and demanding, and therefore his opening question was pronounced with a certain element of annoyance, opening up a dispute and demanding an almost public response.

A similar sense of conflict and tension permeated the entire performance. Efros rejected the moderate "room temperature" and slow pace traditionally associated with Chekhov. Instead, he removed all the pauses and silences, and lost any sense of a cozy conversational style. The actors were directed to shout, cry and moan their lines,[33] were given to frequent outbursts of merriment or anger and to hysterical sobbing. The effect, according to Rudnitsky, was to reproduce the atmosphere of a contemporary communal flat.[34] These characters, brought together in a family reunion, have known each other for decades, and in Efros's interpretation this produced not a sense of mutual kindness, but an opportunity to express deep-seated irritation with each other. In fact, in their constant bickering and petty arguments they were often perceived as "spoiling for a fight," perhaps as a means of relieving boredom and finding scapegoats for their own feelings of purposelessness. N. Ignatova, however, objected to this strident aspect of the production. She argued with some justification that, in making the characters fight over petty things with as much ardor as over such issues as the role of the artist in society, Efros had reduced the philosophical breadth of Chekhov's play. However, as Shakh-Azizova commented, Efros was more concerned with the characters' relationships with each other and their emotional responses to their circumstances than with their aesthetic principles.[35]

The conflicts and continual arguments swamped the lyricism and sadness normally associated with Chekhov's world, and replaced it with a naked drama of disconnected people. The idea that the characters are unable to make contact and communicate with each other has always been a key to the interpretation of Chekhov, but Efros's emphasis was on the fact that the characters did make contact continuously, but nevertheless failed to understand one another.[36] In other words, Efros brought what was formerly regarded as subtext to the surface of the drama, as the substance of the text.

Efros's conceptions of Chekhov's characters were radically different from traditional interpretations, and so confounded the expectations of critics.

Yuri Zubkov, for instance, complained that in their constant bickering the characters lost the gentility normally associated with notions of the intelligentsia. He objected to Alexander Pelevin's portrayal of Dorn. This critic expected to see an erudite doctor whose behavior exhibited a sense of humanity touched by delicacy and a subtle irony, but this Dorn's loud voice and sweeping gestures expressed instead his anger and frustration.[37] He reserved some sympathy and affection for Treplev, but his response to others was frequent angry outbursts. His relationship with his patient, Sorin, lacked all sense of a "bedside manner" and was particularly acrimonious. Thus, for instance, when in Act II he instructs Sorin to take some valerian tablets, the line was delivered aggressively, almost as a threat.[38] Despite Zubkov's objections, Pelevin's doctor was a credible interpretation of the role, and furthermore Dorn's rancorous relationship with his patient was perfectly in keeping with the performance of Arkady Vovsi as Sorin, who, feeling the weight of his twilight years, complained constantly, blaming others for his dissatisfaction with a joyless existence.[39]

Sorin's disappointment with life was matched by that of Masha, whose passionate but unrequited love for Treplev left her both embittered and bereft. According to Poliakova, Antonina Dmitrieva appeared both tired and drained: moving slowly and lazily, she embodied Masha's lines from the beginning of Act II: "I feel as though I was born long, long ago, I drag my life behind me like an endless train."[40]

Yelena Fadeeva, as Arkadina, was vain and self-absorbed, spitefully jealous of Nina and utterly indifferent to her son's plight. Indeed, as Yevseev noted, in Act III her response: У меня нет деньги! (I have no money) to Sorin's pleas to let Konstantin buy a new coat or travel abroad, was delivered not "decisively" (решительно!), as Chekhov's stage directions suggest, but rather with the degree of ferocity which one might expect if Arkadina's very life were at stake.[41]

According to Senelick, in Stanislavsky's production the depiction of the central trio of Nina, Trigorin and Treplev had been relatively simple: "Nina was a pure creature, ruined by that 'scoundrelly Lovelace' Trigorin, and Treplev was a misunderstood Byronic genius."[42] Efros's characterizations deviated greatly from this interpretation. Olga Yakovleva's Nina, most surprisingly to the audiences of the day, lost much of her meekness and naivety. Instead, in what Rudnitsky perceived as "a correction" of her character, she was presented at first as a woman of considerable foresight and self-assurance.[43] In Smeliansky's account, this Nina also displayed an insatiable appetite for fame. In Act I, as she recited her monologue, she deliberately distanced herself through her tone and demeanor from the "decadent" play and its excitable writer. She flirted with his text in the hope of impressing the celebrities from the capital, and when, mortified by the fiasco, Treplev fled, she lost all interest in the sensitive "boy genius" and instead joined her public as a co-conspirator in his humiliation.[44] Later, in Act II, in what was to become the most memorable scene of the production, she turned her conversation with Trigorin into a game of seduction and imbued it with powerful sexual feelings.[45] As the dialogue drew to a close, Yakovleva ferociously and gleefully slashed the air with a thin fishing rod, behavior which, in Smeliansky's view, promised extraordinary carnal delights. In Yakovleva's action there emerged a predatory animal, in a figure traditionally seen as an innocent girl from the provinces.[46] This Nina was a formidable threat to Arkadina, which accounted for the latter's jealousy and their open hostility to one another.

Stanislavsky had played Trigorin in an elegant white suit, and had based his performance on the line "У меня нет своей воли" ("I have no will of my own").[47] Chekhov himself had a different conception, seeing him as a seedy character, who "wears checked trousers and cracked shoes."[48] According to A. Svobodin, Trigorin had also been seen as a vain fop who found country society intolerable.[49] However, Alexander Shirvindt's portrayal differed from all previous interpretations. To the surprise of Marianna Stroeva, Trigorin became the most sympathetic character in the production.[50] Played as a respectable, dignified and serious writer, he spoke with genuine feeling about his work and was honestly aware of his own failings; this Trigorin admitted frankly that he would never write as well as Turgenev.[51] It is impossible to deny Trigorin's responsibility for Nina's fate, but in Efros's production he was seen to have been seduced and used by the aspiring actress, and therefore was not played as a devious villain. Although she was crushed by Trigorin's treatment, Efros refused to see Nina as a victim. Instead, he wanted to show, in her rejection of Treplev and her general demeanor, that she, satisfying her own ego, was at least partially responsible for not only her own downfall, but also Treplev's.

The play's conflict centered, for Efros, on the character of Treplev, and in a major departure from the accepted norm he created from Chekhov's play something close to a monodrama. Arguing that Chekhov's own sympathies lay with Treplev, Efros dismissed the melancholy, morose traits so often associated with this character, and Valentin Smirnitsky, himself a recent acting school graduate, created a different Treplev: child-like, energized and ardently searching for "new forms." The central theme was the fate of the artist of a new generation who is doomed to be misunderstood and unappreciated. Efros saw Treplev as besieged on all sides, rejected by all the other characters with essentially equal vigor. From the outset Efros united them against Treplev and his new art, and ensured that any sympathy they extended to him was fleeting. Thus, he made them all guilty of Treplev's death.

Efros created a new finale. The pace, which for much of the production had been frenetic, was suddenly slowed, so that, in the opinion of G. Kholodova, the new ending also functioned as a requiem for Treplev.[52] In Chekhov's stage directions, Dorn's lines announcing Treplev's suicide are followed by the final curtain; in Efros's production, the auditorium lights were gradually brought up to full, Masha was directed to continue to call the numbers for the lotto game in a meaningless stream of figures, Arkadina sang an old romance, gradually increasing to full volume, and Dom swung back and forth in a rocking chair. Efros was seeking to show that there was no real means of escaping from a senseless life, the only solutions were suicide, or continuing to engage in a pointless game or other monotonous routines.

Rudnitsky's central criticism of this approach, and one that has some validity, was that by concentrating the conflict of the play on a single character Efros lost the "polyphonic" multiplicity of Chekhov's writing, and that the other characters were inevitably weakened as a result. Every character reacted in a similar fashion to the troublesome Treplev. This emphasized his separateness and isolation, but also precluded development and emotional fluidity in the others.[53]

The presentation of *The Seagull* almost as a monodrama was equally clearly to be seen in the set, created by the designers Vladimir Lalevich and Nikolai Sosunov. This, like so many other aspects of the production, was both highly praised and severely criticized. Since Efros's production was meant to generate the bleak atmosphere of a world that was both harsh and unrelenting, on his stage there was no attempt to recreate the magic lake, the leafy trees and glorious sunshine so familiar to Russian audiences. Whereas Stanislavsky had deliberately evoked a sense of life beyond the borders of the set, in Efros's production the stage was surrounded by a fence of old boards, but this, instead of obscuring the natural beauties beyond, was constructed with gaps that deliberately showed the audience that there was nothing but darkness beyond the enclosed world of the characters' lives. For Shakh-Azizova, writing in 1976, this set had the appearance of a prison and expressed the tragic circumstances of Chekhov's characters; they were locked into their lives and fatally conjoined to one another.[54] Writing in *Teatr* in 1980, this same critic saw the set precisely as an expression of the world as seen by Treplev, and – more importantly perhaps – as a realization of the idea of an infinite and empty cosmic space, expressed in the words of Treplev's own play. Moreover, the sense of "nothingness" beyond the world of the estate lent an even greater poignancy and foreboding to Nina's exit into the dark empty space beyond the set.[55]

Zubkov, however, bemoaned the loss of the lake and natural surroundings which, he argued, were so dear to Chekhov. The failure to recreate such surroundings, he maintained, was a refusal on Efros's part to acknowledge Chekhov's intention to use the image of the richness of nature as a deliberate contrast to the inane and absurd life of the characters.[56]

Interestingly, Rudnitsky remarked that Efros succeeded in capturing just this contrast of opposites using a single tree, which in its very vitality stood out against the capricious and unhealthy relationships that developed between the characters. Rudnitsky also saw a thematic link in the contrast between the old boards used for the surrounding fence and the fresh, new planks that littered the stage floor and were used in the construction of Treplev's stage. This was solidly built and he dashed about all over it, fussing and fixing things, balancing on the planks, lying down on his back, leaping up again as he cried out for "new forms." For Rudnitsky, throughout the play in general and in Treplev's performance in particular, there was a sense of foreboding. He remarked that the little stage itself looked like a scaffold and thus gave physical expression to the theme of the martyred artist.[57]

The set for the interior in Act III stood in direct contrast to the stark opening scene. The designers created a room completely crowded with objects and pieces of furniture, a vast variety of different lamps shone from every corner, and every inch of the wooden walls was covered with pictures. However, in what was perhaps a complete reversal of the intention of the MAT production, this set evoked a sense not of comfort and stability, but of gloom and immobility. The characters were so hemmed in by their surroundings that they became absurd and awkward in their movements. Nina was the only one who seemed to be able to move in this atmosphere; in Rudnitsky's image she flitted like a bat from one corner to the next. However, this capacity for movement had by Act III a very different meaning from her activity at the beginning of the production:

> If at the beginning of the production her mobility was symptomatic of reckless enterprise, then by the end it indicated something quite different: she was in her death throes.[58]

The mood for much of the production was aggressively anti-lyrical, but at moments Efros lightened the tension with pieces of pure comedy. At the beginning of Act II, following a short dialogue between Dorn and Arkadina, according to Chekhov's script Sorin enters walking with a stick, accompanied by Nina and Medvedenko, who is pushing Sorin's empty bath chair:[59] in Efros's production, Durov entered without the chair. Later, Sorin and Shamraev are arguing over Shamraev's refusal to provide the party with horses, an exasperated Sorin angrily demands: "Сейчас же подать сюда всех лошадей" (Bring all the horses here right now!).[60] At this precise moment Durov pushed the bath chair violently on to the stage, producing laughter in the audience, who were delighted at the incongruity between the words and the action.

Efros's production raised a storm of controversy that split the Moscow theatre world. As Rudnitsky later noted, the critics of the time ranged between such extremes that on the one hand Efros's champions refused to see any failings or insufficiencies in his interpretation, and on the other his detractors were so blinded by their sense of righteous indignation that they refused to acknowledge the importance of Efros's discoveries.[61]

Zubkov, for instance, considered the scene with the bath chair and other comic moments as gratuitous, and he further charged Efros with altering stage directions to "modernize" Chekhov. Thus, for instance, he objected to the fact that Masha was directed to smoke rather than to take snuff because, he maintained, women of Chekhov's era did not smoke.[62]

Similarly, N. Ignatova suggested that changes made to Chekhov's script in Efros's interpretation demonstrated the director's lack of faith in the play to excite the interest of a modern audience. Writing in *Ogonek*, Ignatova also provided some predictably ideologically charged criticism when she suggested that *The Seagull* failed to send an appropriately optimistic message to the young spectators at the Lenkom:

Muscovites know and love the Lenkom Theatre. Every evening it is crowded with young people, who need to be taught about goodness and truth. The young, more than anybody else, need to know and believe that there is good even in an imperfect world. One leaves this production with a heavy heart. No, this is not Chekhov. This is not *The Seagull*.[63]

Efros's production failed to find approval even from those who had championed his work in the past, thus, it was many years before his former mentors, Maria Knebel and Pavel Markov, could forgive their protege.[64]

The front curtains used for Efros's production had been decorated with the image of a seagull, painted as if by a child's hand. For all Efros's protestations to the contrary, it is difficult not to see in this, and in other features of the production, an ironic commentary on the style of MAT, and Efros was admonished for his audacity by members of that theatre. However, as Stroeva reasoned, criticism from this quarter was hard to justify:

> Naturally, members of MAT were indignant about the liberties taken with *The Seagull*, which they saw as their "rightful property." However, the inglorious failure of their own recent production undermined the "rightfulness" of their indignation.

It is important to note that few, if any, of Efros's critics could have seen Stanislavsky's legendary production of 1898. But Efros was seen to be attacking and indeed destroying a cherished myth. Furthermore, as we have seen, *The Seagull*, both actually and symbolically, lay at the very heart of the history and development of MAT. Efros's assault was therefore also on that theatre's very essence. His challenge upset the sensibilities of those many critics for whom *The Seagull* represented a sacrosanct part of the history and symbolism of MAT.

Interestingly, while *The Seagull* was on tour in the Baltic States and Ukraine, reviews of the production were generally positive, but when it opened in Moscow there was only limited support.[65] A. Svobodin admired Efros's courage for breaking with tradition and Polyakova praised the Lenkom for having staged an innovative but carefully respectful production of a classic which nevertheless explicitly explored Chekhov's ideas in a contemporary context.[66] Mark Polyakov, although he found much to admire in Efros's original interpretation, sharply criticized its excessively strident tone, which in his view reduced the subtle complexity of Chekhov's writing:

> As the voices became sharper and coarser and as quarrelling increased so [also] the sense of a Chekhovian atmosphere was diminished. The symphonic and subtle aspects of Chekhov's dramaturgy disappeared and with them the notion that the tragic fate of Chekhov's characters is many-sided and many-levelled.[67]

Polyakova's comments were justified. Indeed, several years later Efros in his first book *Репетиция – любовь моя* (*Rehearsal is My Love*), criticized his own production and suggested that his Brechtian approach had been misguided and excessively harsh. It had allowed the actors to view the characters objectively but without affection, had reduced the actors' capacity to portray depth and had resulted in a loss of lyricism.[68]

In general, adverse criticism of *The Seagull* outweighed positive commentary, and it significantly failed to find support among the more politically powerful critics. In the late 1960s, at a time when the regime increasingly demanded ideological conformity, Efros's production was simply too radically individual, and it was banned soon after it opened.

There is little doubt that *The Seagull* was very important in the development of Efros's art, but it was also a production about which he had strong feelings for very different reasons. He used it as vehicle of protest at a time when his freedom as artistic director at the Lenkom Theatre was under severe threat. In the mid-1960s Brezhnev's regime oversaw changes in cultural policy that aimed to crush dissent. As a result, Efros's repertoire at the Lenkom was deemed to have failed to meet the theatre's political objectives, and he came under increasing pressure to direct more ideologically appropriate dramas. Efros interpreted this as an infuriating infringement of his artistic integrity, and he began to channel his anger and frustration into his work. He selected plays that featured as central characters creative artists who are misunderstood by the society around them and become martyrs to the cause of artistic freedom. In 1965, he saw a reflection of his own circumstances in Edvard Radzinsky's *Making a Movie*, and in *The Seagull*, he felt drawn to the character of Treplev. The idea of an artist besieged on all sides was clearly close to the heart of a director in the process of establishing his own company and reputation, and producing his first classic work for an adult audience. In 1967 Efros wrote an article for the journal *Teatr*, in which he drew a direct parallel between Treplev's circumstances and his own. He wrote:

> They see a person who wavers, who is not entirely confident because he is constantly searching, and because of this they "shoot" at him from all sides. And when a young, not yet fully-fledged theatre company offers up its new and somewhat imperfect work, they do exactly the same thing.[69]

Smeliansky maintained that Efros did not protest when *The Seagull* was banned, an idea echoed by Senelick.[70] However, this assertion is contradicted by Stroeva's account, and is inaccurate for two reasons.[71] First, Efros tended to register such protest by means of his work. In 1966 Bulgakov's play *Molière, or The Cabal of Hypocrites* was to be Efros's last production at the Lenkom, but the third to explore the self-reflective themes of the Artist and Society and of talent as a crown of thorns. In this final production Efros would forge links between his own experiences and those of Bulgakov and Molière, and give vent once more to his anger at the restrictions placed on his artistic freedom.

Second, while it is generally true that Efros rarely expressed his opinion in print, particularly regarding his troubled relations with the cultural administration, in the case of *The Seagull* he made an exception, and in fact defended his interpretation with no little daring in ways which I can refer to only briefly in the present study.

Significantly, he criticized directly the ideas of Yury Zubkov, who had reviewed his production.[72] Zubkov at this period held a powerful post as an editor of *Teatralnaya zhizn*, and Efros's time at the Lenkom coincided with a "battle" between that journal and *Teatr*. *Teatr*, edited by Yury Rybakov, was noted for its support of more controversial directors like Efros, but in the 1960s came under fire for its liberal editorial policies, and an orchestrated campaign of vilification ultimately led to Rybakov's dismissal. *Teatral'naya zhizn*, on the other hand, regularly published negative reviews of Efros's work, attacking even those productions universally praised elsewhere. It represented such ultraconservative factions as the Russian Federal Ministry of Culture, the All-Union Theatre Society and the RSFSR Writers' Union. Thus, any criticism of the opinions of Zubkov was interpreted as effectively in disagreement with the Party line.

In 1967 Efros was dismissed from the post of artistic director at the Lenkom. It has been suggested that this was a direct result of the controversy surrounding *The Seagull*.[73] Rose Lamont has interpreted his decision to stage Bulgakov's play *Molière* as an act of defiance which led directly to his dismissal.[74] In reality, these productions were only two factors in a complex series of events which I can only summarize here and which resulted in his expulsion. Efros had consistently refused to play politics, had failed to produce the kind of repertoire that the authorities demanded, and had, moreover, created a powerful enemy in Zubkov. More importantly, by the end of 1966 it had become abundantly clear that the Lenkom theatre would not be producing a suitable, newly commissioned play as its contribution to the celebrations in 1967 of the fiftieth anniversary of the Russian Revolution. For the theatre that bore the name of Lenin's Communist Youth this was an intolerable situation.[75]

Dismissed from his theatre, Efros was assigned a lesser position, as a staff director at the Malaya Bronnaya Theatre. Unbowed by the banning of *The Seagull*, he chose Chekhov's *Three Sisters* as his first production at his new theatre. In this he rejected once more the evocation of a melancholy mood and created instead an energetic, fast-paced and openly theatrical production. Through parody and the tragicomedy of the grotesque, he expressed the inherent absurdity and ultimate meaninglessness which he saw in the lives of Chekhov's characters. This production caused as great a scandal as *The Seagull*. Efros was sharply criticized for his allegedly disrespectful handling of Chekhov's hopeful speeches, and for emphasizing what he saw as the play's existentialist and absurdist elements. His production of *Three Sisters* was banned, too.

Efros was to remain at the Malaya Bronnaya Theatre for a further seventeen years. In this period, he produced his most celebrated productions of Russian classic authors: Chekhov, Gogol, Turgenev, Lermontov, Pushkin, Dostoevsky and Lev Tolstoy. In each instance, Efros produced a work of startling originality which upset traditional norms of interpretation. He demonstrated, as he had first done with Chekhov, that these works were neither moribund nor rigidly restricted by a fixed performance style, but vital and relevant to contemporary Soviet experience. Yury Fridshtein, writing in *Ekran i stsena* in 1997 on the tenth anniversary of Efros's death, suggested that it was precisely this aspect of Efros's work that has assured his enduring influence on Russian theatre today.[76]

"What kind of play is *The Seagull*?"

[The following extract is taken from Anatoly Efros, *The Joy of Rehearsal*. (Trans. James Thomas. New York: Peter Lang, 2006).]

It is generally accepted that Chekhov is performed as though the characters were not communicating among themselves.

Vladimir Nemirovich-Danchenko said that it is necessary to dig around for each character in *Three Sisters* separately. And that communication among them is difficult, hidden, and indirect.

But in *The Seagull*, perhaps, everything can be built on stormy communication together with complete misunderstanding of one person by another.

There is the world of Arkadina and Trigorin, a settled world. They know how to describe a moonlit night. They know how to play so they are well accepted in Kharkov. They are successful. They have a routine they love. Life has accepted them, smiled at them, they have everything – they have lived 40 or 45 years as people to whom life has been friendly.

And suddenly there is this 25-year-old person, who cannot even afford to buy a new suit, in whose heart seethes a new world; he does not understand their theatre, their literature. He has his own world, poetry, theatre, love. His world is altogether different.

Trigorin and Arkadina have adjusted comfortably to life; they are residents of the finished world and for them Konstantin is a nobody.

Konstantin puts on his performance and he hopes his mother will understand. He knows in advance that "these people" don't understand what he wants to do. But on this day – they are his audience.

What kind of a play is *The Seagull*? Sharp conflict! A deadly struggle between the settled world and the man in a torn jacket. *The Seagull* is about their incompatibility.

The meaning of *The Seagull* lies in the incompatibility of these different worlds, these different views of life. Konstantin and Nina, Konstantin and Arkadina, and Arkadina Trigorin, Nina and Trigorin – everyone seems oddly to need each other, without each other they cannot "stick" to each other, but this proximity conceals an explosion within it, since everyone has different aspirations.

Arkadina is an actress and she has "backstage" habits. She can adjust her garters in front of everyone and be tactlessly frank. She turns her back on Nina all the time, stressing that she herself has – her own circle. A famous writer interested in some girl! Big deal! For half an hour!

Masha cannot be played as tiresome, even though she says that life pulls her along like a train. Her violent desire is to tell everyone about her condition, everyone! She even enjoys the story of her own misfortunes. Only she is afraid to go to Treplev – because you cannot tell this to him!

For Nina, acquaintance with Trigorin is the same for us as being acquainted with Hemingway. And before that she loved the local poet. Now this boy seems so provincial – with all his manners, obscure verses, and torn jacket. She has distracted, condescending pity for him.

Masha asks Nina to read something from Kostya's play. Everyone has their place, thinks Arkadina. You are here and we can be together, but I will depart with Hemingway.

The Doctor and Sorin – hatred of the patient for the doctor and the doctor for the patient. The Doctor thinks it is disgusting when a sixty-year-old patient wants to be treated. He himself is fifty-five, and it is also time for him to be treated, but he does not want to be a bother to anybody. The patient's life is ruined – he blames the doctor. The doctor's life is ruined – he blames the patient. Dorn is holding a croquet mallet all the time and is just about to clout someone.

The figure of Trigorin is also quite dramatic. Obsessed, he writes everywhere, writes with his notebook held against a fence.

In the third act, everything is subordinate to the departure. I remember in one theatre there was a table, on it were liquor glasses, and near the table was a suitcase. Masha talked with Trigorin, however except for the waiting suitcases, there was no sign of leaving. But the sense of departure needs to be in their blood. Things are all ready to go, and Masha wants to tell him about her life. To repay his good attitude towards her with a high degree of candidness, and what is more, in the atmosphere of this awful pre-departure hustle and bustle. He, too, is restless: he can neither focus nor listen – he needs to see Nina. But how to do it? They are departing in ten minutes, people will be around, it is an interconnecting room, commotion, everyone in front of each other. And during their dialogue, Nina rushes about somewhere nearby, in and out.

And Arkadina is in hurry. She would sooner get out of here and take Trigorin away. As always, she is not ready until the last minute, and she has not completely dressed yet. And with the impudence of an actress, she dresses in front of everybody.

And Sorin – he is the kind of old person for whom a simple act – say, to inform or call or ask for something – is a great event that takes away part of his life. Preparing, worrying etc.

And if we need to ask for money as for alms! Not for myself, for the boy – still it is humiliating, horrible. It is hard to pick a moment, he waited until the last minute of their departure, already understands poorly what he says, is confused. And then suddenly – a blow, not just dizzy, but something terrible – he faints and collapses, drops something, hits his head.

Arkadina forgets about collecting her things, about the departure. And when everything is taken care of, she has a terrible reaction. White as chalk, she lies on the sofa and falls silent.

Konstantin comes in with his head tied up. A sort of elegant black bandage on his head. He asks his mother to change his bandage. This always sounds melodramatic. In fact, his entrance does not need to be played out in this way, but only that his mother is feeling bad after Sorin's blackout. Konstantin is very gentle, very affectionate. He cannot exist without love. Not only in the sense that he must be loved, but mainly the fact that he always needs to love someone. He needs to bestow his tenderness on someone. He always loved his mother. Then Nina. But Nina is no longer with him. And so, he bestows a double tenderness on his mother, no matter what. But his mother has just had this experience, she is pale and haggard. And so, he kisses her, soothes her, as a grown son rarely does.

If only she felt it!

But he says some careless words about Trigorin, and she instantly insults him. He immediately becomes helpless, confused. They don't need to shout at each other – that is banal. He is confused, but he speaks offensive words, too. He speaks not screaming but bewildered: "Go to your precious theatre and play there in those pitiful, clumsy plays . . ."

And then Trigorin asks Arkadina to stay. He cannot leave without Nina now. He needs a woman he could complain to. The scene in the garden with Nina is usually played conceitedly. In fact, he complains like a child. With Arkadina, this would be impossible – she is too busy. But Nina saw such human devotion and commitment that she wanted to be frank and close to him.

And now all this must be properly explained to Arkadina, so that she will release him. How much of Arkadina's feminine charm she needs not to let him go! But this scene is often played roughly. Rather, it needs a high degree of intimacy. Replace this only slightly with an overdramatic path – it falls apart at once.

We will not have the usual scenery – moon, lake, garden pathway, etc. There can also be poetry in a hard-wooden croquet platform.

Isn't it possible that instead of Chekhov's poetry we have Chekhov's psychology – simple modern psychology? The psychology of people who are acclimatized, so to speak, to a completely different way of life? Everyone running around, crowded, etc.

Yes, life today is bad. But how can we get rid of its psychology? And do we need to be rid of it completely? Or maybe, freed from it completely, we would get a Chekhov who is too different from our time? Who can explain this to me?

When all the members of the household gather prior to Treplev's play, there is a conversation about art. Everyone is accepted as a great expert, and speaks about art with assurance. Experts, connoisseurs, experienced evaluators. As is often the way at our opening nights when our experts gather. They talk about art like it is about making borscht. They enter with the crowd and settle in – masters of life and art.

And Konstantin appeals to some shadows and asks them to put everyone to sleep and think what it would be like in two hundred thousand years . . .

But Konstantin is a not just poetic fool in comparison with Arkadina, Shamraev, and others, he needs to find his own concreteness. They are concerned about the borscht, and he is about the spirits, but firmly, courageously and concretely. This is a struggle, and Konstantin is no wimp in this fight. This will need to be shown with the aim of getting this company to listen, and then not to flare up at them, but simply pull the plug, and quietly say, "Enough! Curtain!" He says this softly, and then, like a stooped old man trudges to the stage and crawls under the curtain.

Nina's monologue is like a prayer: a single sound wave. But this "gang" came here to watch a normal play.

Arkadina pulls in her shoulders, she realizes at once which way the wind blows. "This is something decadent," she says, narrowing her eyes and shaking her head. "It would be better to write a play about the way we teachers live, and then produce that on stage," echoes Medvedenko. He is philosopher number one. You cannot, he says, separate spirit from matter!

They listen carefully, hostilely, then they begin to boo, make noise. And when the show is interrupted, Nina, instead of running to Kostya, remains on stage. She wants to know, you see, whether Trigorin liked the play. He gently takes her by the waist and helps to step off the stage. They are both immediately embarrassed, everyone has noticed.

***

Directing *The Seagull*, I was pleased that I tried to expose its Brechtian thematic core. But then it turned out that we only looked at it from one side, which was quite unfriendly to the characters. Trigorin turned into a washcloth. Arkadina – a bad mother and a bad provincial actress. Medvedenko – an arrogant, defiant "little man." While rehearsing, we did not expect things to turn out that way. But, apparently, the basic idea was too schematic, laid bare all the trends, and gave the play a feeling of dryness, stiffness. The vital pollen had departed from the play. It became biased, unpoetic, angry. I would not produce *The Seagull* this way now.

In the first scene between Sorin and Treplev, now I would not only see nervous talking prior to a performance but also friendship between old and young.

Konstantin, smiling, says that his uncle's beard is unkempt, and runs his hand through the beard. He embraces Sorin around and tears off the daisy petals before his eyes, guessing. In fact, we probably don't need to exaggerate Treplev's fear and nervousness before the show. Because the plot immediately prevails over the complexity of the [psychological] life displayed by the characters in the scene.

And Treplev's line about the fact that his mother does not love him and that she is worried and jealous because she will not perform in this little play, and possibly Nina as well – these should probably not be played so literally.

It is one thing to say his mother does not love him and is jealous while nervously running around the platform stage in anticipation of dramatic fate of his play, another thing to say the same thing while tugging at the beard of his beloved uncle.

And he should not say that his mother is stingy so angrily. It is necessary to say this, for example, while lying on his back and tossing a twig to his uncle. Honestly, the serious sense of this will not disappear. However, I'm already leaning too far towards his uncle, but if not his uncle, then something else must complicate, or if you will, simplify Treplev's way of thinking and feeling, giving it a more casual and less unequivocal tone.

It would be interesting to demagnetize my old *Seagull* now, free it from frankness and one-sided intensity.

And it would be even more interesting to produce both *Seagulls* at the same time – the former one – tense, nervous, very modernized, the other – objective, poetic, wiser, more humane. But that, as they say, would be an unnecessary luxury.

Medvedenko would need to be treated less roughly, too. "Why do you always wear black?" – he says to Masha, almost disliking her for her intellectual torments, for her suffering for purely spiritual reasons. He thinks it is only possible to suffer for material reasons. This view of Medvedenko would not be deprived of meaning, but he has an inborn frustration with such people. Now, perhaps, I would remove this frustration. After all, life has really been hard on this man, which would logically make him angry.

We played him in such a way that he knew the kids at school did not like him. But why should it be that way?!

Internally, he was worn-out, boring, uptight, somehow fundamentally limited. "Write a play about teachers who live badly, not some disembodied spirit" – our Medvedenko said maliciously and willfully at Treplev's play. That's exactly how teachers live, and there are a lot of them, and bless them!

But this time Medvedenko could be different – younger, kinder, and gentler.

And what is the line Masha says about her black dress – "in mourning for my life?" Really, is this so irrevocably serious? No, honestly, it should be something more complicated, or, if you prefer, more simplified.

So here is how the new beginning should look.

While on the way, Masha sees Nina's white dress hanging nearby Treplev's makeshift stage and prepared for the presentation.

Masha goes quickly to this dress to see it.

(All of us would want to see the dress the actress will wear today.)

Medvedenko, a bumbling suitor, lags behind, walks in circles in the nearby woods, for some reason jumps over a bench out there somewhere, then leans over through some opening in the trees and at a distance touches, as it were, his beloved again.

– Why do you always wear black? – he asks ridiculously. He is very lanky, tall, awkward.

Masha greets him casually, continuing to examine the dress.

But Medvedenko, at the back of the stage, takes her response seriously. And keeps going over it in his head.

– Why? I don't understand . . . you are healthy, you have a father, though he is not rich, he has money . . . I get only twenty-three rubles a month . . . he even shows her by counting on his fingers how little it is – twenty-three rubles.

Masha again greets him parenthetically, still occupied with Nina's dress.

But to prove to her how difficult it is to live in a big family, he sticks four twigs in the ground – a mother, two sisters, and a brother – then draws a circle around them and repeats, "And all on a salary of only twenty-three rubles!"

Meanwhile, Masha finishes examining the dress, and smiling at how amusingly he tells her about his poverty (because she has been only half listening to him), she walks toward him, indicating the play will begin soon.

Also smiling, he begins to tell her that he loves her, but he meets only with indifference on her side.

And Masha, chuckling and brushing him away, begins to offer him tobacco.

He takes some awkwardly, and even wants to try it, but thinks better of it.

She skillfully draws the tobacco into her nose and sneezes with pleasure, but here she begins to laugh at her foolish habit.

He also quietly laughs, but uncertainly, and shrugs his shoulders. There is no way he will understand her nature!

Masha generally feels all right with him, but she is rather bored, and there is nothing to talk about. Thus, she walks away, seating herself comfortably somewhere, and begins to look up at the sky and in other directions.

"I'm suffocating. It looks like there will be a thunder storm tonight."

He wants to sit down too, but Treplev runs in, and after jumping up on the platform stage, he begins to check and see if it is fastened together correctly and whether it will be comfortable for Nina to perform there.

But Sorin, who is testy from a long nap, he says, comes back in, brushing something away with his stick.

Treplev finishes his master inspection, jumps down, and approaches Masha and Medvedenko, politely asking them to move away.

Then Treplev, expecting Nina's arrival, reclines somewhere near his uncle, and starts some friendly chatter interrupted by jokes, which I already spoke about above.

In the beginning of her monologue, Nina lists many living things. At first glance, she lists them somewhat randomly. According to her own discretion, she selects one or another insect or beast from the whole living world and makes a long chain from everything she remembers. It is as though with this inventory Nina aspires to emphasize something she wants to speak about, it concerns not only one aspect of life, but all, all life, including beetles and deer and lions. And human beings, of course. She names and names and names all these living creatures to say finally that the time supposedly came when all these essences died out. Then, after this entire inventory, she will say that her monologue deals with the fact that no one has remained!

The decadence of Treplev's play is frequently seen in its *form*, in a certain *nonrealistic form* and so forth, the monologue sounds somehow melodiously abstract. A certain woman in white stands on a stage in the moonlight and recites something difficult to understand. But the decadence, if there is any at all, is in the content itself, which, perhaps, needs to be expressed utterly simply, pointedly, maximally prosaic, and then the entire horror of it will be conveyed. We shall hear it, but Arkadina will only be irritated by the form, and the fact that its smells of sulfur!

It could be that Nina addresses the audience with absolute simplicity, completely realistically. She will explain that her monologue deals with the time when everything on earth has died out, as the mammoths died out. Even the simple beetle no longer remains. There is no need for the moon to shine since no one sees it!

No, admittedly, I never clearly heard what was said about this subject before. Like Arkadina, I saw the form as "something decadent," and only that. Naturally, I was too young to see the first MAT production.

But what was it really like?

Let's assume I would have heard about this make-believe future. I would have seen this extinct earth. Then I would have visualized everything, and after understanding everything, I would have heard Nina's terrible cry that it is "cold, cold, cold" and that it is "empty, empty, empty!"

Now Nina's pain would manifest itself as pain appropriate to what was happening.

Usually, "cold, cold, cold" is only a beautiful continuation of the previous "sing-song."

And so, it would be almost quiet: this happened, and then this, and then this. And then after a pause, the terrible pain, "cold, cold, cold!"

Will the earth truly be so empty after millions of years? Who knows? After all, it was like this once before, and perhaps it will be so again. Of course, it is not compulsory to think about this, but, in any case, in the beginning of the monologue, Treplev has written precisely about this. Of course, Arkadina does not begin to consider this. What actress, suddenly for no reason at all, would think about such things, especially when she has become used to a theatre where "people eat, drink, wear their costumes . . . " But Treplev is a poet of another mold, and he presents this kind of play. What should be made of this?

And then Nina begins to develop her thoughts about a "world soul."

All matter has disappeared, and only the "world soul" remains. And this soul is she, Nina! In her dwells the entire memory of everything, from Napoleon to the lowliest leech!

* * *

At the intermission of the new MAT production of *The Seagull* [MAT's third version of *The Seagull* (1980), directed by Oleg Yefremov.], a critic shared his impressions with me. Innokenty Smoktunovsky/Dorn he liked, but the rest, no.

The next week, I read his review in the newspaper. He wrote about Smoktunovsky in one line, but it was only one line, or maybe two or three. The rest of the article was an account of a whole theory explaining why the performance turned out so well.

I agree that there were reasons to praise this performance, only I remember that the critic didn't like all of it that evening, and the memory of this bothers me for some reason.

Obviously, next day, he thought about it and decided he should like the performance, and he should write well about it. It is better to bend the truth a little than to "give up the game."

The critic's reasoning was that after many relatively audacious experiments (more often one-sided), the idea of returning Chekhov to Chekhov was probably a good thing. But what is Chekhov? Furthermore, what is his *Seagull*? The love of an elderly actress for a writer, and besides that, a writer in love with a young actress, who in turn is in love with the writer? This is not enough for *The Seagull*. And the fact that all this occurs against the background of a magical lake is still not enough. Two writers, two actresses, a magical lake, and more . . .

After all, *The Seagull* is a very audacious, disturbing play.

One time our theatre company was in England and everyone saw *The Seagull* there. After the performance, everyone rushed backstage excitedly, and they could not avoid rushing, since that was how the performance moved them. It was about a young man trying to oppose his own art against the prevailing literary style. And he didn't have even a decent jacket. He was poor and dependent.

He elicited enormous tears and sympathy. And everyone had to run and tell the actor about it. Owing to Treplev's performance, the production moved everyone.

One way or another, *The Seagull* should disturb, which is why it was written, but not just to illustrate some issue of literary style. There is so much struggle and irreconcilability in this play . . .

A general Chekhovian atmosphere is good, of course, but atmosphere is not yet meaning. And in each Chekhov play, besides the general atmosphere, there is still a unique meaning.

The Cherry Orchard, The Seagull, Three Sisters. They have much in common, but is it possible to understand anything if the very thing that distinguishes them is not understood? For me, that evening at MAT all the characters in *The Seagull* had merged into one impression. I only noticed that it really was a magical lake, and that everything was very gloomy and mysterious, and each thing was beautiful its own way. It could be that at some moments I even experienced something like a nostalgic feeling for that departed art when they used to play everything equally well and precisely, when there was big scenery and calm, spacious staging. But there was no meaning.

They say the time has passed for the rigid, unilateral interpretations of Chekhov, which defined the [artistic] searches of the preceding years. That the time has come for a soft, volumetric, lyrical Chekhov. Perhaps. But why? This is what I would like to learn. Could it be that time and life have correspondingly changed? And does this require another Chekhov? But what exactly has changed in time and why is another Chekhov required, one different from previous years? Or does this requirement for a softer Chekhov rest in the art itself: one-sided experiences are simply boring; a polyphonic approach [equally distributed character voices] is wanted now. Or maybe some of the people who are engaged in theory have grown old and want a lyrical respite, whereas youth possibly dreams of an impudent Chekhov now? Or maybe it is not necessary to invent anything. Because both a severe and a softer Chekhov will always be wanted, if only each of them will be produced with sense and talent.

It is even better if it could be both rigid and soft simultaneously. I reflect and I wish to hear the reflections of others, but when they tell me, without any special proofs, that the time for one interpretation has passed and the time for another has come, I perceive this as obstinacy or idle fabrication.

It is necessary to love art, instead of theories about art.

After Treplev's suicide, all the beautiful scenery of the new MAT *Seagull* grows dim, the stage becomes colorless, mournful, the central gazebo becomes dark, gloomy. Just before the curtain closes, Nina, in a black dress, repeats her earlier monologue, which now sounds like a graveside eulogy. This ending emphasizes the entire performance as gloomy, but in a strong light. A requiem. Dying. A very strong ending. But nevertheless, *The Seagull* cannot stand upon its ending alone. Prior to this there is a great deal of volume in it. But the main thing about this new interpretation is that it is too far from the way people live today. Sometimes the blasphemous idea even occurred to me that this production is not very good. Old-fashioned. Pre-Chekhovian. Flaccid melodrama. This is not true, of course, but perhaps *The Seagull* demands a certain, strict reading, not like any other play. It is impossible to build everything on the issue of slow dying. This is life, and it is full of conflicts. When Stanislavsky-Trigorin and Meyerhold-Treplev performed in it, this fact alone probably said very much. It already bore within itself a state of great conflict. Such different types of art, such different paths. True, all this had long-term effects that were to be revealed in the future. But even at that time, it was probably already possible to recognize something. Yet in this new [MAT] performance, the difference between Treplev and Trigorin is almost erased. And yet this difference is just what art reveals. Different worlds! Perhaps this is what Chekhov's play is really about: that it is not feasible to persist in this "general Chekhovian atmosphere."

"*The Seagull* is very difficult to produce"

[The following extract is from a speech of Efros's at the Anton Chekov Museum, December 27, 1973 and transcribed by Marina Zajonc.]

The Seagull is very difficult to produce. This play was written as a dotted line, very sparingly, like the outline of some huge object. Regardless of whether Chekhov had not yet developed his style, or whether the play was well-conceived.

What is *The Seagull* about? Nina was going to be a wonderful actress, thought about the theatre with Treplev, and his play is far from senseless. It is a serious monologue: matter disappears, but spirit is eternal. Konstantin is a philosopher.

These are wonderful people. But Nina's fate is not so wonderful. She performs badly. Arkadina triumphs, Konstantin is shot, Trigorin feels like a hunted fox. It is not the way one would want life to be.

In life, things don't go as they should, it is not perfectly arranged – in this lies Chekhov's meaning.

Humanity needs not only positive examples. Just that fact alone creates a lot of thoughts and worries. Chekhov saw that people would not want to live like this, but he arranged it so everything turns out ridiculously. This is the sick, painful theme of a person who understands that things are going wrong in life. This idea functions as more than an active thought.

You cannot dismiss the questions about art raised in the play. There is always an art of something settled, a position won, a young man in a torn jacket favoring new forms and a mother laughing at him. But it is he who moves the art. Chekhov knew how terribly difficult it is to resist the conventional. I think this is a play about Treplev. The story of Nina is contrived. She betrayed him at the worst possible moment, both humanly and artistically.

And she paid strongly for it. She must be played very realistically, without romance and a white dress.

The Seagull is a tragedy. There is nothing funny in that. Many theatres produce *The Seagull* in terms of Trigorin. Treplev is ridiculed. But *The Seagull* is a ruthless, terrifying drama. The end of the play strikes with sharpness and horror . . .

You need experience for everything. For the severe environment of *The Seagull*, you also need experience. I directed my first Chekhov play and my third classical play without any preliminary laboratory. I wanted to emphasize the sharpness of the play, not to spiritualize its life and display its [historical] details. To take this style as a basis and make a tough, ruthless thing, stressing its [thematic] framework. The dryness of my *Seagull* angered the public in 1966. Everything was wooden. All the characters were incompatible. Croquet court, gambling, loud smacking croquet balls . . . In this play, almost no one is successful.

There may be another way, a different approach to the play – it is, relatively speaking, like a skull on which you need to restore the face. Everything needs to be [developed] slowly and carefully . . .

All the major plays need to appear on stage. A brilliant play must also be delivered brilliantly. The Seagull should be produced four times. If you have a theatre, you should produce four versions of *The Seagull* . . .

How I would begin to direct it now [i.e., 1973] – I don't know.

Notes

1 Yelena Poliakova, "Ereticheski-genial'naya p'esa" (A Heretical-Genius Play), *Teatr* 8 (1966), 38.
2 Edward Braun, *The Director and the Stage* (Methuen, London, 1987) 65.
3 Laurence Senelick, *The Chekhov Theatre* (Cambridge: Cambridge University Press, 1997) 28.
4 It should be noted that Stanislavsky did not work alone on *The Seagull* but with Nemirovich-Danchenko. However, in essence, Nemirovich-Danchenko supplied an interpretation of the written text, which Stanislavsky then embodied in theatrical form: see Jean Benedetti, "Stanislavsky and the Moscow Art Theatre," in Robert Leach and Victor Borovsky, eds, *A History of the Russian Theatre* (Cambridge: Cambridge University Press, 1997) 259.
5 It is generally acknowledged that Stanislavsky's development of an approach to staging based on a total design concept was influenced by European companies such as the Meiningen Theatre. However, he is sometimes credited (erroneously) with introducing the idea to the Russian stage. In fact, his ideas and practice also had native antecedents: the playwright Alexei Tolstoy, for instance, reacted in a similar fashion against the standard practices of much nineteenth-century theatre when in 1866 he elaborated a new approach to staging for his play *The Death of Ivan the Terrible*: see Cynthia Marsh, "Realism in the Russian Theatre, 1850–1882," Leach and Borovsky, 155.
6 In 1905 the production was revived in the company's new and fully equipped theatre; this permitted Stanislavsky and Simov to construct the set in greater detail: Braun, 64.
7 Konstantin Rudnitsky "Chaika" – 1898" (The Seagull), in *Chekovskie chteniya v Yalte: Chekhov i teatr* (Chekhov Readings in Yalta), edited by V. I. Kuleshov (Moskva: Kniga, 1976) 65.
8 Braun, 64.
9 Braun, 65.
10 Term coined by Meyerhold to describe the Moscow Art Theatre's production style for Chekhov's plays, for which see Vsevelod Meyerhold, "The Naturalistic Theatre and the Theatre of Mood," *Meyerhold on Theatre*, Trans. Edward Braun (London: Methuen, 1969) 23–53.
11 In 1939 Solodnikov, then Head of the Theatre Directorate, addressed the first national conference for theatre directors; he exhorted those present to learn from the Moscow Art Theatre, for the Moscow Art Theatre learns from life itself: N. Velekhova, "The Link of Time: Directing in the Soviet Union," 3 *Theatre*, (1989), (Fall), 32.
12 Following a heart attack in 1928, Stanislavsky spent increasingly long periods away from the theatre he had founded, rehearsing, developing his "system' and working on opera.

13 Poliakova, 38.
14 *The Seagull* was not the most popular of Chekhov's major dramas. In the Soviet Union, between 1917 and Efros's production of 1966, there were 48 professional stagings of the play. In the same period there were 55 productions of *Three Sisters* and almost twice that number of *The Cherry Orchard*. The latter could be most clearly reinterpreted in accord with Soviet ideology and propaganda, and this accounted for its popularity. For a full list of professional theatre productions of Chekhov in the Soviet Union, see V. Berezkin, *Postanovki pes A. P. Chekova v sovetskom teatre 1917–1986 gody* (The Production of Chekhov's Plays in the Soviet Theatre 1917–1986) (Moscow and Prague, 1987).
15 Poliakova, 38.
16 Konstantin Rudnitsky, "Vremya, Chekhov i rezhissery" (Time, Chekhov, and Directors), *Voprosy teatra* (Theatre Questions) (Moskva: VTO, 1965) 139–40.
17 M. Turovskaya, "Ustarel li Chekhov? (Is Chekhov Outdated?)," *Literaturnaya gazeta* (26 July 1960) 3.
18 Senelick, 202.
19 One of Chekhov's writing precepts. In an 1886 letter to his brother, Alexander, Chekhov explained his self-defined requirements for good writing: 1) the absence of lengthy political socio-economic embellishments, 2) continuous objectivity, 3) truthfulness in describing characters and objects, 4) severe brevity; 5) courage and originality and escape from stereotypes; 6) kindness of heart.
20 Tatyana Shakh-Azizova, "Dolgaya zhizn traditsy" (The Long Life of Tradition), in *Chekovskie chteniya v Yalte* (Chekhov's Readings in Yalta) (Moskva: Kniga, 1976) 25.
21 Shakh-Azizova, 27.
22 Anatoly Efros, "Kak bystro idet vreraya," *Teatr*, 2 (1967) 69.
23 Konstantin Rudnitsky, *Spektakli raznykhlet* (Moskva: Iskusstvo, 1965) 145.
24 Anatoly Efros, "Premera sostoitsya v Vilnyuse, *Sovetskaya Litva* (10 March 1966) 3.
25 Anatoly Smeliansky, *The Russian Theatre after Stalin*, trans. Patrick Miles (Cambridge: Cambridge University Press, 1999) 64.
26 Efros, "Kak bystro," Efros appears to have had an idealized view of the English stage in the 1960s. His suggestion that the works of Shakespeare are more readily accessible to English actors is debatable; Dennis Kennedy appears to suggest that the opposite is the case; see Dennis Kennedy, "Introduction; Shakespeare Without his Language," *Foreign Shakespeare* (Cambridge Cambridge University Press, 1993) 1–17.
27 Efros, "Kak bystro," 68.
28 Anatoly Efros, *Repetitsiya–lyubov moya* (Moscow: Panas, 1993) 141.
29 Anatoly Efros, "Energy, Enervation and Mathematics of Intrigue," in discussion with Spencer Golub, *Theatre Quarterly* 26 (Summer 1977) 30.
30 Z. Vladimirova, *Kazhdyi po svoemu: tri ocherka o rezhisserakh* (Moskva: Iskusstvo, 1966) 111.
31 Efros, "Kak bystro," 69.
32 B. Yevseev, "Na puti k Chekhovu," *Moskovsky komsomolets* (10 June 1966) 3.
33 This is probably Rudnitsky's opinion. In fact, the rehearsal records do not indicate Efros's actors were ever "directed to shout, cry and moan their lines . . . ." Such instructions would be contrary to Efros's Stanislavsky-based aesthetic. [jt]
34 Rudnitsky, 147.
35 Shakh-Azizova, 31.
36 Anatoly Efros, 'Anatoly Efros repetiruet . . . i rasskazyvaet' *Moskovsky komsomolets* (23 January 1966) 3.
37 Yu. Zubkov, "Razvedka chekovskoi temy" *Teatralnaya zhizn* 13 (1966) 14.
38 Poliakova, 40.
39 Rudnitsky, 147.

40 A. P. Chekhov, *Chaika*, Act II, in *Sochinetyya: Pesy 1895–1904* (Writings: Plays, *Polnoe sobranie sochineny i pisem v tridtsati tomakh*, Vol. 13 Moscow: Nauka, 1978) 21; Poliakova, 40.
41 Yevseev, 3; Chekhov, *Chaika*, Act III, 33.
42 Senelick, 40.
43 Rudnitsky, 149.
44 Smeliansky, 65.
45 Poliakova, 41.
46 Smeliansky, 65.
47 Chekhov, *Chaika*, Act III, 42.
48 Jean Benedetti, "Stanislavsky and the Moscow Art Theatre, 1898–1938," Leach and Borovsky, 261.
49 A. Svobodin, "Chekhov bez pauz," *Moskovskaya Pravda* (21 May 1966) 3.
50 Marianna Stroeva, "Anatoly Efros: molodost," unpublished chapter (Moscow, no date) 369; cited here with permission of the author.
51 Svobodin, 3.
52 G. Kholodova, "Tri chekhovskikh spektaklya," *Teatr* 1 (1968) 17.
53 Rudnitsky, 148.
54 Shakh-Azizova, 30.
55 Tatyana Shakh-Azizova, "*Chaika*" segodnia i prezhde," *Teatr* 7 (1980) 91.
56 Zubkov, 14.
57 Rudnitsky, 146.
58 Rudnitsky, 152.
59 Chekhov, *Chaika*, Act II, 23.
60 Chekhov, *Chaika*, Act II, 25.
61 Rudnitsky, 145.
62 Zubkov, 14.
63 N. Ignatova, " Chekhov drugoi i 'Chaika' drugaya," *Ogonek* 23(1966) 27.
64 Stroeva, 370.
65 See I. Kashnitsky, "Chaika" prodolzhaet polet," *Sovetskyia Litva* (22 March 1966) 3. Later there were also positive reviews in the following newspapers outside Moscow: M. Brusilovskaya, "Chekhovskim klyuchom," *Komsomolskoe znamya*, Kiev (12 July 1966), and S. Lerman, "Chaika' vchera i segodnya," *Sovetskaya Estoniya* (11 December 1966).
66 Svobodin, 3; Poliakova, 3.
67 Mark Poliakov, "Zapiski bez daty," *Nash Sovremennik* 4 (1967) 106.
68 Efros, *Repetitsia*, 163.
69 Efros, "Kak bystro," 67.
70 Smeliansky, 65. Senelick, 214.
71 Stroeva, 373–5.
72 Zubkov wrote two articles in which he criticized Efros's interpretation of *The Seagull*. The first, published in *Teatralnaya zhizn*, has already been cited in these notes. In "Kak bystro" (66–7), Efros challenged the ideas that Zubkov articulated in the second article, Yu. Zubkov, "Sovremennost I klassika," *Izvestiya* (1 August 1966) 5.
73 Birgit Beumers, "Performing Culture: Theatre," in Catriona Kelly and David Shepherd, eds, *Russian Cultural Studies* (Oxford: Oxford University Press, 1998) 104.
74 Rose Lamont, "The Taganka of Anatoly Efros," *Performing Arts Journal*, 10: 3 (1978) 97–8.
75 Archival document dated simply "February 1967": *Gorodskoe obedinenie moskovskikh arkhivov*, f. 429, op. 1, del. 1053.
76 Yury Fridshtein, "On muzykantom byl, no ne ostavil ne not," *Ekran i stsena*, 2 (1997) 5.

Chapter 2

Efros's preliminary thoughts on *The Seagull*[1]

I have wanted to direct *The Seagull* from the first time I detected a generation gap. I wanted to "take a shot," to show that Treplev is the clear-headed one and that Arkadina is the silly woman. However, gradually everything became complicated. And now I have moved away from this initial thought. We are still going to play it from Treplev's point of view, though not the Treplev in the play, but the Treplev of life today.

1   Treplev is outwardly languid. He is inactive in conversation. A feeling of complete loneliness.

Trigorin and his Mother arrive. It will be necessary [for me] to show how to play them.
 His answers are verbose, but casual, thinking of himself.
 Despair from loneliness. He waits for Nina, worries that she is late.
 Internally terribly nervous, but he is reserved and talks unwillingly, looking away from his interlocutor and moving away from him.
 Sorin feels Treplev's mood. He would like to dispel it somehow, therefore he starts talking to him.
 So, we will handle the scene more truthfully than it is usually handled, when Treplev is open, active, and says what he thinks, forthright about both the theatre and his mother, etc. Then he looks like such a "cock of the walk," a "debunker," and his depth disappears.
 Because we have never seriously listened attentively to his reasoning. This is not an excited and talkative Jimmy Porter.[2] Treplev's melancholy is a serious and deep despair.
 When Nina arrives, he changes absolutely, contrastingly. Nina is a unique person, not part of this clique. She is the only person with whom Treplev is open. This openness and affection sounds especially contrasting alongside the previous scene.
 But Treplev's drama is aggravated because Nina does not answer him with the same openness. If Treplev looks skeptically at the possibility of success for today's performance, and Nina only thinks about its contents for today and

tomorrow's evenings, etc., then Nina possibly refers to the performance and its success with jealousy. She is concentrated and abstracted, like an actress before an opening night.

She is concentrated because now she must be; moreover, she is in the presence of the well-known actress and the writer, and she is abstracted by Treplev, of course, but politely abstracted.

2   Usually in the first scenes of *The Seagull* Nina involves some kind of foolish actress, a rather fussy, very young and infatuated girl. At the same time, she has one love – art.

She was out of breath, but does not behave in a fussy manner; on the contrary, somehow steadily, like a runner before the start.

3   And at this point, Treplev's performance begins.

For Treplev the performance is less important than communication with Nina. He does not count on its success. His announcement at the start of the play does not sound solemn, as it usually does.

To show the performance to Arkadina would be the same thing as showing an abstract painting to naturalists. Nevertheless, both he and Nina knew what he wanted.

And then comes the monologue that says matter is mortal and spirit is eternal. Nina reads it carefully and precisely, not as a little girl infatuated with art, but as a young woman aware of the type of art she is now preaching.

At the Moscow Art Theatre, this scene usually employs the customary mise-en-scène: in the distance Nina is on a platform and in the foreground the audience grumbles. And Treplev hangs about somewhere behind.

The viewer in the auditorium understands Nina's monologue as the viewers on stage do, and consequently there is little intellectual sympathy for Nina and Treplev.

In fact, everything should be constructed differently.

We should not only understand the monologue as clearly as Treplev did when he wrote it. We should also see that Nina is aware of what she is performing (after all, Treplev it explained to her, and she is young and lives with new ideas).

We must consider her acting "close-up," so there is no impression left of something blank and abstract.

And Treplev must be seen in detail, how he behaves, when his [nonrealistic] picture is shown to the convinced naturalists.

As for the onstage audience, having been pushed into the background, they can be played traditionally, but with that special subtlety, of course, handed down by MAT tradition.

Usually Treplev shouts very much when the performance breaks up. And he should disrupt and shout here, but he should still seem quiet. Firmer and more closed than his mother, who, after he leaves, will start shouting just as older people shout and get rattled, sensing there is already another generation who considers them out-of-date, ridiculous, and backward. Arkadina shouts in place of Treplev, protecting her right to life.

What is important to Nina is the impression made on Trigorin. Let the play fail, but how did I perform? There is no pettiness in this egoism, on the contrary, there is refinement from her remarkably exciting devotion to the art.

4   The essence of the second act is revealed mainly in two scenes. Treplev and Nina, and Nina and Trigorin.

Treplev killed a seagull and drops it at Nina's feet. Usually they play this scene as a nervous and jealous reproach for her internal withdrawal from him. It is also possible to assume that Treplev shot himself at the end of the second act in a rush of nervous excitement. In fact, Treplev has a feeling much more terrible than jealousy. For him Nina is now – one of *that* clique. She has moved over there, and there is absolute emptiness surrounding Treplev on all sides. Treplev does not run to Nina with his feelings [as in the past], he is now as painfully renounced by her as by his mother. He has placed Nina among those who are strangers to him. He adjusts rather philosophically, he is in cruel despair from a clear awareness of his loneliness, and in this condition of cruel despair – he shoots himself.

In the second act, Nina is filled entirely with new impressions. She is at the house of the well-known actress, and becomes acquainted with her and with Trigorin. She, in turn, is alienated from Treplev's experiences, so that his experiences and his behavior seem remote and almost ridiculous to her. But Trigorin is here, and Nina instantly becomes trustful, both open and absorbent as a sponge. But this is not simply the enthusiasm of a young girl. It is a deep, open impressionability.

Trigorin can be perceived as Treplev's opposite, as a person whom Chekhov treats badly, derisively. In fact, Chekhov speaks only about Trigorin's weakness, his submissiveness. But in general, Trigorin is a gentle person, soft, sincere, and intelligent. Even talented. He lives for literature and can be considered quite a decent writer. He has everything, but his everything – is his cross, vaguely disturbing, and he is afraid of his readers and does not understand them, is afraid to offend Arkadina, etc. Nina's understanding is essential to him, he needs to speak about his weaknesses, about his work, and it is necessary to speak to a new and energetic person. Everything has already been discussed with Arkadina long ago. But Nina is like a fresh clean sheet of fine paper.

5   After his suicide attempt, Treplev makes a last wild attempt to communicate with his mother. He is full of caresses and tenderness. Except that nobody wants his caresses and his tenderness, everyone is occupied with something else. It is not even important to him that they love him, at

least that they should accept his love, but nobody cares about him. When his mother, who is upset with the quarrel that just occurred with Sorin, remains alone in the room in a hysterical condition, Treplev is tender and gentle with her. But this time, when his caresses and his tenderness are rejected – the most terrible of all scenes in the play occurs, a scene more terrible than suicide, a scene of frenzied confusion and mutual insults.

One more attempt will be made by Treplev for a reconciliation with Nina – in the last act. And then, having finally understood there is nothing, that nothing remains and nothing will change, having already felt emptiness and absurdity in the fullest measure – he will go off to be shot again, only now he will try to aim more accurately.

Nina, having felt the passion of devotion for Trigorin, not simply as a man but also as a writer, as a person of art, comes back in the fourth act tormented and broken, without wishing to accept defeat, and yet ready for it, clinging to it all the same.

Notes

1 From his notebooks at the Anatoly Efros archives. Efros began his first conversations with the actors about a production of T*he Seagull* during the tours of the Lenin Komsomol Theatre in in July 1964. A final cast list did not yet exist. In Efros's diaries and notebooks from this time, the name of one or the other character of the play is frequently encountered, also under each character is a rather lengthy listing of the surnames of the actors, along with incomprehensible marks and the notations of the director. It was not possible to decipher them successfully. Unfortunately, in the archives of the theatre the directive about the beginning of work and the cast list was not preserved. Work on the play began in December 1965.
2 Volatile idealistic character from John Osborne's 1956 play, *Look Back in Anger.*

Chapter 3

Rehearsal records of Anatoly Efros's production of *The Seagull* at the Lenkom Theatre, 1965–1966

About the transcripts[1]

These records were written more than 40 [now 50] years ago, solely from interest in the work of the director.

> It has been known for a long time how it difficult is to transfer the secret of the birth of a production on paper. Nevertheless, such attempts do not cease and, as it happens, they appear to be reasonably useful. Sometimes theatre rehearsals show a special creative universe that is difficult to comprehend until the end, but living inside it is akin to good luck personified.
>
> (Gnessa Plyatskovska)
>
> It is very difficult to communicate the features of Efros's method of work. Everything is very simple – he simply talks to the actors about life and the play, simply shares his feelings, but gradually you are taken prisoner by the special world built by Efros, where there is no place for either literary or theatrical stereotypes, where the exposed nerves of a subtle, clever artist respond to the pain, injustice, rudeness, and disrespect for a human being. He feels a part of everything that he wants to tell the audience. And he infects the actors with this feeling. The process is subtle and difficult to perceive.
>
> But maybe to embody what occurred at rehearsals of *The Seagull* at the Lenkom, even in the most imperfect way, will allow us to touch the secret of the creativity of one of the most talented directors of the twentieth century.
>
> (Inez Sidorina)

Cast list[2]

Irina Nikolaevna Arkadina	Elena Fadeeva
Konstantin Gavrilovich Treplev	Valentin Smirnitsky, Valentin Gaft
Peter Nikolaevich Sorin	Arkady Vovsi
Nina Mikhailovna Zarechnaya	Olga Yakovleva

Ilya Afanasyevich Shamraev	Vladimir Solovyov, Leonid Kanevsky
Polina	Zoya Kuznetsova
Masha	Antonina Dmitrieva
Boris Arkadevich Trigorin	Alexander Shirvindt, Vsevelod Larionov
Evgeny Sergeevich Dorn	Alexander Pelevin
Simeon Semyonitch Medvedenko	Lev Durov
Jacob	Nikolai Kashirin
Cook	Dmitry Goshev
Maid	Nina Gorshkova
	§
Director	Anatoly Efros
Designers	Vladimir Lalevich, Nikolai Sosunov
Assistant Director	M. F. Rutkovskaya

13 December 1965[P]
Table rehearsal
Rehearsal hall
Act I

EFROS. The first act does not begin with Masha and Medvedenko, but with Treplev. He runs on stage and walks around for a long time, wanting to concentrate.

Efros demonstrates.

Then Masha enters, she is frank, she shows her love for Treplev almost impudently. She looks at him fixedly, internally saying: "Our souls do not unite because of Nina Zarechnaya . . . Because . . . "

Sorin asks her to tell her father to let them unchain the [barking] dog.

> **MASHA**. Talk to my father yourself, I will not do it. Keep me out of it, please. *(To Medvedenko.)* Let's go . . . [3]
> **EFROS**. *(To Dmitrieva–Masha.)* Imagine you are contemplating a beautiful picture, and someone tears it away from you and wants to give you two kopeks for it. Masha has something like this reaction to Sorin's request.

If we grasp this pivotal point very strongly from the very beginning, then we will have what we need. We know nothing about Chekhov, about traditions, about Chekhovian poetry. Here is a play – we need to play it without knowing anything. An "anti-Chekhovian" performance begins. People step on stage, make a fuss, absorbed in themselves.

> He reads the beginning of the first act rapidly.

For us there is no Chekhov yet, there is no first dialogue, there is [simply] a medley of natural passions.

> Scene: Treplev, Sorin, Nina

(To Vovsi–Sorin.) Imagine that you see a person who is dear to you, whom you love, and you see that he is loaded with explosives to blow himself up. You need to defuse him.

Treplev's "multifocal" conversations are not conversations at all and not dialogue. Treplev is entirely involved in the preparation of the performance. Even his well-known monologues – "We need new forms" – are not monologues either. This whole scene is for him – a burden. The following scene, when the performance will begin, is actually what is important to him. But the present scene should be mundane that "she loves me, she loves me not" has nothing in common with guessing about a flower, he is simply marking time. All his conversations are a protection against the moment all of us are familiar with: waiting for the full-dress rehearsal or the opening night. This is just the beginning, and the heroine is not present. The scene should be played as if she is *not present*, but actually she *is present*. Moreover, very intensely. Sorin sees all this: something is going on with Treplev, it is necessary to get him to talk, otherwise he will die.

Then Nina arrives. She lives only for the performance, and there is no love for Treplev; there is friendship, sympathy, but not love.

In this scene Nina turns into Treplev, and Treplev turns into Sorin. Treplev tries to get into her soul, but Nina uses cunning and changes the subject: "What kind of tree is that? Why is it so dark?" All the first scenes go very quickly. Then the monsters appear – the stage audience . . .

> Entrance of the stage audience.

Slowly the first spectator enters. He does not hurry up, he whistles. Dorn and Polina enter. Her love for Dorn is shown literally in the form of physical attention, guardianship – like a grandmother and her granddaughter.

Nothing must be known beforehand. Yesterday I saw a performance at the Mossoviet Theatre, and I knew everything beforehand – not only the plot, but even the scenery, byplay, and staging.

(To Pelevin–Dorn.) In the second act, we will have a croquet ground. Here you will have croquet balls in your hand. And you will toss them in the air all the time while you are talking.

> Efros demonstrates this, energetically turning his body, as if throwing a spear, he sings: "Do not tell me my youth was wasted . . . "

The movements can be different. The point here is that the movements show Dorn discharging a buildup of nervous energy.

Do not play melancholy or dreaminess. And none of the women's lines should be played for atmosphere, environment, or poetry. This is the biggest challenge.

> His uses an example from the second act for an explanation of the style of the performance as a whole.

At all times, we will reach for moments of full, decisive aggravation, instead of pensiveness, hopelessness.

It is not necessary to render the sense especially. We live, and you and the audience already draw conclusions from our own lives. We know the sense, of course, we know it is feeling, emotion, but we do not play it.

We will do away with Nina's foolish white dress. Let's dress her somehow differently. She murmurs her monologue as though it were a prayer and does not say it like a monologue.

And as soon as the performance begins, Arkadina understands at once that it is a performance opposed to her life and opposed to her art. Enraged, Treplev literally pushes Nina off the stage.

Today the relations between fathers and children is different from that of Chekhovian times. Formerly fathers were quiet, and children fumed. Now, it is just the opposite. Therefore, Treplev pushes Nina off the stage: we will not act the clown before them. These Philistines understand nothing.

Arkadina is opposed to the terrible questions raised in Treplev's performance. They frighten and revolt her. He, this youngster, dares to teach her?! This is a scene of grandiose outrage. "What is the matter with him?" Arkadina asks. Not "What happened?" But "What is the matter with him that he dares to teach me?" This remark has to be prepared for by everyone on stage.

"Nobody has the right to separate spirit from a matter . . ." Interestingly, Medvedenko addresses this to Arkadina. She was at the highest point of her anger against avant-gardism and she was championed by, let's say, a bus driver. Then it became disgusting to her, and she said ". . . Let's not talk about plays and atoms. The evening is so nice!"

Nina and Trigorin's acquaintance scene. He is struck by the fact that she is young, beautiful, it is possible for him to fall in love, it is impossible for him to fall in love. This scene lasts an uncomfortably long time. Then a pause so long it seems like everyone forgot something. It makes everyone feel strange. Then Dorn says: "I believe the curtain can be raised now. Otherwise, it feels strange." Even Shamraev says something because of the uneasiness. They live through all their loves in this pause.

They ask Nina to remain. She speaks tearfully: "It is impossible."

When she leaves, everyone starts talking at once: they have to smooth over the scandal somehow.

If all the scenes of [characters' internal] assessment are played economically, they will have an enormous importance.

Dorn remains alone and thinks: what was this, he has to understand what just occurred. Words are always more primitive than feelings. After all, something happened that could not be expected in advance. It was impossible to expect such works as *Waterloo Bridge* or the English performance, *Look Back in Anger*, in advance – they amazed you.

Treplev returns. Dorn rushes to him, uneasy, with tears. But Treplev is in a different world: Everyone has fled, the swine. Only after five minutes pass does Treplev realize that Dorn ran to him, and in what manner he ran. He silently embraces him. Dorn continues to speak to him, but Treplev immediately remembers: "Excuse me, where Nina Zarechnaya?"

> Efros performs this passage with the actor Gennady Saifulin.[4]
>
> Further coaching of the scene: Masha watches over Treplev.

> **MASHA**. You should go home, Konstantin Gavrilovich. Your mother is expecting you. She is upset.

He has run away, escaped.

And the following scene [with Dorn] is based on what has just happened.

> **MASHA**. I suffer. Nobody knows my sufferings! *(Puts her head on Dorn's breast, silently.)* I love Konstantin.
> **DORN**. How nervous they all are! How nervous! And so much love . . . Oh, magical lake! *(Tenderly)* But what can I do, my child? What can I do?

Masha says to Dorn: Tell me, what I should do, tell me, what? And Dorn answers: What you are asking of me – I do not know the answer.

With this ambiguous ending, the first act comes to an end.

The second act begins with everyone taking out croquet equipment and arranging it.[5]

Arkadina is energized by yesterday's events, she feels all of it, she boils with this energy.

Is anything not clear?

Should we play the first act?

> The actors smile confusedly.[6]

Really, some days we will get up on stage right away. We will not play things correctly, of course, but we will sketch out the act and then deal with what is needed after that.

Our task is not for us to experience the poetry or even for the spectators to do so. We need to feel the clusters of human interweavings, nervous textures. But in this, I think, there is also the poetry of Chekhov.

I have thought about the role of plasticity [i.e., bodily mobility] in modern theatre, about the plastic side of psychological theatre. We can analyze everything wonderfully, but if we do not lay all this out with the necessary plastic expression – it will turn out to be nothing. So, I also want to jump on stage a bit earlier.

However, this plastic expression needs to be totally different from the best MAT productions of Chekhov.

VOVSI–SORIN. But how can we understand the plastic side of psychological art?

EFROS. I have said it is necessary to play a scene so it is clear that the most important thing is the next scene. The beginning of one is embedded in the other, the subsequent is embedded in the previous, plastically embedded. But the plasticity of the actor – this is only one side. The entire space needs to fit around you, so there is continuous unified motion!

14 December 1965[P]
Table rehearsal
Rehearsal hall
Act II

EFROS. There is something interesting here. Nemirovich's best discovery about Chekhov was "Contact without communication." But it has already been seen in so many Chekhov performances that it has ceased to awaken any emotion from infinite repetitions. Now, [our production will show] complete misunderstanding [among the characters] with absolutely stormy communication.

In the first act, we need to understand there is no Chekhovian "Impressionism" or poetry. It is absolutely different: dramatic collisions. Nina is played along these lines: "I fell into the society of Hemingway [i.e., Trigorin] and Marlene Dietrich [i.e., Arkadina]. I am 20 years old, I am living in enthusiastic ecstasy, adoration. And suddenly I see that he is afraid of betrayal, or they secretly make things up, or some other nonsense that is absolutely not right for a genius. And I have come to know this [for myself]." An icon comes to life, in the flesh. This is knowledge of the world and it is always dramatic. That it is possible to fall in love with an icon, love is possible in the flesh. Assessing, learning. Therefore, all the remarks and stage directions – [such as] "enthusiastically"– are nonsense.

She "grew thin from knowing" [so to speak].[7] On the scales are Treplev and Trigorin. "Hemingway wins this fight," since childishness and romanticism grow pale before the depth and complexity of life. And we should play this. Then there will be meaning. In current Chekhovian theatre, instead of an iron framework of meaning they provide "Impressionism," but this is incorrect. I said to you at the previous rehearsal that we will have a croquet ground and all the events will be accompanied by the blows of wooden mallets on croquet balls – a harsh accompaniment to the life of the characters.

We are all filled with ourselves, but we are made up of simple events. To understand them, to catch them, what these *events* [sic] are – not physical actions, drinking tea etc., but events – they are the key to unlocking Chekhov.

What occurs to the characters in the play? What do they want? What do they leave the first act with?

Arkadina, all torn to pieces because withering time is catching up with her, and so by means of super-coarse means of communication she will prove: "I am better than Nina, the little girl who has something that attracts my Trigorin." And she proves it! She reads Maupassant, showing that even he understands nothing about love, and nobody understands anything. Also, there is nothing of the aristocrat in her. She can adjust a garter and be frankly tactless.

Masha remarks elegiacally that her life drags on endlessly "like a train," she has nothing more than the rough desire to tell everyone, to explain her personal situation to everyone, everyone, clutching at everyone, everyone. She is only afraid to approach Treplev, she will not tell this to him.

There are few places where there would not be direct communication in the play. Also, the second act does not begin with a pause to create a mood, but from the brutality of everyone getting in each other's way. A bundle of energy. Everyone needs to interrupt each other.

When Nina arrives, Arkadina actively rushes to keep Nina out of their world, and from this [desire] comes her demand: "Where is Trigorin?" This is like saying "Where is my man?" From this [same desire,] very coldly: "I am reading Maupassant," but behind this is: "I am reading, but you are not allowed yet."

Then she attaches herself to her son instead of Trigorin. And Masha asks to read something from his play. How is this perceived by Nina? Nina thinks: at Hemingway's house, it is as if they are asking her to sing a melody that Konstantin played on an accordion at the local club yesterday. This is absurd beyond belief. She wants to understand what is happening. But Arkadina and Masha insist. And all this is aggravating.

The Doctor and Sorin quarrel. The doctor hates the patient and vice versa. To Doctor Dorn the fact that a 60-year-old patient still wants to be treated by a doctor is absolutely disgusting, that he still wants to live. And Dorn finally exclaims that I am 55 years old too, and it is time for me to be treated, life goes on – how can you stop it? But none of this is interesting for Masha because Treplev is not present. Meantime Dorn plays croquet and sings "Oh, speak to her, you flowers," while thinking: "I will throw this mallet and somebody."

Efros demonstrates.

And further. At the theatre, they always do this in *The Seagull*: before Shamraev's arrival there is calm, hot weather, then he enters, blusters comically, gets the same in return, and nothing is clear. But Chekhov has reinforced concrete logic. All of them live dreadfully, and in this scene about horses, Shamraev spills everything out about how he lives: "To hell with your horses. Get yourself another manager." And as for Nina, "Hemingway asked for a car, and they refused him," and "Marlene Dietrich washes her own linens and has no money." It is a nightmare. Enter Treplev, who sees everything differently, for him Trigorin is Anatoly Sofronov, and Arkadina is Vera Maretskaya, and them cleaning their own linens and their tragedy are phony. They and Nina do not understand each other at all. They speak different languages. Treplev regards everything like this: "There is this fat type, and she is already past the time when they applaud for her anymore." He cannot breathe from the weight of the truth he has found. He lashes out at her with the cruel truth of her behavior. He is boiling over.

And now, if we do not look at Trigorin from Treplev's point of view, he too is a dramatic figure. He too [like Arkadina] is not simply rich and plump. But here it is more complicated. Let's get hold of him. He writes on fences. I remember how I once visited Alexander Volodin at his vacation home, and I witnessed this scene. He came up to greet us. He was somehow overcome internally, then he suddenly rushed into the bathroom. And when he came out, I realized he ran in there to write down some thought, some flash of an image, because he was afraid it would become obscured, stopped up, and would escape. It seems to me something similar exists in Trigorin. He is a writer first, and he seizes on Nina: "Tell me everything about yourself, young women never turn out right for me [in my writing]. Talk to me now, and I will write it down."

And only when they both understand everything, at the end, they need to exit. A whole life is lived in three minutes.

It seems to me that when the second act comes to an end, we need to clearly see that a cycle has come to an end. Everything is clear, the characters were distributed. They met and dispersed. And this should force us to think further. It is as though we do not know this Chekhov. We take a breath, and then – come what may.

I saw *Three Sisters* recently. The beginning, as usual, was contact without communication. It seemed to me a feeble imitation. I would have wished the characters to specifically remember that a year ago the moon was the same, that they sat here now as they did before, but everything was different back then – father had died, and we had to start to live. Remember Vershinin and Masha, their well-known "Tram-tam-tam," after which he said, "Let's philosophize." However, it was played like this: they paused and then began to philosophize. Chekhov was transformed into philosophy. It was boring, and basically the "Tram-tam-tam" [the love interest] had gotten so lost that it would have been better to talk about what would exist after a thousand years. It is psychology, not naked philosophy. So far, I think we can only aspire to this. The audience's reaction should be three seconds behind the events on stage, not ahead of them.

In *The Seagull,* I would like us to escape from the captivity of traditions and feel concretely, inside the flesh of these characters, to understand what sort of irritations define their life, to understand what excites them now, this minute. And then there will be no more efforts to see and hear and want to criticize everything, but something different – to prove to everyone how good it is.

FADEEVA–ARKADINA. The psychology and passion will be modern, but won't [the essence of] Chekhov's era disappear?
EFROS. In [Pushkin's historical play] *Boris Godunov* the boyars depart very quietly, and everything comes to an end. We all [tend to] oversimplify an era, but we should bare its nerves, its action. *Three Sisters* at the Moscow Art Theatre was a tremendous production. But the spectator [of the era] just before the war could not accept it anymore, since those were some else's cares, someone else's troubles, unintelligible.[8] But I am convinced *Three Sisters* can convey everything, and can do so for today. Only we need to find different keys to unlock the essence of the play.

14 December 1965[S]
Rehearsal hall
Table rehearsal
Act II

EFROS. The second act is very complex, and it looks as if it is elegiac, as if everything happens *impressionistically*, as it were. But the poetry is not exactly *impressionistic;* there is something else – a battle of wits, of characters.

Imagine I am 20 years old, I am young, enthusiastic, and I have fallen into the company of Hemingway and Marlene Dietrich. And suddenly I see that Hemingway, let's say, is afraid to knock on a door, and Marlene Dietrich suffers from rheumatism. Instead of being icons, they have turned into ordinary people. This is the first awareness of the drama and complexity of life. And Nina says: "Hemingway is afraid of knocking on a door, he is like everyone else." But it is a strange thing. An icon cannot fall in love, he can only delight in love, and love makes demands of the flesh. Nina loves the real Hemingway. Therefore, she falls in love with him rapturously. She grew thin from this knowing [so to speak], she began to belong to their world.[9] Treplev became a stranger to her. He has neither fear nor despair, no [exciting] past life, for Nina, he is – a boy.

Chekhov has created steely logic, but instead of that, [to some of us] it appears that he has given us *impressionism*.

All of them, the more they are fully fledged heroes up till now, up till our own time, the less they are fully fledged – the more they have lived, the less they continue to live. But yesterday something happened. Arkadina had a quarrel with her son, and Trigorin behaved shamelessly, in front of everyone, with the girl.

After everything that happened, when Trigorin and Arkadina went to their room, they spoke reluctantly, exchanging dry remarks to each other.

And then this morning she got up, got dressed, went out, and began to show her superiority compared to Nina: look here, which one of us is better, younger looking, who is more interesting, I am spry as a chick, I am always in shape, etc.

And Masha is the opposite: how badly I live, my soul is torn to pieces, I have no desire to live. She needs to explain the story of her fate.

A third member of this scene – Dorn, vigorously knocking croquet balls around, redirecting his strained nerves, singing: "Tell her, my flowers . . . "

> Efros demonstrates this point: his movement is full of nervous energy, which is contrary to the neutrality of his intonation.

There is a cluster of nervous energy here, which is what we need in this first scene of the second act.

Then Sorin and Nina enter.

Interestingly, there is no direct communication in Chekhov. Pauses arise, but they are unclear. To Nina, yesterday's play was quite uninteresting. Today, now, she is at Hemingway's house and suddenly she is reminded that everyone saw her yesterday at the club [so to speak], on amateur night, beautifully playing the harmonica.

Scene with Sorin and Dorn.

In the next scene, Sorin and Dorn show doctor vs. patient hostility. Wild hostility. But behind this hostility something quite different is hidden: Dorn mocks Sorin, who wants to be ministered to at 60 years of age, and because Dorn himself is 55, he feels it is also time for him to be ministered to. And the finishing stoke is a scene for Nina.

> **ARKADINA**. Well it is nice to be with you, my friends, it is nice to listen to you, but . . . to sit in one's room and study a role is much better!
> **NINA** *(enthusiastically)*. Yes! I know exactly what you mean.
> **DORN** *(sings)*. Go and tell her, my flowers . . .

On his line Dorn strikes the croquet balls again. Shamraev enters and refuses to provide the horses for Arkadina to go to town.

For Nina, this is unbelievable: they are refusing a carriage for Hemingway and Marlene Dietrich. And at this moment Konstantin enters, for whom Trigorin is not Hemingway, but some [scribbler] Sofronov, and Arkadina is not Marlene Dietrich. And Nina has betrayed Treplev by moving into their camp. He speaks to her about it, but Nina is not strong enough to understand and listen to his words. She does not hear half his words.

Trigorin appears and Konstantin leaves. In my opinion, Trigorin is a colossal personality: he continually writes, cannot not write, "smokes and drinks vodka. Always in black. Is loved by her teacher . . . " He is ready to record your thoughts directly on a fence [nearby, if he had to]. Once I was at a writers' retreat with Volodin. Visitors continuously annoyed and bothered him there. And I noticed that he ran to the bathroom to write something down.

Trigorin and Nina want to obtain an understanding of each other, but in different ways.

The path of their thinking is something like this: Trigorin: "Nothing succeeds for me, everything I write is superficial. Tell me about your life, I want to be able to describe it." Nina: "But you are famous, loved, you ride in a chariot . . . " Trigorin: "What do you mean, what chariots, what celebrity. I am suffering, I am a failure." In three minutes, they live their entire lives. This comprises their entire conversation.

After the second act – the plot line is full of knots for Nina and Trigorin, full of loose ends for Nina and Treplev. But as they were fully fledged heroes before, so they are fully fledged heroes now. This [circumstance] provides further knots.

Playing *The Seagull*, we must forget this is Chekhov, we just have to breathe and live. And the audience should understand something quite different, really beautiful, that they once understood at the Moscow Art Theatre . . .

FADEEVA–ARKADINA. But if we all play modern people will it turn out to be Chekhov?

EFROS. It will.

FADEEVA–ARKADINA. But it was a different era . . .

EFROS. The hell with that, the era. Everything will turn out if we live the essence and not merely deal with external physical actions. We all filled with lots of everything, but our actions are composed of the simplest of events. To understand them, to grasp what a [given] event is – not physical actions – drinking tea, etc., but [inner] events are the key to unlocking Chekhov.

Three Sisters at the Moscow Art Theatre was wonderful, magnificent, but, after all, there were things [in the play itself] they were not looking for. When the characters dreamed of "work, work" – I could not help thinking: What the hell! – really, but we [here] cannot wait for Sunday.

In the *Three Sisters* currently running, everyone lives, lives, but when they get into disputes – "let's dream a little," – everything is switched off, everything becomes different, but I think this [dreaming] should be an extension of their life, they are also passionately searching, solving the problems of their life in these disputes.

> Ultimately, Efros does not so much tell but – in a manner peculiar to him – perform the lives of the characters through the episode in question.

The most important thing is that the memory of our performance should not be its external manner of behaving, but everything that happened with the characters, their emotional upheavals.

> They play the second act. Where all the major events live, exposing the nerve tissue of the action. It is hard to describe.

In our performance, I would like no one to notice how the characters are dressed, or the furniture, or the wigs, or the hats. I would like everyone to be involved in the breathing [consciousness] of these people.

16 December 1965[P]
Rehearsal hall
Act III

EFROS. Interestingly, they always emphasize departure when analyzing this act, departure – everything is subordinated to departure. But this is only words. We have to find what to express them through. I remember in *The Seagull* at the Mossoviet Theatre there was a table, liqueur glasses and suitcases. They sat, talked to Masha, but except for the waiting suitcases, nothing was said about departure, and the result was nonsense. What is the secret? They analyzed the scene and said that Masha talks about life. Where did the boredom arise from? I think we need to feel Chekhov as a breath of wind, instead of a solid mass. Movement, instead of mass. One can play departure, but perhaps the pulsation of departure should be in their blood.

They are carrying things away, disturbing everything, but Masha wants time to tell Trigorin all about herself. [What is really happening] here is wanting to have time, and then there will be departure, departure in the blood, instead of theatre fiction. The tree leaves begin to rustle from the draft created by the departure.[10] The words are the same, the setting is the same, but in a few minutes, nothing will be the same . . . I am convinced that the issue is not in the table and not in the liqueur glasses, and it has nothing to do with the lyrical atmosphere of a "Chekhovian" farewell conversation. That's all wrong here.

Efros performs as Masha, bursting out with her story convulsively, aggressively, hastily: "I am speaking to you as to a writer" – there is so much frankness! But only to a writer, after all, because it might be useful for him.

Efros performs as Trigorin. He is completely in motion – he is very restless, damn little time, he needs to see Nina, he can neither concentrate nor listen. Only a few words of hers occasionally break though into his consciousness. He reacts to them. So only the illusion of a dialogue is created.

EFROS. And during their scene, Nina, who is rushing around somewhere nearby, enters and exits. And since this is a walk-through room, everyone walking through is in full view, it is impossible to talk, it is impossible to say what you want. And everyone lives absolutely in different ways. Trigorin needs to hold something within himself, to withhold something from the others, a piece of himself, a few seconds remain, and soon everything will come to an end. Everything that we talked about is the same, but we need to get this feeling of departure into our blood.

In all the earlier performances Trigorin has moved about and spoken suggestively, sufferingly. The same with Arkadina. But Arkadina is in an awful hurry: the hell with it, the sooner we are out of here the better. She gathers her things. Always the actress, she is never ready until the last minute, she is not dressed, and with the shamelessness and exposure of an actress, she is doing this in front of everyone. The issue is not that this is frankly rude, but that it is a blatant maneuver. And there is ease and lightness in it. Like fluff that does not settle to the ground.

> **SORIN**. *(whistles, then speaks hesitantly).* I think it would be best, if you . . . gave him a little money. First, he needs to dress properly, and so on. He has been wearing the same suit of clothes for the last three years, and he goes outdoors without a coat . . . *(Laughs.)* And it wouldn't hurt for him to have a little fun . . . To go abroad, or something . . . After all, it does not cost much.

Now for Sorin . . . There are old men for whom an elementary act – to telephone someone – is a grandiose event that occupies half a lifetime. He prepares, he worries, he changes his mind, etc. And if he needs to ask for money, it is like begging for alms.

It is for the boy rather than himself – which is even more humiliating, even more awful. It is even hard to choose the right moment, everything is public here. He does not quite understand what he says, but splashes out everything all together – "I feel bad," "Give me some money." Then he cannot hold anything back. And he faints!

His head begins to spin. He is weak, but not sick. It is something terrible, as though he will fall to pieces. Arkadina forgets about collecting her things, about her clothing. And after everything settles down – she has a severe reaction. White as chalk, she lies down on the sofa.

In the turmoil of Sorin's recovery, Treplev enters. Nobody [in the audience] should think that this is a tragic entrance for Treplev to "explain" everything [to his mother before she leaves]. Absolutely not.

The son consoles his mother and, consoling, explains that his uncle cannot live in the country and he needs money. He does not know that this is the worst thing he could say to her. She shouts, and then Treplev sees that this is even worse for her than his uncle's collapse. Therefore, he asks her to change his bandage, wants to slow her down, return her to everyday life.

Treplev consoles Arkadina, he wants her to depart happy. This seldom happens with children. They do not speak this way with their mother, do not talk so openly about love. But he cannot give away the only thing he had left – "her." And therefore, he needs to continue this declaration of love, even when the words do not come easily any more. So, when his lines are about Trigorin – it is a wound, but not conscious. And already Arkadina starts to consider how to offend him more strongly, how to pay him back. Therefore, her insults should be measured at the beginning.

Then the frenzy, the fuse is lit, when it is no longer so important what to say. What is important is that it causes pain. And then mother consoles the son: "Do not cry. There is no need to cry . . . "

It is challenging, how can we negotiate the pauses? How do we maintain the momentum, get away from the pauses, move forward to the next scene without stopping? And what follows is – Trigorin. First, he wants to explain: "I fell in love, can't you really understand that?" But she really does not understand.

> **ARKADINA**. Am I really so old and ugly that you do not mind talking to me about other women? *(Embraces him and kisses.)* You are mad! My fine, marvelous . . . You are the last page of my life! *(Kneels.)* My delight, my pride, my joy . . . *(Embraces his knees.)* If you leave me for one hour, I will not survive, I will go mad, my amazing, magnificent, my master . . .

She explains they are so close that she is the only one who understands him, reads his works and understands. This is almost without emotion – a catalog of proofs. This is also a modern twist – to deprive everything of emotional suffocation, as it were.

Some are inclined to rattle on about departure in general. What is needed here is concreteness: Trigorin enters and calls offstage: "I forgot my cane!" So that everyone would know and suspect nothing. Like getting on a bus and saying [offhandedly], "I have a pass!"

And now let's question everything and try to figure it all out once more.

When departure is "in the blood" – the eyes start wandering, and those who were only visiting are [mentally] already no longer here. How will Trigorin and Masha's scene be played? Simply talk?! But the [overall] rhythm is different, it is established by the [ongoing] departure. This means that other motives force Masha to talk about herself. I think Masha needs to speak with unusual precision about what has happened to her.

FADEEVA–ARKADINA. When Eduardo de Filippo spoke about what happened in the front lines [of the war], I understood him. He did not repeat himself. Why does the same thing happen here? She does not want anything except relief from her unhappiness.

EFROS. There are people with a fixation (they are unfortunate people), afflicted with a passion to prove how unhappy they are, to reveal all their spiritual problems. This makes them happy.

DMITRIEVA–MASHA. But she wants them to help her.

DUROV–MEDVEDENKO. No, it is simply important that at least one person is aware of her destiny.

EFROS. If she just asks for help, concretely speaking, it would be less [interesting] than what we have come up with. After all, she speaks to the writer because she is convinced it is interesting to him.
DUROV–MEDVEDENKO. She gets pleasure from this?
EFROS. Yes, yes! These unfortunates are proud of their misfortunes. It gives them relevance. I would make sure they run from her. We are going in the right path. After all, as soon as she leaves, they say terrible things about her.
DMITRIEVA–MASHA. It is clear. Her life is empty and uninteresting. Suffering makes it more interesting for her.
EFROS. And in the fourth act everything comes to an end. Everything interesting. And then boorishly, swinishly, [Masha says] to her husband: "Go. Get out of my sight." Maybe she has stopped living.

What do we do so often? We take some characterization, put a case around it, and give it to the audience. No sort of revelations. We already know in advance whom to give role to and how to play it: black dress, she drinks – and all the rest . . .

But let's return to Arkadina and Treplev, to their scene. Let's try to do an etude. Imagine that I have finished the business of Dorn fainting, I am upset, and you Sasha [Shirvindt–Trigorin] know that I often like to rehearse with you, to distract myself.

> Shirvindt–Trigorin persuades her to rehearse and consoles her.
> 2nd variant. She declares her love to Efros–Trigorin and accuses him of changing places with Gaft–Treplev. From here on, naturally, there are insults.

FADEEVA–ARKADINA. Everything is good [in the etudes], but they are strangers [to each other].
EFROS. True, they are strangers.
FADEEVA–ARKADINA. But it is more terrible if they are friends.
EFROS. Wait a minute. Here we are insulting each other, trying to discover each other's sorest spot. For example, I could shout at Sasha–Shirvindt: "You would be better off doing trivial little skits instead of real theatre." This hurts the most. Then I hurt back even more. And suddenly I see – he is trembling! My son! And immediately everything comes back as it was in his childhood.
FADEEVA–ARKADINA. Wouldn't it be more interesting to reach for her son?
EFROS. No. She only pays attention to her son when he starts talking about Trigorin. Before that, her child's love was not important enough compared with what was happening to herself.

The third act should begin as if we entered an apartment at the moment of departure. Everything comes out in this moment of departure – Masha wants to express her life, Nina wants to establish a connection, Sorin wants to decide and request, then he faints. All in ten minutes.

Now we have one quality – confusion. This is invaluable because from this comes movement. But we also need to disturb the layout on stage and advance everyone forward towards their goal.

In the third and fourth acts, there are more traditional scenes. Therefore, it is more difficult.

Consider the structure of the second act. Everything leads to the thought: How can they live? How can they live?! One cries, and then another one, one's life breaks down, another's was broken long ago, and nobody understands each other. They are irritated by each attempt of someone to break through this misunderstanding. I want someone to understand me, but I do not want to understand anyone else. Alexei Popov continually repeated in his directing course that, when analyzing a play, [too rarely] directors study the era that generated the play or the artist who created the [play's] point of view, but [only] the record of commentaries about the play. Thus, theatrical experience, instead of life experience, becomes the basis for the new performance, creating generalized, second-hand work and clichés. We're trying to get away from that.

We're already doing the first and second acts absolutely unconventionally, without "impressionism." As when shadows fall over our wooden croquet court, and then there is a song, which is both lyrical and a counterpoint. And Nina's hard modern assessments – her sudden horror of knowing "They are just like everyone else." And Treplev's monologue, which nobody wanted to listen to when it was not related to anything, will begin to sound absolutely differently if it is related to Treplev's desire to hold onto Nina at all costs.

And all this occurs along with the sounds of the wickets and mallets and wooden knocks of croquet balls. This is the first two acts.

And the third and fourth acts are "turmoil." Scenically, this is less effective. The locale is a room. And the [third act] action of a tuning fork – with two liqueur glasses. We all sit at different ends. Everyone is occupied with miscellanies. Masha is tearing through her own story. This is the tuning fork of the act, and everything should be in harmony with it, without letting down, without discharging the tension. Sorin and Arkadina – there is anger in their eyes, since they have been placed in circumstances where general conversation is impossible. It is like you are acting at the mad speed of Goldoni, but you still need to talk with your wife.

Arkadina's chair needs to be inconveniently low. This creates the awkward position required.

LARIONOV–TRIGORIN. It is the psychology of a communal apartment. But in a hundred square meters of space.[11] What are they like when they're in an open space?

EFROS. Not ruling out the psychology of a small area, a narrow space, we need to understand Chekhov. For us, the actors, it is the little physical feelings of the moment!!!

Actually, Larionov's question is absolutely typical and very precisely defines the relation of actors to the classics – "they," "them over there." But not we, us over here. If there is no movement in time, there will be no birth of a living performance either. But for this to take place, I should feel myself in circumstances close to the circumstances of the play. But I have no circumstances close to the circumstances of characters who are so distant in social position and actuality. I have other circumstances . . .

16 December 1965[S]
Table rehearsal
Rehearsal hall
Act III

EFROS. I remember the third act of *The Seagull* at a certain Moscow theatre very well. Masha was talking with Trigorin. He is in traveling clothes, they drink, she tells him about herself. Then Nina enters, again there is conversation, etc. Everything was boring, trite . . .

In Chekhov, you need to catch the puff of a breeze, not a large mass. These are my usual words, they are inadequate, but I cannot find any others. Imagine that a breeze blows by, only a breeze, but all the foliage stirs, changes direction.[12]

What happens in the third act? Checking out, but this departure is in the blood. We must feel that in 15 minutes everything will change, different communications will start to become operative. Perpetual motion, an endless breeze that rustles the wispy bushes. And everything is driven into the blood.

The first scene is Masha and Trigorin. She hurries to announce that she has decided to leave with Medvedenko, she will tear out the love from her heart. In 15 minutes, there will be no one to tell this to.

And in the important meeting scene with Nina and Trigorin – extend the moment of their meeting, 15 minutes later they will have to part.

Arkadina, as a seasoned actress, dresses herself, gets herself ready to go. As an actress, she has no shame of doing this in front of others. The kind of thinking that happens when you are not yet dressed and are late for a train, and you are overwhelmed with thoughts. Something happens, you are beset with all this, and furthermore continuously occupied with something [else].

What happens to Sorin here is what happens in older people when they need to do something that is difficult for them, to request something. In such cases, they reach almost to the point of fainting. This faint is what happens to Sorin – it is so difficult for him to talk to Arkadina about money for Treplev.

There must be something like that happening, so that afterwards Arkadina needs to stop dressing, lie on the sofa, and grow pale, everything has stopped.

And when Treplev runs in just as Sorin has fainted, he also finds her pale, she is turned away to the wall. He does not know what to do to get her out of this state, and then: "Mother, change my bandage. You do it so well." He wants to turn her attention back to domestic things. She gets up slowly, pulls her legs off the couch, and returns to life. The main thing here is not the scene itself, but the change from what was before – from Sorin's fainting. Therefore, Treplev started talking about childhood memories, the laundress, about the dancers who visited them to drink coffee. He wants to calm down his mother. This is an unusual situation for children.

And besides, he can no longer give his love to anyone else. Now he has no one, except his mother.

When their exchange turns to Trigorin – he has no strength to continue this topic. He walks slowly, reluctantly. Gradually, the scene switches to the fact that Treplev does not wish to annoy her.

At first, you need to do everything very steadily . . .

> **ARKADINA**. Decadent!
> **KONSTANTIN**. Go to a nice little theatre and play in the pitiful, inept plays there!
> **ARKADINA**. I have never played in such plays. Leave me alone! You are pathetic and unable to write even a vaudeville. Kiev bourgeois! Parasite!
> **KONSTANTIN**. Cheapskate!
> **ARKADINA**. Beggar!
> *Konstantin sits quietly crying.*

EFROS. Then: "Do not cry. There is no need to cry . . . " – This is deeply internal for Arkadina.

Trigorin reaches for Nina at this point because she offers a clean, fresh feeling. He grabs at a thread capable of revitalizing him.

Arkadina's task is to convince him it is impossible, that he cannot leave her, "You and I are so close that what you ask is impossible. I alone know what you mean, every day I read your works." And for him to lose Nina is to lose his moment of rebirth. With a modern approach to *The Seagull*, an emotional turnabout is needed.

> **TRIGORIN** *(coming back)*. I forgot my cane. It seems to be out there on the terrace.

This statement of his sounds loud and unnecessary, like a person who, entering a tram, declares [offhandedly]: "I have a pass." For Trigorin, this is a cover. Returning for his cane, he actually wants to see Nina.

Interestingly, the characters are filled with each other in these moments. They are filled with each other before parting. All Trigorin's words at the end, "these wonderful eyes" and "modest features," "gentle smile" – it all sounds like a spell that they must invoke.

Now let's call everything into question.

> Back to the top of the act, reexamining it, and dwelling on some points.

EFROS. Masha needs to tell others everything going on with her, thoroughly and in detail. For her, others need to know. For her relief. This is a mania of unfortunate people – to tell everyone what they are going through. She pours herself out to Arkadina, pours herself out to Dorn, pours herself out to Trigorin.
DMITRIEVA–MASHA. Or maybe she is waiting for help from those people?
EFROS. It is impossible to help her, and she knows it.

Besides if you set yourself such a task, it will be concrete, but flat. Her disease is loneliness, her illness is misfortune. Three acts go on like this, but in the fourth, everything will change. I think they even run away from her. After all, it is reasonable for her to go away, they say terrible things about her: she drinks.
DMITRIEVA–MASHA. She likes it that she suffers?
EFROS. I think she does not realize it, she is not aware of it. You know what is interesting? Usually we think of Masha as a cook, dress her in a black dress, and present her in this nutshell. That is all. And there are no internal discoveries. Even Maretskaya played her this way. But, oddly enough, Masha has lively eyes, she wants to live.

> Efros and Shirvindt perform etudes on the theme of the quarrel and reconciliation of Arkadina and Treplev.

FADEEVA–ARKADINA. Everything is good, but you had a conversation between two strangers, and they are not strangers.
EFROS. But they did extract from this scene what is [usually] impossible to extract. And so, in the process of the scene a shift occurs when everything can be expressed.

I remember the English play, *Look Back in Anger*. They know the laws of expressive movement much better than we do. There is an episode when the insulted wife leaves her husband. The girlfriend remains. She gives Jimmy Porter a slap for everyone – for his wife, for herself... And suddenly she gets confused and sits down. Then she rushes to him and starts kissing him. She understands that he hurts everyone because he himself is harassed to the extreme, he is a Robespierre who was born out of his era. Expressive movement can reveal a lot. It is interesting how a farewell scene can be performed when everyone is in such a state of extreme confusion.

> Efros shows how Arkadina exits, "I gave the cook a ruble. That's for all three of you." The servant is crushed on the spot, slowly retreats. All the confusion is conveyed in expressive movement.

The third act should begin when everyone is completely scattering. Masha tells Trigorin her life, and at this moment Trigorin thinks he sees Nina. Then Sorin painfully asks Arkadina for money for her son, then Sorin faints, Arkadina quarrels with Treplev, her explanation with Trigorin, the meeting with Nina. Imagine everyone's state if all this is going on ten minutes before departure?

The act should be without scenes, it cannot be played like individual scenes between Masha and Trigorin, Treplev and Arkadina, Arkadina and Trigorin, Nina and Trigorin. It must be played continuously, "without scenes."

In the first and second acts, I sense complete clarity. The third is complete clarity with complete uncertainty.

The third and fourth acts are a mess.

The tuning fork of the third act is Masha and Trigorin. This is not a story, but just the opposite. She seeks to tell, but all his thoughts are on Nina. So, the third act is knit together, and goes on and on up to the fainting.

The entire third act is performed.

The Sorin–Arkadina scene is unusual, not only because it is difficult for Sorin to ask for money but also because their dialogue takes place in an absurdly difficult situation. Imagine this: you spend your most important explanation on an elevator or moving escalator before you scatter in different directions. I think, maybe, here Arkadina is placed in an uncomfortably low chair, where it is difficult to see ... This provides the necessary sense.

20 December 1965[P]
Rehearsal hall
Act IV

Efros reads the fourth act.

EFROS. What will happen if we follow all of Chekhov's stage directions? Medvedenko and Masha enter. Masha calls Treplev. He is gone. Pause. Masha and Medvedenko exchange a few remarks. Again, a pause, etc. In fact, this approach is impossible now. It would be straightforward and primitive. From our point of view, it would simply be an illustration – two years have passed, and everyone is unhappy.

But this act should be long, difficult, without pauses, and without moments of reflection, so that everyone's unhappiness would be disclosed gradually. If it is based on the premise that none of the characters notice anything, do not understand what is happening – in that case after the third act there could be a big pause and a voice saying: *"Two years later"* – then the curtain opens, and everything proceeds in the usual rhythms of life. The daily routine goes on without pauses, i.e. without moments when the characters reflect on what is happening. In life, this is reasonable. Sorin, for example, no longer gets out of his chair. Instead, someone pushes him. After all, this has happened to him over the course of two years, and gradually he has managed to get used to it. It should be the same for everyone: the conversations between Masha and Medvedenko, Polina and Treplev.

Efros demonstrates.

There is a routine, a shroud over everything: in the conversation about the plot for a short story, in the story about Genoa, in Trigorin and Treplev's meeting. Everything flows, flows without understandings, neither yours nor that of the characters. But we, the audience, will look at you from afar and understand.

I think when Treplev remains alone in the room – this is the first pause, the first moment of understanding. Then the meeting with Nina. I do not know whether it will be possible for us to do this scene as I said before, Treplev and Nina conducting the whole scene without separating from each other.

DMITRIEVA–MASHA. I understand there is routine in the fourth act, but after all, they have changed internally. Take Masha, aren't there internal changes in her?

EFROS. The circumstances have changed, but they still struggle with them just as before. She has a husband, a child, but her eyes are still on Treplev, and her husband and her child are a vicious circle for her. When Medvedenko asks Masha to return home, and she does not want to go, there is no need to play it with a dramatic awareness, as if it occurred today for the first time. It happens every day, and it needs to be played as an ordinary everyday conversation. There is no need to finalize anything: neither Arkadina's arrival, nor Shamraev's refusal to provide horses for Medvedenko. They do not know what is happening to them, since no one knows it. Day after day, day after day people lead this life. Not a single moment is static. This is a continuous intermediate stage between time and space. Everything that occurs is an intermediate stage: It is an intermediate stage when Masha married and gave birth to her son, it is an intermediate stage when Trigorin arrived there. Even when Treplev shoots himself it is an intermediate stage, and what Dorn said about that event is an intermediate stage. Only very seldom are there separate moments of understanding: "How easy it is to be a philosopher on paper, Doctor, and how difficult it is in practice!"

Horribly, people do not want to be stopped. Shamraev says to Trigorin: Remember, you asked to get the seagull stuffed? – I do not remember, I do not remember – he answers hastily. And Arkadina speaks unceasingly about her success in Kharkov. Everything is transpiring like this. This is how we should approach the so-called "Chekhovian action" and "Chekhovian stiffness." *No moods on stage, the moods should be in the auditorium* [sic].

I even think, except for Nina and Treplev's scene, all this is easy to play. But this scene is difficult: it connects to their past. Remarks like: "I am a seagull . . . No, not that." – can be said impudently, without any sense. That is not the issue. You may like to finish something, but is Chekhov something complete, something finished, something defined? And if you do finish something, you will just get a little moral platitude, [something merely] comprehensible, useful . . . In my opinion, however, this something is an eternal concern, a vicious circle.

> Efros shows the ending: a shot, a fright, a big pause resulting from the fright, and then: "Well, what is next, let's play lotto."

EFROS. I am nervous and afraid of commonplace interpretations. Understanding the absolute incompleteness, the sheer routine of life – this is the understanding needed here.

Misfortunes, maladjustment, incompatibility: Arkadina and Trigorin, Trigorin and Nina, Treplev and Nina, Nina and Arkadina, Dorn and Sorin's incompatibility, the doctor and the patient, the patient and the doctor – everything is incompatible. It is life with its infidelities, incoherencies, misfortunes. This, roughly speaking, is a summation of *The Seagull*. But it disgusts me, and I do not like to talk about it. Let others talk about it. But on stage we should forever live truthfully.

YAKOVLEVA–NINA. How is it possible to play the big scene with only one physical action?

> Her question is about Nina and Treplev's scene in the fourth act.

EFROS. In love, there is always something physical. For example, you talk to your mother, and she does not listen to you, but she looks to see whether your hair has turned gray or whether your wrinkles have increased. And in this scene, it is Treplev's continuous physical perception of Nina. No matter what she says, he looks to see how her lips move, how her eyes change. He is not listening, but seeing, absorbing, drinking in. It is impossible to take a breath, impossible to completely make up for their two-year separation.

And for her? She has no joy. Only he has it. Coming between her and Treplev is her child with Trigorin. There is so much about her hair, her eyes, that he cannot bear to look at everything. Her big monologue needs to be spoken under his close examination.

Certainly, it would be possible to translate all this into literary-scenic language, but I want to translate it into physical language. After all, he does not know that she is just about to leave, but she knows. She cannot resolve everything. This is all that matters, and the entire text is only like the rustle of leaves, it has no value.

We should not play even one moment as they usually play it, but play an infinite chain of moments with the greatest physical truth. Igor Kvasha plays like this in *Look Back in Anger* at the Sovremennik Theatre. He is one entire united bundle, one piece. For me, he is an example of the best modern actor. He plays every moment with remarkable physicality.

Maybe all this is nonsense? But if it is nonsense, I cannot do otherwise. Tomorrow at 11:00 in the morning we will go on stage.

21 December 1965[P]
On stage
Setting for Act I

> A partition is on stage. The scenery is on stage left. In the center is drapery. Before it are placed benches and a platform for playing croquet.
> Treplev enters on the left, jumps across the croquet platform, jumps onto the platform stage at the right, and walks around on it for a long time.

EFROS. *(To Smirnitsky–Treplev.)* At this early point, we will do everything quietly. Move slowly, slowly. Gradually enter the rhythm that will prompt your entrance.

> They repeat. Smirnitsky–Treplev runs on from the left, jumps across the croquet platform.
> He comes on stage, jumps across a bench, and stands quietly on the stage.
> Masha enters from the left and looks at Treplev. Then Medvedenko enters.

MEDVEDENKO. Why do you always wear black?
MASHA. I am in mourning for my life. I am unhappy.

(To Dmitrieva–Masha.) You should cut him off so you cut short his desire to ask. You are giving him too much attention. Cut him off quickly, and that's all.

MASHA. *(looking back at the platform stage.)* The performance will begin soon.

Masha addresses this remark to Treplev. She wants something to release the tension within him.

> They repeat the scene.

EFROS. Treplev should do everything a hundred times more slowly during his entrance. He enters gradually, with the rhythm of an exhausted person. He walks around and walks around, then up and leaves. Not with a jerk, not on purpose, but without purpose.

> **MASHA.** Trifles. *(Takes tobacco.)* Your love touches me, but I cannot love you in return, that's all. *(Offering the tobacco.)* Help yourself.

Masha says all this in one continuous phrase and goes to Medvedenko, extending her hand with the tobacco. He already understands that she will offer him tobacco. He refuses. "I do not feel like it."

> Durov–Medvedenko, grasping the director's idea, refuses Masha's offer hastily and abruptly, with an internal protest against her smoking and against his rejected love. His answer to the recognition and the tobacco places them on equal footing.

Masha says everything brusquely, but internally she is very active in this scene, just as though it has a lot of text. She is preoccupied with Treplev.

Treplev reenters: "My friends, we will call you when the play begins, but you should not be here now, please." Masha promptly leaves, Medvedenko after her. Sorin calls to her: "Masha, please ask your father to have that dog untied . . ."

Masha sharply returns, literally shouts to Sorin: "Talk with my father yourself, I will not ask him . . ."

> They repeat the scene.

(To Smirnitsky–Treplev.) Move aimlessly around on the platform stage, hang about. You walked around, but I did not feel the aimlessness.

(To Durov–Medvedenko.) "Why do you always wear black?" This question resonates with his [characteristic] sophistry. And at the same time, when Masha answers him: I am in mourning for my life . . ." – he seems to speak internally, "So . . . " – he knows the answer in advance and is prepared to object. And after that follows his long reply.

This scene should contrast with Nina and Treplev's scene, contrast is necessary between them, Nina and Treplev's frankness, and Masha and Medvedenko's, isolation.

> **TREPLEV.** My friends, we will call you when the play begins, but you should not be here now, please.

Treplev's remark almost kicks them off the stage.

> Efros shows the internal intensity, Treplev's misery bursts open in his separate remarks. They can be used to judge his internal condition.

EFROS. To Sorin's question, "Why is my sister in such a bad mood?" he answers mechanically, no need to talk sense, he is thinking of something else while speaking the words.

(To Smirnitsky–Treplev.) Let's change this circumstance. Tell him everything about your mother as if for the first time, it is your first conversation about it.

> **TREPLEV** *(listens).* I hear steps . . . *(Embraces his uncle.)* I cannot live without her . . . Even the sound of her steps is beautiful . . . I am madly happy. My enchanter, my dream . . .

On these words Smirnitsky–Treplev lies down on the platform stage, listens for the sound of Nina's steps. She comes nearer, he jumps up. Nina enters out of breath and greets him.

> **NINA**. I am not late . . . I hope I am not late . . .

> > Efros suggests that she offer one hand to Treplev, another to Sorin. Both arms crossed over her breast.

Treplev runs off: "It is time to begin . . . We must go and call everyone." Sorin responds, "I will go, and that is all there is to it."

They remain alone. Nina is on the platform stage. Treplev approaches her. Embraces her. Some noise offstage. Treplev listens: "It is nobody." He tries to kiss her. She is in his arms, looking around. "What kind of tree is that?" She shies away from a love scene. Jacob appears. Treplev crosses to him.

> > Nina and Treplev are on opposite sides of the platform stage. So is their dialogue.

> **NINA**. It is difficult to act in your play. There are no living characters in it.
> **TREPLEV**. Living characters! You must not show life as it is or as it should be, but life such as it appears in dreams.

He parries her from the other side of the platform stage.

> > Dorn and Polina enter.

EFROS. Dorn enters first. Aims and strikes a croquet ball. He whistles ironically. He gathers his energy and discharges it in another strike.

> > Trigorin, Arkadina, and Shamraev enter. The men arrange the benches. Now they are arranged as a place for the audience in front of the stage platform. Everyone sits down facing the platform stage.

"My dear son, when are you going to start?" – Arkadina impatiently approaches the benches. Treplev: "In a minute. Please be patient." Returning to her place, Arkadina quotes from *Hamlet*: "My dear son, Thou turn'st mine eyes into my very soul, And there I see such black and grained spots as will not leave their tinct." Treplev, coming out from backstage, answers her from the same passage: "And why did you succumb to vice, seeking love in an abyss of crime?"

Nina appears. Approaches the edge of the stage, kneels, reads the monologue like a prayer. Treplev is behind everyone's backs now, standing stiffly at the opposite wall.

Arkadina interrupts: "This is something decadent." Nina rises, changes her position. Treplev rushes to Arkadina: "Mother!" Nina continues. Jacob is standing behind her, holding out a stick with the "red eyes." Arkadina interrupts again: "It smells of sulfur. Is that really necessary?" Treplev rushes forward again. But he barely manages to calm her down when Polina says: "You took off your hat. Put it back on, or you'll catch a cold." It happens as she says, "Wait a minute . . . All right, now we can continue." Everything is important except the performance.

Treplev leads Nina backstage. To Arkadina, he wanted to say, "I am too disgusted to even talk to you." But he only said: to "Me . . . I . . . I hate you." He wanted to say something more, but told only "I . . . " comes out. Arkadina shouts, "What is matter with him?"

(To Fadeeva–Arkadina.) Do not sit down, it is still early. Sitting will calm you down.

Nina appears. Arkadina conducts her to Trigorin. Acquaintance. Nina is on the stage. Trigorin below. Arkadina between them: "Do not be embarrassed, darling. He is a celebrity, but he has a simple soul."

(To Fadeeva–Arkadina.) Do not smile. You noticed the eye contact between them. Her face is serious, almost terrifying. Dorn turns away, as if to say, "Does everyone feel uncomfortable, or is it only me?" This is the source of his remark, "I believe we can open the curtain now; it feels strange."

After a big pause, everyone starts talking at once: we need to feel something has happened.

25 December 1965[P]
Rehearsal of Act I[13]

EFROS. We are changing the acquaintance scene between Nina and Trigorin. Yesterday Arkadina brought Trigorin to Nina. Now Nina is still on the platform stage, but Trigorin remains on the opposite side of the stage. He bows to Nina from afar.

> Everyone sitting between Nina and Trigorin is now involuntarily included in this scene.

DORN. The angel of silence just flew by.
NINA. It is time for me to go. Goodbye.
ARKADINA. Where? why so early? We will not let you go.

NINA. Father is waiting for me.
ARKADINA. Oh, that's not right . . . *(They embrace.)* Well, it cannot be helped. It is a pity, though, a pity to let you go.
NINA. If you only knew how hard it is for me to leave!
ARKADINA. You should be seen off with someone, my child.
NINA. *(frightened).* Oh, no, no!
SORIN. *(beseeching).* Please stay!
NINA. I cannot, Peter Nikolaevich.
SORIN. Stay for another hour, and so forth. What about it? Please . . .
NINA *(having thought a moment, through tears).* It is impossible! *(Presses his hand and quickly leaves.)*

(To Yakovleva-Nina.) Nina directs her lines to Trigorin. She speaks only to him. The conversation between them began over the heads of everyone.

(To Fadeeva-Arkadina.) Arkadina comes in with her line – "Oh, don't say that to him. Whenever they say nice words to him, he feels embarrassed"– on Nina's line. This conversation needs to be fastened together. This is an active scene for her.

In this scene, everyone should only speak with Nina, and Nina should only speak with Trigorin.

> The whole scene is changed for the sake of this close communication at a distance, so it is even more obvious.
> They repeat the scene.

EFROS. Let's move ahead. After Nina's exit, there is a long pause. In this pause, everyone looks at Trigorin, at Arkadina, again at Trigorin. "Unfortunate girl, really" Arkadina says, approaches Trigorin, takes him by the arm, and withdraws to another place. With this conversation, she seems to close the previous scene. Then with outstretched arms she holds Trigorin at a distance, looks at him attentively, and assesses the impression made by Nina.

At this moment Dorn simultaneously remarks, "Yes, to tell the truth, her father is a real swine." – he strikes the croquet balls again.

> They repeat Act I.

(To Gaft–Treplev.) When Masha enters, he sees her and internally brushes her off. He thought it was Nina, since he is waiting for her. But Masha tags along behind him incessantly. She notices his reaction. Medvedenko approaches and starts his usual quibbling conversation. Masha cuts him off. But he continues. At once this dramatic knot is tied. Treplev exits. Masha: "According to you, there is no greater misfortune than poverty, but in my opinion, it is a thousand times easier to go in rags and beg, than . . . " At this point her look is directed at the platform stage, where Treplev just was, the idea is that hers is a one-sided love.

> Scene between Sorin and Treplev.

EFROS. Sorin starts to speak to calm down Treplev and to calm himself down.

Treplev says to him, "Here is the theatre. The curtain, the first set of wings, the second . . . " He wants to distract Sorin with something. When he speaks about his mother, he is thinking about something else. He has already spoken a hundred times about this. He makes unexpected pauses. From this it is clear he is not saying what is on his mind.

The monologue about modern theatre: ". . . these great talents, priests of sacred art show how people eat, drink, love, walk around, wear costumes . . . " The implication for Treplev here is as follows: they think there is meaning in their art, whereas they only eat, drink and wear costumes on stage. At the end of the monologue, Treplev lays down directly on the platform stage: indignation passes to fatigue. But, hearing Nina's steps, he quickly and abruptly rises.

Nina's monologue.

ARKADINA *(silently).* This is something decadent.

(To Fadeeva–Arkadina.) Catch her on this. Incidentally, say it as someone might say it is anti-Soviet.

(To all the actors.) Now we need to do everything without any effort, simply do it technically.

When the play comes to an end, they draw the curtain. Treplev is fatigued, extremely physically fatigued.

Medvedenko's remark in dispute about the play: "Nobody has the right to separate spirit from a matter . . . " He means that nobody dares to do it because matter is primary and spirit is secondary. Additionally, he presses the need to write a play about our brother the teacher, since we work hard but receive little. He is accusing Treplev of self-display and foppery.

28 December 1965[P]
Rehearsal hall
Rehearse Act I

>Reading of the first act, starting from Shamraev's remarks.
>
>Arkadina enters arm in arm with Sorin, Trigorin, Shamraev, Medvedenko, and Masha.

SHAMRAEV. At the fair in Poltava in 1873 she was amazing. What a delight!

EFROS. What is distinctive in this scene?

They all feel themselves to be great experts in art. Broadly speaking, they all stick their noses in. They consider themselves among the elect who really understand art. They are having a serious business conversation.

Shamraev speaks about Pavel Chadin with the self-assurance of a great critic.[14] But for Arkadina, Chadin is merely some nasty, provincial, antediluvian actor. In her opinion, the circle of her actor–colleagues includes greats

such as Maria Yermolova and Polina Strepetova. Both Shamraev and Arkadina are confident in their infallibility.
(To Fadeeva–Arkadina and Solovyov–Shamraev.) Let's begin this scene.

> They perform the scene.

(To Fadeeva–Arkadina) There is no need to listen to him so attentively and for so long. She speaks, turns away, and leaves. If he were speaking about Yermolova, then she would respond. But it is not interesting for her to talk about Chadin.

> Efros demonstrates this moment. He takes Arkadina's place, walks, laughs indulgently, and talks carelessly.

But throughout all this, it needs to be a conversation about art. The more the conversation is about art, the sillier it will seem to us.

Arkadina: "My dear son, when are you going to start?" This remark, regarding the whole previous scene, should sound emphatic and demanding.

The quote from *Hamlet* "My dear son, Thou turn'st mine eyes into my very soul . . . " means: Let's go. Show us the art. We are waiting for your Shakespearean art.

TREPLEV. In a minute. Please be patient.

Treplev should try to calm the entire group, he should physically stop them – he needs to say the entire line as one phrase.

Nina enters. She begins her monologue. Everyone talks about art, but Nina prays to art. But nobody notices this. They are all occupied with their own interests, they have no time to listen to her.

Imagine: you need a shot for a film. The director announces that the most poetic scene in the film will be performed now. The general reaction is, Let's go, give us the poetry. But in this truly poetic scene the only ones who pray are Nina and Treplev. All the rest – theirs is the practical business activity surrounding poetry.

(To Yakovleva–Nina.) Nina's monologue needs to be a prayer, but only for her alone.

TREPLEV. All right, then we will show what that nothing is.

He wants to talk about genuine unreality.

POLINA ANDREEVNA *(to Dorn)*. You took off your hat. Put it back on, or you'll catch a cold

(To Kuznetsova–Polina.) There is no need to wait for Nina's remarks. Speak at the same time she does.

Treplev needs to show tremendous strength of will to listen to these hoodlums.

ARKADINA. The doctor has taken off his hat before the devil, the father of eternal matter.
TREPLEV *(flaring up, in a loud voice).* The play is over! Enough! Curtain!
ARKADINA. What are you so angry about?
TREPLEV. That's enough! Curtain! Close the curtain! *(He stamps his foot.)* Curtain!
The curtain falls.
I am sorry! I forgot that only a few elite can write plays and have them performed on stage. I broke up the monopoly! Me . . . I . . . *(Wants to say something more, but waves his hand and goes out left.)*
ARKADINA. What is matter with him?
SORIN. Irina, you should not hurt a young man's pride like that.
ARKADINA. What did I say to him?

In her opinion, she did not do anything wrong. Furthermore, Treplev thinks: now I will calmly rebuke all these vermin – "Me . . . I . . . " He wanted to say, "I hate all your ugly faces!" but he restrains himself.

There is no need to be malicious. If Treplev is malicious, then everything disappears. It all comes from his terrible fatigue. Between "me" and "I" there should be hour of pause.

They repeat the scene once again.

EFROS. The conversation between Arkadina and Shamraev is, let's say, a conversation about Stanislavsky's etude method carried on at the level of some country village.

They feel so competent about art and are so sure of themselves that they form a wall against Treplev and Nina's stage performance. You need iron strength to break through this wall. The "shadows" from the play need to be stronger than all these jerks. The onstage audience should simply be a curiosity, a meaningful counterpoint to the performance.

(To Yakovleva–Nina.) The text of your monologue is basically a prayer.
YAKOVLEVA. But after all, there is meaning in this text, which needs to be preserved.
EFROS. No, we do not notice this meaning. Many have tried, but nobody has been able to explain it. We are switching the meaning of the monologue in another direction – the opposition between "praying" to art and the self-confident "experts."

Later in the course of work, Efros will try to explain the meaning of Nina's monologue.

But Nina's monologue should make an impression of shock upon the stage audience. They are waiting for a normal performance, but instead, a strangely costumed person appears on stage and commences to show the eyes of the devil. They start to exchange glances and whispers, and shift around in their seats.

Everyone wants to get away from this place. Someone catches a moth, someone breaks a leaf from a tree.

Treplev tries to prod everyone back in their seats. He only just sets them back down and they begin to listen quietly to one paragraph, when a further disturbance arises: "This is something decadent." shouts Arkadina.

> They repeat the scene once again.

EFROS. Let's try this. I think it will be good. When Nina is kneeling, everyone begins to shift slightly. Medvedenko suddenly slaps a mosquito and for everyone this is like a signal for action. Everyone gets up and changes places. Nina clutches her head and moves to another position. For a minute, everyone calms down and listens attentively, but this is merely indulgence; that, let's say, they are here for a kindergarten performance. And then everything shifts to frank hostility: this is something decadent. During the pauses, Nina looks to see whether she should continue or not.

In Stanislavsky's director's copy, it says that when Nina stands near the background of the moon, everyone says "oooh, oooh, oooh." Let's make this a general "oooh."

TREPLEV. The play is over! Enough! Curtain!

Treplev is absolutely exhausted, has no strength, and hardly speaks. Now he is offended, but everyone only sees this as bitterness. And Treplev must throw insults at them: "Me . . . I . . . "

> The scene of Nina and Trigorin's acquaintance.
>
> Today there is a change in the stage setting. Trigorin approaches the platform stage. He helps Nina step down to the ground and moves to the opposite side.
>
> Solovyov–Shamraev talks about "the church chorister," looks at Nina, then at Trigorin.

EFROS. *(To Yakovleva–Nina.)* Imagine this is a field and you are alone in the field, only Trigorin and you. "it is time for me to go. Goodbye." Speak only to him.

ARKADINA. Where? Why so early? We will not let you go.

(To Fadeeva–Arkadina) You should hide your false discontent with her departure more deeply, not so frankly.

> They repeat the scene.

You remember Fellini's film [*La Strada*]? There is a scene in the countryside where the circus entertainer prepares for a performance. This situation is very like us. Now we do not notice anything beyond the commotion [of rehearsals], but there is something familiar to us and clear. I, you and me, have similar moments of expectation before a performance, before a new performance. One thing moves ahead to the next thing, and to the next thing, and everything is fastened together, everything goes forward, nothing must slow down. In this entire scene, from beginning to end, everything aspires towards the discovery of spirituality and prayer in the theatre: "Horror, horror, horror . . . Empty, empty, empty . . . " – Nina speaks and thinks, how horrible, nobody understands, and yet I need to continue.

Everything should be the opposite of prayer, of spirituality in its purest form.

Everything strives towards it, but it does not happen – "The play is over! Enough! Curtain!"

"I broke up the monopoly" – this is complete desolation.

Arkadina's reaction to Treplev's "prank" is not tears, but blaming others.

Trigorin and Nina ignore all this.

Efros plays through the whole act in his inimitable manner.

EFROS. What is clear from all this?

It is as if not one person understands himself. And not one person is capable of understanding anyone else. Complete turmoil on stage. And complete exposure of their primitive lives.

Let's go over the entire act once again, and at the table we will question what is not clear in all this. Now the most important thing is to do everything without movement, but in terms of meaning.

They play the act once again.

Treplev *(viewing the stage).* Here is the . . .

EFROS. *(To Gaft/Treplev.)* You need to start over. Everything up to now was the preface, and now is the beginning [for Treplev].

The pauses need to be there in the monologue about your mother. Here comes the monologue about your mother. But keep silent until the next thought comes. When the text surfaces but the thought does not, it turns out empty, and then life does not proceed on thoughts, but only mechanically.

(To Pelevin–Dorn.) All of Dorn's lines to Polina mean: get away from me, for God's sake. All your lines say, Go! And all her lines say: you are mine, go home, put on your galoshes.

They repeat the scene.

Any remarks?

LARIONOV–TRIGORIN. It was interesting for us to watch Efros's face, there was such pain in it.

EFROS. Well, it is still too early to suffer. After all, this is the beginning of work and it is natural the performance is still not how it needs to be. You remember when we rehearsed [Viktor Rozov's play] *Wedding Day*, you were also in despair that we were not doing what was considered essential. Nevertheless, at the last rehearsals everything burst open. The same thing can happen here.

> Someone says everything is very interestingly planned, but it is too early to demand results. Someone else says humorously, quoting Dorn's words: "It is fresh, it is naive." Efros answers, It is not fresh or naive, because everything was done mechanically.
>
> The following are Efros's remarks to individual actors.

(To Durov–Medvedenko.) For Medvedenko the earth is higher than the sky. To eat and drink is all a person needs. But Masha has all this. This suggests to him that Masha wears black because of the weather and not because she lacks enough bread.

(To Vovsi–Sorin.) Sorin needs to be a nurse, a gentle nurse. To live with Treplev all the time. To me, Sorin, needs to talk to him to remove the wild tension.

(To Gaft–Treplev.) In the scene with Sorin, Treplev wants to tell the story, although he is living in another dimension. Take as many pauses as you need. All the action is seen in the pauses.

Nina's arrival – this means there will be a performance. It has been planned correctly. But you need to perform it more courageously. I, Treplev, cannot surrender myself to a love scene, because I have a mass of unfinished matters. I digress, I speak with Jacob, then I come back to the love scene. Ideally, this scene should proceed like that of Chatsky and Sofia.[15] Treplev wants to embrace and kiss Nina. She tries not to offend him, submits formally and absent-mindedly, and tactfully avoids the kisses.

(To Pelevin–Dorn.) In Dorn and Polina's scene, the issue is not in the nature of his temperament, but in the accuracy of everything that happens.

In the first scenes up to Nina's exit, there is a lot of severity and awkwardness, but there is no truth. And in the scenes after Nina's exit, i.e. after the end of the onstage performance – "Obviously, the play will not continue, and I can leave." – there is truth, but there is no severity. There is only some whining.

Trigorin should do everything quieter. He should help Nina from the stage more quietly. They are introduced, connected. Everyone notices they are embarrassed, something has happened. This awkwardness should be a little restrained, but everyone should notice something. Let's go over the first act once again.

> Rehearsal began at 11 o'clock in the morning.
> At 3:08 they repeated the first act.
> After the run.

EFROS. It seems to me something is there. A long, disturbing overture . . .

28 December 1965[5]
Rehearsal hall
Act I

> They read the text of the scene where the audience enters for Treplev's play.
> After the reading, Efros and the actors try to understand what is happening.

EFROS. Everyone comes in convinced of his own right to judge. More "specialists" in art. And everyone sticks their noses in, everyone believes he is entitled.

A surprisingly business-like conversation – like a doctor making a report, and all doctors, as everyone knows, both prepare for and speak about such subjects.

> They rehearse the scene where the audience enters.
> Solovyov [Shamraev] tries to become more active.

Arkadina enters hand in hand with Sorin, Trigorin, Shamraev, Medvedenko and Masha.
SHAMRAEV. At the fair in Poltava in 1873, she played wonderfully. A delight! A miracle. But the acting! Would you please let me know where Chadin,[16] the comedian, is now? Paul Semyonitch? As Rasplyuev,[17] he was outstanding, better than Sadovsky,[18] I swear to you, my dear. Where is he now?
ARKADINA. You are always asking about some antediluvian. How should I know!
EFROS. *(To Shamraev/Solovyov.)* Okay, but let's have even more self-confidence – like Belinsky. [Shamraev thinks] he is an expert and that she is not.

(To Fadeeva–Arkadina.) She needs to react with complete amazement from what they toss at her, and then reject it.
And Treplev is businesslike, "We should start."

> They repeat the scene.

SHAMRAEV *(sighs).* Pasha Chadin! There are none like him anymore. The theatre has gone downhill, Irina! Before there were mighty oaks, and now we see nothing but tree stumps.
DORN. There are fewer brilliant talents, that is true, but the average actor has become much better.

SHAMRAEV. I cannot agree with you. However, it is a matter of taste. De gustibus aut bene, aut nihil.

EFROS. *(To Pelevin–Dorn.)* And you chime in too – "the average actor has become better."

(To Shamraev–Solovyov.) And you say that his taste is simply worse – a debate of specialists in the study of drama.

> They repeat the scene.

(To Fadeeva–Arkadina.) You are irritated. But that is not necessary. If he had asked about Yermolova, you would answer. That's all.

> They repeat the scene.

Still irritated. You are participating in a conversation about art, in the dispute as a matter of principle.

> Efros tries it for Fadeeva.
> They repeat the scene.

EFROS. Already better, but Solovyov [Shamraev] should not lower the tone of the dispute. He needs to prove himself to everyone. Shamraev approves of Pasha Chadin's theatre! And the others – some other theatre. But what is important is that this is a fundamental debate about modern acting skills.

> Treplev comes out from behind the stage.

ARKADINA *(to her son).* My dear son, when do you start?
KONSTANTIN. In a minute. I beg your patience.
ARKADINA *(recites from Hamlet).* "You have turned my eyes into my very soul, and there I saw such black and bloody spots that there is no escape!"
KONSTANTIN *(from Hamlet).* "And why have you given in to defect, looked for love in an abyss of crime?"

(To Arkadina/Fadeeva.) She needs to challenge her son to compete with Shakespeare.

> They repeat the scene.

EFROS. Yet all three of you are still lying a little bit. How can I make this not happen?

> They repeat the scene and move on.

KONSTANTIN. Gentlemen, start! Attention, please!
I am starting. *(Knocks with stick and says loudly.)* O you, respectable old shadows, who rush over this lake at night-time, lull us to sleep and let's dream what will happen in two hundred thousand years!

> **SORIN**. In two hundred thousand years there will be nothing
> **ARKADINA**. Let it. We will sleep.
> **KONSTANTIN**. Then let's portray this nothing.

EFROS. (*To Treplev–Smirnitsky.*) Appeal to the shadows without poetry. And reply to "two hundred thousand years there will be nothing" without irritation.

And yet, how can I say it . . . here are all these terribly commercial and prosaic people, and against this background is a true prayer. Konstantin is the priest who prays.

(*To Fadeeva–Arkadina.*) Do not be irritated. It is just a dispute about art not being at a certain level.

> They repeat the scene.

EFROS. I want the meaning to be clear. They are all awfully terrestrial and yet really demand poetry. Everyday material activity amid poetry. All the lines about sulfur, etc. – Common sense [people], yet they demand poetry. Only Nina and Konstantin escape from the terrestrial.

(*To Fadeeva–Arkadina.*) "This is something decadent" – the subtext: this is what they expelled him from school for. A remark, not an assertion.

(*To Smirnitsky–Treplev.*) "Mom!" – quietly. This is not solemn. Simply a request not to disturb.

(*To Yakovleva–Nina.*) Olya! Not accusatory – even if the words are not clear. As if in prayer. One continuous sound wave.

". . . Let's portray this nothing" is also without irritation – simply [ask], why the objection?

> They repeat the scene.[19]

Treplev should have the willpower to force these hoodlums to listen. Damn it . . .

The play is over – you cannot force them.

Everything collapses. There is no pathos here.

He should quietly tell them all to go to hell.

> They try the scene.

> **KONSTANTIN**. It is my fault! I failed to see that only the select few can write plays and act on stage. I broke up the monopoly! I . . . I . . .

I see your nasty faces. This is not anger, but terrible fatigue. Every day, these same mugs.

> Gaft improvises: "I am more talented than all of you."

EFROS. Precisely. He is tired. Too tired even to talk to them. He waves them off and leaves.

> **ARKADINA.** What is the matter with him?
> **SORIN.** Irina, my dear, you should not hurt his young pride like that.
> **ARKADINA.** What did I say to him?
> **SORIN.** You hurt his feelings.
> **ARKADINA.** He warned us earlier that it was a joke, and I treated his play as a joke.
> **SORIN.** Even so . . .

EFROS. *(To Fadeeva–Arkadina.)* Your reaction is not drama, but indignation, "I have been on the road, you old fool, and this is how you have raised him here!"

Now, first: they are all occupied with one thing – a dispute about art. This is their unity. They go to the play like a wall you cannot break through. Powerful shadows are necessary for Treplev to silence these idiots. Treplev should understand all this. He took a desperate step. And then he realized it was madness. He begins to define his relationship to these "elite." It is not pathos, but a specific attitude towards them.

Imagine we are going with this attitude to see brilliant actress: "Come on! Let her show us that she is brilliant." We have no curiosity, only business sense.

[Treplev's] performance should shock everyone. Unfamiliar stage settings, whispering [among the audience] even before Arkadina interrupts. Then everyone listens, and there is indignation at the beginning – "Shocking." And play it strongly. Up to the point of absurdity.

> They repeat the scene.

EFROS. When things subside and they start to listen, they listen very carefully, but hostilely. Then they get bored, they fidget, and then the hell with being interested – ironically. Kindergarten. And only then, openly – they do not accept it.

Against this background, "Cold, cold, cold. Empty, empty, empty." sounds very different.

After Treplev leaves, the scandal must begin at once – "What is the matter with him?"

The actors try this on stage and go further ahead – the entrance of Nina and her introduction to Trigorin.

> **NINA** *(coming from behind the stage).* Obviously, we will not continue, so I can come out. Hello! *(Kisses Arkadina and Pauline.)*

> Break.

EFROS. We must remember Fellini's film, *La Strada*, although there is no direct connection. There is a scene in the middle of nowhere with a traveling circus. They sort out their relationship, and there is something tragic, in the underside of our business.

Everything goes on and on. Everything is screwed in place, but nothing is being given back, nothing is happening below.

They play the whole act.

EFROS. Amid all this prosaic vanity is pure, clean spirituality – prayer. We pray for the life of people in general, but we spit at the person next to us.

Their vanity is different. Some are hostile, but Sorin and Dorn – they suppress this hostility.

And everything is opposed to this prayer. Everyone aspires to it, but it does not happen. [Treplev:] "That is it! The end"

Treplev can even throw something.

And then he says politely, sweetly: "I forgot that [certain] people cannot understand this."

Arkadina should not have to go on crying, but take charge of everything.

Trigorin says importantly that it is not necessary to impose restrictions [on writers]. Everyone writes as he can and as he lives. Everyone is tired of instructions.

Efros demonstrates.

Here I am showing, telling, and from this it should be clear: no one needs to be an island unto himself. Totally in communication, totally active, but nobody understands each other. Let's do it once again. The main thing now is *without the motor* [without being mechanical].

They repeat the scene between Konstantin and Sorin.

KONSTANTIN *(looking around the stage)*. See, here is the theatre. The curtain, then the first wings, the second and beyond that, open space. No scenery. Directly overlooking the lake and the horizon. We open the curtain at exactly 8:30, when the moon is rising.

EFROS. *(To Gaft–Treplev)*. Valya! Up to now was the preface, but now is the [real] beginning [for Treplev]. Everything needs to move further and further ahead. "Here is the theatre, now it is time for me to concentrate."

Konstantin cannot find any peace before the show and while waiting for Nina. Sorin wants Treplev to talk. Treplev internally dismisses his uncle about the question of his mother. He dismisses Masha. He switches his uncle's attention to the theatre, to backstage. Convince someone that Nina being late is like death. This is the most important thing here. He takes it out on his uncle's beard a little.

Asked about his mother, this question pricked, hurt, so for the first time he starts to tell his uncle something, with pauses to return to waiting for Nina. But in the same pauses there are new thoughts about his mother, which he also wants to express to his uncle strongly, fully, and clearly. After Nina's arrival, Treplev is no longer in the second plan [thinking about his mother].[20] A complete switch. He wants to hug and kiss. Nina, trying not to offend him, moves away from his kisses. Play it in human terms, without hurrying, but not slow.

Do not forget Sorin opposes Treplev's views about writers.

> They try the scene, then move on.

EFROS. Doctor – all the lines with Polina Andreevna must say: "Leave me alone, get out of here."
And Polina: "Go back inside, put on your galoshes." It is a nightmare!

> They play the whole act up to Dorn's line, "It was fresh. Naive . . ."

But ours is not fresh and not naive. Because it is mechanical. Let's take another look at what is going on! What is it about? What is missing in a big way?

Lev [Medvedenko] throughout should be a confirmation of his philosophy – the earth is the earth and the sky is the sky. Masha needs to be more clearly in opposition – this is "nonsense." This is her position.

The path of Sorin and Konstantin. Sorin should subordinate everything to the task – to be a good nanny. Now you are living separately, fixing on the words of the text.

Then Konstantin arrives. His purpose: first – to drive everyone away, and second – to share [with Sorin his fear] that everything will be ruined if Nina is late, third – to share his thoughts about the theatre. The basis of the pauses is not that scenery is missing. The basis of the pauses – there *is* no scenery. This is what he lives by. The basis [of those pauses] is also his mother. Then the following piece of action will be correctly planned, but it needs to be played courageously, and slowly: "I was waiting for her" – as the most important thing. But he has a pile of things [to do]. Therefore, he hugs Sorin, and for Jacob – instructions.

(To Pelevin–Dorn.) The doctor – the issue is not in the power of his temperament, but in specificity.

Konstantin finishes everything and begins a new piece of action in the presentation of the performance, forgetting [for the moment] whom he is showing [this to]. And then a pause – "I forget who you all are and that it is impossible to show you anything."

In the scenes before Nina departs there is a lot of cruelty, but no truth, but in this scene, there is truth, but no cruelty. That is not my interpretation. It is mawkish. There should be no poetry in the way Trigorin helps Nina down [from the platform stage]. "Hemingway" is quiet in front of the girl. Then embarrassed, both he and she, and everyone notices. Not a frontal attack, but the fact that something has happened. It should probably be tougher.

They repeat the scene.

EFROS. Durov [Medvedenko] caught the "seed" – "plain sense" – and carries it through the whole scene.[21] And Treplev does not connect the requirement for new forms with his own performance.

The overall conclusion – it is noisy. But there is little belief that you know everything. You should watch and move formally, without disconnecting from Nina. Durov asks to write a play about teachers, like a spectator at a conference.

I want thought, not words. We need to search further.

30 December 1965[P]
Rehearsal hall
Act I

EFROS. Let's try to look once again at all the events in the act with detachment, from the outside. For a person such as Treplev, the arrival of Arkadina and Trigorin is practically the same as Dietrich and Hemingway's arrival. Treplev is engaged in literature, but lives in the countryside without ever leaving the place because he has no money. He hopes to show a performance while they are here – for him this is a unique possibility to prove himself somehow. As for them, they treat this situation as a lark, a skit. They do not consider the idea that this young man has something to teach them – Dietrich and Hemingway. For them this is childish. But for Treplev and Zarechnaya, who live in solitude and aspire to art, just about any person from their domestic environment has seen more than they, even Sorin and Shamraev, and so they are desperately worried. And here is an additional complication – love with its attendant difficulties. For Treplev everything came to an end when they did not understand, a wall exists between him and the audience of his performance, they do not have the power to understand him. For them everything came to an end when they saw that Treplev was engaged in a sermon about some unfamiliar art, unknown and unnecessary to them, a sermon about anti-forms, a sermon about some *Rhinoceros*.[22] This is the assessment of Arkadina, Shamraev, and Medvedenko. However, a fool is capable of discrediting anything. Here the fool is Medvedenko. The sense of his position is as follows: nobody has the right to be engaged in art for art's sake when people are poor and teachers are starving, nobody. But he went too far, and Arkadina had to say that's enough, we will not talk about it. But their opinions generally coincide.

Only Trigorin and Dorn treat the performance differently. Trigorin is the person who lives for an art wider than that of Arkadina, and he thinks differently from her: nowadays everything is much more difficult, there is no one unique truth, Madam, everyone writes as he can and as he wishes. To Dorn something [in the performance] seemed new, interesting. He does not know exactly what it is. Perhaps, it is some type of *Rhinoceros*. Nowadays we already know rather a lot about Ionesco. But Dorn's reaction can be compared with the moment when *Rhinoceros* reached some of us for the first time: how or why it seems interesting to me or whether there is anything there exactly – I do not know, but there is something. Perhaps, I can see traces of Alexander Blok? But I, Dorn, know well enough how similar experiments have come to a tragic end, I want to warn him, I want to help him with advice: he needs to write about big important things, I want him not to be lost . . .

But we also need to convey that Hemingway and Dietrich have arrived, that Dietrich introduces her son's girlfriend to Hemingway, and he takes her away.

Nina is met by a company of self-involved people who revolted against the fact that *Rhinoceros* was shown to them. They treat her in a business-friendly manner: darling, you have talent, you should go on stage. This refers to Arkadina, by the way. The way she introduces Nina to Trigorin. Placed next to each other, Nina and Trigorin are unexpectedly confused. Owing to this confusion. Nina also speaks quite coolly: "I am so glad . . . I always read you . . . " This confusion should be played during a pause. During their remarks, it should remain hidden. They try to hide it, but nothing happens, the thread of the conversation sags, and everyone notices. I, Arkadina, see it and consequently I do the opposite: "Why do you hesitate, he has a simple soul, he is embarrassed." Everyone furtively hides the fact that something has happened. Therefore, we will change this situation: Nina leaves because it would be impossible to do otherwise.

Everyone leaves, Dorn remains alone and reflects: "Why do I think there is something in this play?" Everyone has already forgotten about the performance except him. But Treplev is not present. Therefore, it depends on Dorn to carry this thought forward to the end of the act.

I have said nothing about Masha and Polina Andreevna. They are included here as well. And we will talk about them now. There is one important theme in Masha's role: she comprehends everything. Yesterday I saw *The Adventures of a Dentist,* and this theme is very strong in there.[23] It also appears in *The Appointment,* especially the scene where the character of Lyamin faints, which is so well performed by Oleg Yefremov: "I had a rest . . . " In general, this is a splendid vital theme . . .

Masha looks literally for physical contact with Treplev, and she has a general desire to make the other persons listen to her.

> Then Efros reads the separate requirements he formulated about Act I.

EFROS. Medvedenko considers himself a representative of the people who can act on their behalf, he behaves in a clever but unsound manner. His final paragraph of claims: "Nina and Treplev are in love with each other, but we are not in love because I earn too little."

The main thing for Sorin is to get Treplev to talk, to distract him with conversations about literature, about diseases, about anything, if only to work off his energy.

As for Treplev – before the conversation about his mother – he internally waves Sorin away, does not enter a dialogue with him: "If you want to be occupied with something, be occupied by what I am offering you here, the theatre, here is the stage." To distract his uncle's attention. But the main thing is to convince someone that Nina's delay is like death to him.

After the subject of his mother is mentioned, he enters a dialogue with Sorin. But the question of his mother is a terrible question, a sore point. It turns over continuously in Treplev's consciousness: she arrived recently, and again I am depressed by her, I am struck by her avarice, her meanness, her relationship with the fiction writer, she is simply some psychological curiosity. In the pauses during this conversation he remembers the impending performance: "There will be a chair here, a table here." – but he comes back again to the conversation about his mother. The most important thing is, "She does not love me because my age reminds her she is no longer young."

When he speaks about Nina, he needs to tell his uncle everything that he feels now: "I hear her steps," etc. Treplev's idle talk works out like this: when he speaks about the performance, the main thing is today's performance; when the conversation is about his Mother, the main thing is his Mother; when the subject of Nina arises, Nina becomes the main thing.

In Dorn and Polina Andreevna's scene we will make a technical adjustment. Dorn leaves earlier than she does. This provides an opportunity to separate one scene from another, and the rhythm will not be lost.

Dorn should dispatch Polina Andreevna more aggressively. That is the meaning of all his lines: "I am 55 years old," "What do you want me to do?" "It is called idealism." Dorn should be more aggressively matter-of-fact.

Then there are the "experts" on art. One is Shamraev, who is for older art, another is Arkadina, who is for current art. Dorn supports Arkadina. This scene connects Arkadina's line at once: "My dear son, when will you start?" And further on, quoting from *Hamlet*, she playfully reminds Treplev that she is waiting for a Shakespearean penetration into the soul from him.

He, answering also with a quote, parries: "I know everything you can say to me, your cruelty is already known to me."

Treplev addresses the "shadows of olden days" and asks that they lull them all to sleep. When he is interrupted, he insists on continuing this thought.

In Nina's monologue, there is a sense that everything is clear: there is a world soul, there is only spirit, I pray and I want you to hear – matter is secondary, and spirit is primary, and when spirit is not present, everything "will be empty, empty, empty, terrible, terrible, terrible."

"This is something decadent," Arkadina interrupts Nina. This is like the remark of a teacher directed at a schoolchild. Arkadina is not aware that Nina's entire monologue is a prayer.

When Treplev shouts to close the curtain, it means all his hopes have failed, nothing is left of his aspirations: "I forgot that only the elite can be engaged in art." And all that is left for him is to go around in his shabby jacket until next summer. If Nina's treachery is added to this, it is truly possible for him to shoot himself.

After the failure of the performance, everyone stands with their backs to us. And from their backs we, the audience, feel something coarse is there, all of them feel guilty. And suddenly, facing them and us and understanding nothing, Arkadina indignantly asks: "What is wrong with him?"

Everyone disperses. Dorn and Masha remain. They cannot recover. They may have seen a young Blok, who read his poem, was booed, and even took away his girlfriend. Dorn, without knowing what to say, says: "Youth, youth!" To this Masha responds with the splendid line: "When there is nothing more to say, people say: youth, youth . . . " Specifically, people say these words in the most tragic cases. People perish, destinies collapse, and we can only say: "Youth, youth."

Break

Rehearsal hall
Act II

EFROS. Arkadina begins the second act. She should be very active, should prove her youthful appearance.

> Fadeeva–Arkadina begins the first scene. Efros thinks she does not satisfactorily show that she is as sprightly as a young girl. Therefore, in parallel with Arkadina's lines, Efros tosses remarks at her during small pauses: "Old, old, still old." The actress should try to disprove this, to silence him, therefore she becomes more active, and each of her arguments becomes stronger in her favor than the previous one.

EFROS. When Sorin comes in with the words "Are we happy? Are we enjoying ourselves today?" he does not need to be touched by the meaning of these words, but to convey these words actively to Nina.

Nina embraces Arkadina: "I am so happy! I belong to you now." Arkadina coldly releases herself from the embrace, and continues to read. Nina: "What do you have there?" – "Maupassant. 'On the Water,' darling." Arkadina says the name fluently, assuming it is unknown to Nina.

> Rehearsal of Act II continues non-stop up to Nina's monologue: "How strange it is to see a famous actress crying, and for such a trivial reason!"

EFROS. Very rough, but more or less correct. The meaning of this scene is not that they, these great talents, own life, but that life completely owns them. And Nina draws the conclusion they are the same as mere mortals, life holds them by the scruff of the neck too.

2 January 1966[P]
Rehearsal hall[24]
Act II

> Rehearsal begins with the Nina–Treplev scene.

EFROS. Treplev finds Nina when she is absorbed in a cruel discovery, a cruel knowledge about this circle of people, these intellectuals. She does not have the strength to perceive Treplev's drama.

Then I want to do this: let it sound vulgar – "to pour out all the bile and frustration."[25] Treplev's path: my performance failed, and you turned away from me, how clear everything is to me now. But Nina lives with things that are larger and more difficult for her: to her eyes a child [Treplev's play] has just been killed [so to speak], and they are using foul language to talk about it. She lives absolutely on another plane.

> **TREPLEV** (*enters without a hat, carrying a gun and with a dead seagull*). Are you alone here?
> **NINA**. Alone. (*Treplev drops the seagull at her feet.*) What does this mean?
> **TREPLEV**. I had the meanness to kill a seagull today. I put it at your feet.
> **NINA**. What is matter with you?
> **TREPLEV**. One day I will kill myself the same way.
> **EFROS**. Treplev needs to find a tone of quiet awareness of the tragedy of life to pour out all his bile, all his disappointment. Look here, now I killed a seagull, and one day I will kill myself the same way . . .

Trigorin appears. Trigorin hooks into Nina. In ten minutes, he needs to learn everything about her, about her life.

In the same ten minutes, Nina lives in complete harmony with him to help him find out what he needs. Three quarters of this scene proceeds unconsciously for them, and only during the last instant do they realize they are holding each other by the hands, that this is a coming together.

Finale of the act: Arkadina leaves without noticing Nina or that a sense of fate appears here: "We are staying." And Nina turns: It is a dream!"

GAFT–TREPLEV. In this scene, does it not seem to you that Treplev wants something from Nina, seeks contact?

EFROS. I think, no. It is possible, of course, and perhaps true, but it seems to me more interesting if played differently. After all, he has observed Nina continuously for some time.

GAFT–TREPLEV. So, this is his conclusion already?

EFROS. Yes, a conclusion, I would even say a particular conclusion. "I have burned everything, everything, to the last scrap." A measure of despair that has crossed over to self-flagellation. Then all this changes his nature, his idiotic vanity. He did not shoot himself from disappointment, but from a true understanding of things. In addition, no matter what he says he encounters

Nina's vacant look: "I will talk to you next time willingly, but today I cannot even listen to your words." Trigorin approaches – and there is complete communication with him. A full separation [from Treplev], then complete communication [with Trigorin], unity, togetherness.

This communication arises not without some difficulty. They slog towards it through words, through a heap of words. They reach it at last and both feel this communication and are embarrassed. Their last words already sound like a declaration of love.

The writer Yuri Olesha often came to the Café National in his later years. There was a waitress with whom he had a certain special relationship. He always looked slovenly, almost dirty, but he wrote the most poetic language. Alexander Pushkin was outwardly like Volodin, the same strangeness. Nina understands all this.

She sees only a scrap – one episode – but she realizes the full depth [of Trigorin's soul].

Nina and Treplev are a pair in their knowledge of the moment, but they do not interconnect.

(To Yakovleva–Nina, Shirvindt–Trigorin, Treplev/Gaft) Please enter together and play it without stage settings. That is the main thing required now.

3 January 1966[P]
Rehearsal hall
Acts II and III

EFROS. Before beginning the third act, I want to summarize the second act. Be super attentive.

When I think it over for myself, I see a harmonious concept. Perhaps I do not always explain the meaning of this concept, but it exists nonetheless. I have thought everything over self-critically many times. Yesterday I telephoned two guys, Smirnitsky [Treplev] and Gaft [Treplev], and we rehearsed at my place, in the bathroom [sic].

2 January, New Year's Day!

What do they carry over from the first act to the second?

Arkadina is tormented by the fact that she feels [her] time is fading. And she comes to the second act with a need to prove to herself and others that her time has not come yet.

Masha needs communication, conversation.

Dorn needs to put an end to his old connections, his old life. All three come to the second act with a distinct action. This is all before Nina's appearance. From this point on Arkadina creates a void around Nina. To separate Nina from herself and from what is "hers." Nina feels the dramatic futility of their lives, something is going on there.

In this futility, Masha only has the desire to read more of Treplev's play, she leaves when this becomes impossible. Dorn mortally hates his patients, his old loves, everything old. Medvedenko has a casuistic desire to notice everyone's shortcomings, to direct everyone to the correct way: "Do not smoke." Arkadina needs to care for her family: "You need to have a treatment, Peter [Sorin]." It proves to be impossible to read Treplev's play, and so Masha leaves. Everything ends with the fact that they will not provide horses for Hemingway and Dietrich.

Chekhov not only shows the futility of this world but also shows it through the soul of an observer – Nina. Nina observes and gives flowers to Dorn, to those who live dramatically.

Treplev has an oversupply of betrayals. And the day is not over yet. He wants to show Nina her treachery. This is new – what we tried last night. His lines deal only with the extent of this disclosure. One disclosure after another, she does not even manage to understand one when another follows straightaway. And this is terrible and cruel for Nina, this misunderstanding! Then Trigorin appears.

> **NINA.** See that house and garden on the shore over there?
> **TRIGORIN.** Yes.
> **NINA.** That is the estate of my late mother. I was born there. I lived my whole life near this lake and I know every little island on it.
> **TRIGORIN.** It is very nice here *(Seeing the seagull.)* But what is this?
> **NINA.** A seagull. Konstantin Gavrilich killed it.
> **TRIGORIN.** A beautiful bird . . . *(Writes in his notebook.)*
> **NINA.** What are you writing?
> **TRIGORIN.** Oh, just some notes . . . A subject crossed my mind . . . *(Hiding the book.)* A subject for a short story: on the shore of a lake there lives a young girl like you, she loves the lake, like a seagull, both are happy, and she is free, like a seagull. But a man happens to come by, sees her, and having nothing else to do, kills her, just like this seagull here.

EFROS. The starting point here is so terrible, tragic, and fatal. Nina – "I live in this house" – this is like an pledge. I will love you all my life, but I will also demand the same from you. He says, "a seagull," and, like a wise man, he tells her the story of her future life: he killed a seagull.

> Once again, the story about Yuri Olesha. "And this young little girl [the above-mentioned waitress] comprehended for the first time that he [Olesha] had no home, he sits in a small restaurant, he drinks, and his sole pleasure is the waitress."
> They perform an etude. Efros is Nina. Smirnitsky is Treplev.

EFROS. The extent of what she did, the measure of what she made, is [for Treplev] the measure of female ordinariness – "Women do not forgive failure."

The more accurately this action is established, the more subtly it can be performed. Treplev exposes her as "a love boat crashed against life."[26]

But Trigorin – he is the beginning of everything, he ennobles her. There is a contrast between these two scenes here – and not from the fact that both men are yearning for her.

(To Shirvindt–Trigorin) There is a sum of sufferings in a person such as Trigorin. When Nina comes to him, he lays out the sum of these sufferings to her. Therefore, he clings to her. They cling as friend to friend. He holds onto her as a person – and they keep hold of each other for God knows how many months. What experiences have you had, what secrets, you reveal all this to her in the course of a few minutes. And she is so interested in you that she cannot get enough, she aspires to learn even more about you.

> They play the scene Nina–Treplev–Trigorin.

Let's understand what was correct what was wrong.

(To Yakovleva–Nina.) As soon as he, Trigorin, comes near you (there is no specific moment in the text when he notices her), you rush to him before saying, "Hello, Boris Alekseevich." His response is even stronger: "And I thought we would not meet again." They rush to each other, who is stronger, who is sharper. So much for the scene with Trigorin.

Treplev was about right, but you *(to Smirnitsky–Treplev)* were a little inside yourself. He throws a stick. The orientation was correct, but it was done timidly.

It would be unnatural for Nina not to notice this in Treplev. No, she notices. She gets away from it.

Is it clear, guys? Really, I am sure they have not performed Chekhov this way before. If we do so, it will be very healthy.

We spoke about the first and second acts, but in the third act the intensity is even greater.

The third act is departure in the blood.

The third act begins with the fact that Trigorin is already leaving. His eyes are distracted, he does not see Nina anywhere and does not know whether he will see her. And during this moment the most essential things of his biography are spoken. This is done by Masha. The concreteness of her story in such circumstances: write the book and sign it this way [she asks]. There are people who do not notice the other person is distracted, and psychologically cling to him. Departure is "in the blood." The sweep of the eyes is "in the blood." Departure is inevitable, they know it. There is a need to find a connection that makes them unable to leave: therefore "odd or even" [Nina's teasing question to Trigorin] rise and fall feverishly, as in children.

Arkadina is absolutely not ready, and Sorin has to ask her for money. It is awful.

And to do something when she is not ready, when she is hurrying to leave – is three times as awful. Sorin struggles with himself because asking her for money at this moment is like asking for alms from a running horse.

> **SORIN**. It seems to me the best thing would be for you . . . to give him a little money.
> **SORIN**. If I had the money, I would clearly give it to him. But I do not have anything, not even a suit.
> **SORIN**. You are kind, my dear . . . I respect you . . .

He tries one approach, then a second: "If I had the money, I would give it to him." A third approach: "You are a generous woman, you are lovely, noble-hearted." And here something snaps in him, and he faints. His departure is finished because something more awful has occurred. Everything instantly changes. Arkadina becomes pale, not completely ready yet, she falls on the sofa from tension. A huge pause.

Treplev lives only by the fact of his mother.

He loves her very much at such moments, he does not love her when she shows off. And again, there is a conversation about money. She cries: "I have no money. I am an actress, not a banker." Meaning, "Can't you see I am about to faint?"

And there is further conversation with her son. Everyone sticks a knife into the breast of someone else. It is necessary to endure this knife and stick it in even deeper next time. They choose the most hurtful places.

No sooner do things calm down when Trigorin enters: "Page 121 . . . lines 11 and 12 . . . " After a conversation with Nina, he is on fire too. They are all burning with something. In spite of the fact that Arkadina just made a scene, she does not forget to remind him: "They will bring the horses soon. Do not forget."

> **ARKADINA** *(looking at her watch)*. They will bring the horses soon.
> **TRIGORIN** *(to himself)*. "If you ever need my life, come and take it."
> **ARKADINA**. I hope all your things are ready.
> **TRIGORIN** *(impatiently)*. Yes, yes . . . *(In thought.)* Why is there so much pain in this appeal from someone whose soul is so pure? "If you ever need my life, come and take it." *(To Arkadina.)* Let's stay one more day . . .

This enormous scene between Arkadina and Trigorin needs to be played savagely sober.

Arkadina's purpose is to be protected from blows. "All of you have arranged to torment me today."

Then comes Trigorin's crisis – everything, a wall, she does not understand. And then Arkadina immediately changes – "I am the only one who understands you."

> **TRIGORIN**. I have no will of my own . . . I've never had a will of my own . . . Lazy, soft, always obedient – really, how can this be pleasing to a woman? Take me, take me away, only do not let me stray one step away from you . . .

EFROS. He only wants to survive. Then, "I heard a good expression this morning: 'A maiden pine forest . . . ' It could be useful" – he returns to his habitual path.

And then the departure, which is not difficult to play, except the scene between Trigorin and Nina, of course. He does not know that she has news for him. He only thought to briefly say goodbye during her appearance. Let's take a break. And then etudes for the entire act. A little suggestion was made to me that previous etudes were not in sequence [internally], and so, with books in hands.

Break.
They rehearse Act III.

EFROS. There should be no raw nerves here. As soon as there are raw nerves, the characters' internal turmoil disappears.
The scene with Nina arises in the middle of the scene with Masha. Masha sees this, but continues.
Her dishonesty can be seen in this. There is such density of communication here. Contact is initiated just when it is impossible, 15 minutes prior to departure. The next scene is Arkadina–Sorin.
(To Fadeeva–Arkadina) Do not sit down. You walk and conduct the scene with Sorin in motion.

They try the scene.

Almost right, but with some comment. There should be a strong contrast between the way Sorin hesitates and finally decides to ask for money from Arkadina.

They perform the Arkadina–Treplev scene.

EFROS. Treplev began with a very restrained communication with Arkadina, but actually he needs to search for a way to bring her out of her condition.
Children reach into one's soul. But her son's love does not soften Arkadina: "I too live with other things." This scene will succeed only if everyone chooses the most hurtful insults, blows aimed at the sorest points. There is a first time in everyone's life. She offends him terribly. He needs to endure it to say something even more terrible to her. Otherwise it will only be a heated argument, laughter in the audience, and nonsense.

The next scene is Trigorin–Arkadina.

Arkadina is on the defensive, as if five guns were aimed at her. Then he realizes she does not understand. And then she properly, slowly, and quietly seems to elicit something from him: "Well, give me a pencil." The scene leads to a declaration of love: "You have no pencil with you? Oh well, I will write with this piece of charcoal: 'A maiden pine forest . . . '"
(To the actors.) Any questions?

FADEEVA–ARKADINA. I have a problem with Arkadina's relation to her son. She is not a mother at all.

EFROS. It seems to me too that she is absolutely not a mother. Remember in the film *The 400 Blows*, the mother steps across her sleeping son two nights in a row, it is a tiny room and he gets in her way.[27]

And besides, at any given moment we live in what occurs in the present, until something stronger begins. But in this case, she is not experiencing the tragedy. It is his tragedy, not hers. In general, she has no time to think about it. He, the son who shot himself, calms her down when she is naughty.

4 January 1966[P]
Rehearsal hall
Act III

EFROS. We will take a walk through all the scenes of the third act once again. Note: "Trigorin is having breakfast, Masha stands at the table."

If we work according to [Stanislavsky's] lexicon, what is the action here? She talks about her life. But this is not yet action. What is the action here? The only participants in the scene are those involved in the conversation.

DMITRIEVA–MASHA. She says goodbye to him.

EFROS. Well, probably. But that is not enough. It is interesting to look for some secret here. It is because everything is so clear that the [actual] force is not as clear.

YAKOVLEVA–NINA. Perhaps, she wants to change her life and looks to him for support?

EFROS. But she asks for nothing and does not receive any advice. There is something specific in the fact that Masha talks to Trigorin. I wonder what is happening in this scene. On the literary textual side, she tries to shut down an old love. But after all, it is possible to say this in different ways, depending on the action. Words about this subject alternate here with words about Trigorin. How can we make this scene appear super-necessary and super-specific? Why does she say specifically to him, "I am telling you all this because you are a writer"? I want you to be grateful for this super-natural frankness [of mine]: "You are a very good person." This is some sort of human longing: "My teacher [Medvedenko] is not very clever, but he is a kind person, and poor, and loves me strongly. I feel sorry for him. And I feel sorry for his old mother."

The search for a connection, the need for a connection.

To repay his tremendous sincerity with the maximum degree of frankness, confession, sincerity – this is Masha.

But Trigorin is in a devilishly difficult position. He lives for Nina, of course, but he also sees what is happening to Masha. His task is not to offend her. To live super-concretely in the life of another. Let's play this scene.

> Dmitrieva and Gaft rehearse (both performers of Trigorin are ill).

EFROS. Behind that door Nina stands and waits. But Trigorin cannot get away from Masha. Do you know what would be interesting to build this scene on? Trigorin considers each of her words is the last, that now she will finish, and he can exit. But each time Masha needs to return his attention to herself.

> They play the scene.

Any comments?
And he – I know this for a fact since I often behave much more unscrupulously myself – connects extreme attentiveness with an extreme desire to end the conversation. She re-adjusts every time, approaches from another direction, and begins again. Both in their own rhythm. It must be kept hold of. She is in her own rhythm: to treat him with affectionate frankness.

There is one danger. Do you know why I do not do etudes at this point? Because the super-psychological truth achieved in etudes does not provide the opportunity for sharp character drawing.[28]

DMITRIEV. When we do performances with etudes, we are your creative accomplices.

EFROS. In the West, I think, they discovered the secret of Chekhov long ago. And we should reveal it. To find Chekhov today in direct, rough, violent communication, when, in spite of everything, nobody understands anything. Life runs ahead with madcap speed, it is impossible to concentrate – this is today's Chekhov. Not to lose the actor and the humanity in this communication, but for the actor to live truthfully and the same time as though he were an artificial figure.[29] Not to reduce it to level of mood alone. The cruel, sharp, brutality of each situation enters his living blood.

Well, let's move ahead.

> He reads the text of the scene between Nina and Trigorin.

NINA *(holding out her hand with fist closed to Trigorin)*. Odd or even?
TRIGORIN. Even.

EFROS. This is interesting. Let's all get up. Walk around together in the tired-out rhythm of Nina and Trigorin. They struggle to communicate, but cannot. They do not approach each other. Their communication is based on looks. It is utterly impossible to achieve perfect harmony and contact. Along with this complete artificiality there needs to be complete truth. This is the manner of Nina and Trigorin's scene.

Thus, we create more than the play. We create associations with our own life and something more.[30]

And then you think: wow, how all this reflects life, even unconsciously, by physical behavior itself.

> Rehearsal comes back to the beginning of the act again. Efros performs it himself. Quitting the conversation with Masha, he tries to bang his head on a heating pipe.

Interestingly enough, most of us live this way. This is the seed of our life.

And when this is not present, performances can be magnificent, but they are not about this, our life [today]. So, the objective is to live in these two scenes according to the same truth as the etude's action, but under nightmarish circumstances.

And what is in the third scene?

> **SORIN**. You are going away, and it will be hard for me to stay at home here without you.
> **ARKADINA**. But what is there for you in the city?

What is Sorin's action? I need to ask her for money. But this is the most humiliating thing that can be. This request should be put into action: to evade the request, to keep himself away from it.

And what Arkadina's action? To gather her things together, to decide to leave, she needs to be disconnected from Sorin. At the same time try [so to speak] to solve the calculations – 250 divided by 14, 125 times 12, to extract the square root of 12,5000 – and to list everything that you put in your purse, to think of Trigorin's next meeting with Nina, and still say the text of the scene.

> They perform an etude. Efros is Sorin, Fadeeva is Arkadina.

EFROS. When she is very, very concentrated on something, suddenly she says something contrary to everything – suddenly she is hysterical: "I am an actress, not a banker." The main thing is that her internal concentration is on 15 things that do not relate to the ongoing conversation.

> The next scene: Fadeeva–Arkadina, Smirnitsky–Treplev.

EFROS. His purpose is to melt her heart, to hold onto her as in childhood.

As for her, she knows it is impossible to refuse him, for him it is an extreme expression, but she responds to him mechanically. Physically she turns her attention to him, but psychologically she is not present.

What was right and what was wrong in the etude?

DMITRIEVA. First, everything was correct up to the point when they start to offend each other.

EFROS. Yes, at first everything was correct up to the ultimatum. After that everything should be quick and sharp. And now Treplev gets into an argument with her. She demands silence from him. After the episode in which Treplev has tried to bring her out of her swooning condition, this is a huge offense to him. It is possible to be silent as much as necessary, until too much evil and insults have been accumulated. Let's do it once again, only do not get involved in a discussion, beat each other up more hurtfully.

They repeat the scene once again.

In general, of course, it is certainly there. But neither one of you finds an ultimate insult. You offend each other, and then you begin to ramble on. At first there is no defense from these hurtful words. Therefore, you are going in the wrong direction when you try to reach the ultimate insult. They both strike at the maximum sorest point. You need to be aware that a mother is speaking of her son and a son of his mother. If this was said by strangers, the insults would be meaningless.

Trigorin's scene with Arkadina.

EFROS. How can we define what he is doing more precisely?

I am convinced we need to find some very rational basis for this scene. He needs to ask her to release him. To implore her for his sake, for the sake of that specific reason.

As for her, she needs to be physically protected from the horror that has swept over her. Let's play this part of the scene.

Fadeeva–Arkadina and Gaft–Trigorin play the scene.

DMITRIEVA–MASHA. He did not explain to her, and she did not protect herself.
EFROS. That's true.

Dmitrieva plays Trigorin, and Yakovleva plays Arkadina.

EFROS. The foundation is correct, she is physically protected. She feels like five rifles are shooting at her.

And now the shift: "Am I really so old and ugly already that you can talk to me about other women?" She, of course, wants him to respond with caresses. She wants to change his mood to super-happiness and honesty, but to change him deliberately. To change him with hundreds, even millions of specifics, their personal specifics: "You are the best writer." She can prove these: "You cried when you were abused by the critics, I was the one who brought you round, I am the only one who can appreciate you." Let's play directly from this transition.

Fadeeva–Arkadina and Gaft–Trigorin perform.

(To Gaft–Trigorin.) Turn away from her all the time, evade her so she needs to watch you and follow along.

This seems correct. Interestingly, in this episode you can force him into submission, continue with the same text, and keep the same objectives.

Let's do the final etude.

> **TRIGORIN** *(coming back).* I forgot my cane. It is on the veranda out back. *(Goes inside and meets Nina who is entering.)* Is it you? We are leaving . . .
> **NINA**. I had a feeling we would see each other again. *(Excitedly.)* Boris Alekseevich, I have decided once and for all, the die is cast, I will go on the stage. Tomorrow I will not stay here anymore, I am leaving my father, leaving everything, I am beginning a new life . . . I am leaving, just like you . . . for Moscow. We will meet there.

EFROS. Nina comes to report her decision, but he does not know this. She comes in, and he embraces her to say goodbye for the last time. She tells him about her decision. Their last words are like a promise of love.

I would like very much to include a moment of external direction here, as in a film. We cannot leave everything to the actors alone. They can do their parts magnificently, but there should still be the door, the telephone, and the lamps [to focus on].

4 January 1966[5]
Rehearsal hall
Act III

> Efros reads the beginning of the act.
> Scene with Masha and Trigorin.

EFROS. What is the real action here?

Interestingly, Chekhov's stage direction says: "Trigorin has lunch. Masha is standing by the table." Judging by the logic, by everything that is written, she talks about her life, but that is not action. What is the psychological action?

Let's see how it is written.

> Efros reads again with all the periods and other punctuation marks.

> **MASHA**. I am telling you all this because you are a writer. You can take advantage of it. I tell you honestly that if he had injured himself seriously, I would not be able to live a single minute. And yet I am brave. I have made up my mind and decided: I will tear this love from my heart, I will tear it up by the roots.

EFROS. What is going on?
DMITRIEVA–MASHA. She is saying goodbye to him. The introduction was long, and now this is the end.

EFROS. Is this really enough?
DMITRIEV–MASHA. If you toss something different in, I will take it.
EFROS. This is the logic of the text, but it is not action. What is the actress doing here with Trigorin? Some kind of secret must be found. But now everything seems clear, horribly clear.
YAKOVLEVA–NINA. She wants to seek advice.
EFROS. Let's suppose so, but if that's true, then the secret problem is – to get advice. And did she get it? No. But she is not disappointed. And yet there is still nothing.
SMIRNITSKY–TREPLEV. Sometimes it happens that when people are deciding something, they talk to convince themselves.
EFROS. It does happen sometimes, but I am afraid this may lead to mechanical acting. It seems to me the literary side is clear. But the dramatic action – no. And this – as they always say – contains the meaning.
Let's look again.

Efros reads the text.

> **MASHA.** I am telling you all this because you are a writer. You can take advantage of it. I tell you honestly that if he had injured himself seriously, I would not be able to live a single minute. And yet I am brave. I have made up my mind and decided: I will tear this love from my heart, I will tear it up by the roots.
> **TRIGORIN.** In what way?
> **MASHA.** By getting married. To Medvedenko.
> **TRIGORIN.** Isn't he the teacher?
> **MASHA.** Yes.
> **TRIGORIN.** I do not understand what the need is.

The alternation here is interesting. The words about Trigorin and Medvedenko occupy the same amount of space. How can this scene be made super-necessary and super-individual?
DMITRIEVA–MASHA. She chooses two listeners –Trigorin and Dorn. These two can understand. And she says goodbye to them too.
EFROS. Why Trigorin? He is a very good man. We must decide to give him something, "I will be super-frank with you."

Efros performs.

"I am telling you, as a writer – everything, everything, everything I can about myself and about the whole lot." And during this time his attention is scattered.

Efros plays, emphasizing her frankness.

Masha wants to thank him for his amazing warm-heartedness with the highest degree of openness, closeness, and intimacy. And what is Trigorin's action? He lives totally for Nina and he cannot see Masha and her situation. But so as not to offend her, he behaves super-correctly towards her.

Gaft and Tonya *(Dmitrieva)*, try an etude.

(To Gaft). Valya! What is important for Trigorin is this: every time he thinks the conversation will end, she – returns him to her desired frame of mind.

> They do an etude: Gaft–Trigorin looks around very actively. Dmitrieva is trying to tell him about herself. Quite sincerely and quietly.

EFROS. What is wrong? It is very important to sustain the rhythm of the third act throughout the whole time, so there is no sadness in their departing, no Chekhovian requiem. What is more important is narcissism, a mad, intense rhythm. For some it is a departure, for others it is a need to meet. Masha must "attach herself" to Trigorin.

DMITRIEVA–MASHA. And do I have the same rhythm?

EFROS. Probably different. Your own. But also, intense, since it goes from him. And it is impossible for Masha to lose the rhythm of the act. We need to think of something to overcome this calmness. Do you know why I am not doing etudes? It seems to me that in our searches in the field of psychology, super-psychological truth can really destroy sharp character drawing, it smooths out the corners, prevents sharp highlighting of what is most important. Subtleties, nuances shut out the essences, preventing disclosure of the main thing in all its sharpness.[31]

Now we lack excitement in our desire to say what is important. We are drawing an objective picture here. I would like it to be more uncertain, rude, clumsy, overdone, but loudly and subjectively about the most important things.

At this point I would like to try and wade through what we already know, and get to what we still do not know. Hence, all our searches, even in methods of work. Now it is very important for us to achieve a realization of our understanding of Chekhov. I am convinced that Chekhov is direct communication, but without understanding, since each character is occupied with something different.

Just today my son and I met up with a boy, a friend of his. As we drove, I was painfully irritated by everything: their questions and their chatter, since I knew I also had to deliver them somewhere, and then drive to the theatre and rehearse. I replied to them while trying to think of the third act, to understand it, to feel what is important in it. And somewhere in there I caught the essence of the third act. This happened when I felt an illogical pattern – the tiny clink of a glass amidst all the commotion of the party. We must live in this illogical, silly picture [I have been speaking about], because it is something from life, from the alogisms and complexities of our time.

The profound significance of the situation makes my heart pound. Now I am scared. I suddenly thought: now that I know it, I can already see how this third act should go. I do not want to go down those old familiar paths. That is not truthful and not today's atmosphere, everything needs to be looked at with fresh eyes and seen all over again, refusing what is already known.

> Efros reads the next scene between Nina and Trigorin.

NINA *(holding out her hand with fist closed to Trigorin)*. Odd or even?
TRIGORIN. Even.
NINA *(sighing)*. No. I only have one pea in my hand. I was trying to guess: should I become an actress or not? If only someone would advise me.
TRIGORIN. It is impossible to give advice in this situation.

It will be interesting to try this piece of action. Everyone stand up. Let's go, and watch closely. The point is these people have not met up so far today. Keep your eyes open. And nevertheless, they must meet up to get into the correct rhythm. Let's go, quickly.

> They do an etude.

EFROS. There are no crowds as in a train station, but everyone's hearts are pounding: everyone is unsettled, but they do not have time. Therefore, communication and contact are honest but with complete detachment, exhaustively honest communication. How can this be done? It should be full of emotional behavior to reveal the whole truth. Fragmented, compelled to pretend, to hide what is important, and to do so with openly emotional behavior. They oppose each other, and at the same time they manage to be psychologically accurate and live life truthfully. But only if we create something bigger than the play, only when associations with our own lives arise – and, by the way, only then will the characters speak as a reflection of our era. Accurately. After all, there is no need for a museum restoration, it is all in our lives, in our sensations. And this is very important – in our own feelings. It is possible to play everything, but without barrels of dynamite exploding. It needs to have a feeling of something impending.

(To Dmitrieva–Masha.) Tonya! All this is necessary for you too, in this scene with Trigorin. It is interesting. Remember – all day long we are living as if in a train station, a state of extreme confusion, countless levels of activity. I do not know anyone, maybe that person lives differently, better than I do. But this is true of all life today.

The feeling of the rhythm of today's life is not merely necessary for the performance of modern plays, since today's plays are performed for today's audiences. For people living in the nervous rhythms of today, it is impossible to apprehend a performance taking place in the rhythms of the last century, even when the basis of the performance is a play written in the last century. A modern interpretation of the classics is impossible without injecting the nerves of our own time into it, the tensions and internal dynamics of our own time.

These two scenes – their difficulty here lies in the fact that even under these extraordinary circumstances it is necessary to live truthfully.

And when four people live this way, it is even more difficult, even more nightmarish. Jacob asking Trigorin to pack the fishing rods can already begin to get the point across. Arkadina says to Sorin: "Then just remain here." How come? After all, he said he was going to the city. She probably does not hear what he says.

Efros reads the act further.

> **ARKADINA**. Oh, the grief he brings me! *(Thinking.)* Maybe he should go into the civil service or something . . .
> **SORIN** *(whistles, then hesitantly)*. I think it would be best if you . . . gave him some money. First, he needs to dress like a human being, that's all. He has been wearing the same jacket for three years, and he goes around outside without an overcoat . . . *(Laughs.)* And it wouldn't hurt for him to get away once and awhile, go abroad . . . or something . . . it is not that expensive.

Sorin's action: "I absolutely have to ask her for money for Treplev. I know what his life is like here; afterward, without money – it would be horrible for him.

"I understand this request is a terrible humiliation, and I am trying to get out of it. All the time I am doing whatever." And suddenly I blurt out everything at once, and then I leave at once to get away from this, and I withdraw my request. We talked about Arkadina accurately: to gather herself, to pack, she has to disconnect from everything, but when they start interfering with everything – leave me alone!

FADEEVA–ARKADINA. Why is she crying?

EFROS. Every phenomenon is always born from concrete facts, and behind this – is everything else. Getting your thoughts together, not in the sense of getting your head around them now, but in the sense that the thoughts are no longer there. She is thinking about sitting on the train with Trigorin, but here is – a suicidal son, Nina and her relationship with Trigorin. At the same time, she is trying [so to speak] to solve the following problems: $250 \div 14$, 346×3 and the square root of 546, collect her suitcases and remember the strange words Trigorin was muttering to himself.

In the morning when I was delivering my son and going to the theatre, I thought about six things at the same time. Everything was confused – in the first plan was Masha's first line: the rehearsal starts with this. And then I had to explain to my son that they should use the underpass instead of crossing on the street. This conversation was torture for me. Now I have this creative task – to reconstruct our entire conversation. And I am focused on it, but then it was a nightmare – I needed to give him money for lunch and tell him not to scramble around back stage. And I was angry with him. But if he was greedy and said he only had a few kopeks, then I would take them away.

Let's try to do an etude aloud, saying everything we talked about.

> An etude with Fadeeva–Arkadina. At the same time, each of her actions contributes to the frenzy.

How should the scene be constructed? You can enter, sit down, then sit down at another place.

And it is not necessary to deal with everyday things. You just need to focus on the fifteen things that are not related to the conversation.

> The scene with Treplev and Arkadina.

ARKADINA. He frightened me!
KONSTANTIN. It is not healthy for him to live here in the village. He is bored. Now, if you, Mama, could suddenly become generous and loan him fifteen hundred or two thousand, he could live in the city for a year.
ARKADINA. I have no money. I am an actress, not a banker.

What is important for Treplev here? To melt her parental tenderness. She understands this development cannot be denied since he is the most important one, but she responds to the development unconsciously. Mechanically, physically, she departs from her previous position, but psychologically – she is not here. But this does not interfere with her main action. This is nothing. Avoid talking about Trigorin while you can. When this is not possible – an ultimatum, he – replies, she is even angrier, he – and so on.

> They perform an etude: Fadeeva is Arkadina, Smirnitsky is Konstantin.

EFROS. What are they doing right and what is wrong?
DMITRIEVA–MASHA. At first, everything was right up to the second piece of action, when they begin to insult each other.
EFROS. Right. From the ultimatum onward, everything should explode. The more tender everything is up to that point, the more fragile everything is.

So, an ultimatum – Smirnitsky [Treplev] needs to respond precisely to the ultimatum and not join in the debate, but in the fracas.
SMIRNITSKIY–TREPLEV. But she hurts me later, when she calls me a mediocrity.
EFROS. No. Before. You offered her the maximum of a child's openness, and she betrayed you, she delivered an ultimatum. Strike at once! And be silent if necessary to save up for the next blow. Try it again.

On the first attack, Fadeeva–Arkadina opens her eyes and looks at him severely, albeit quietly, "I will not speak . . . I will not."

> She becomes sharper.

EFROS. They are sort of there, but they are not finished insults. You insult and then become soft again. You should not react so quickly, since it is necessary to understand what he said, and figure out how to strike back. I can imagine how I would react if my son said to me: "Go, see your own lousy performances." It is the same result here as in life.

Let's consider what is next, the last scene. Arkadina and Trigorin.

Two persons are in the scene. How do we determine what he is doing? I am convinced we need to find some rational basis, and then the emotional outbursts will come. And then it would be more logical than emotional. To beg for freedom, concretely, for just that. To talk about concrete facts, and for Arkadina – physically to defend yourself, to escape from this concreteness.

(To Gaft–Treplev and Fadeeva–Arkadina.) Do an etude. Valya, spell it out, explain.

Gaft plays Trigorin. They do an etude.

DMITRIEVA–MASHA. He needs to explain more precisely, and she needs to defend herself in different ways.
EFROS. And Fadeeva–Arkadina, in my opinion, is not defending herself.
(To Yakovleva.) Olya, try Arkadina, and Tonya (Dmitrieva) – do Trigorin.

They perform.

EFROS. Correct seed. You need to defend yourself, to physically hide, as if he were trying to take five rubles from you.

It is like this: we watch a foreign performance, not knowing the language, and we watch this scene – and we understand. We check with the translator, and he confirms: "He tells her he fell in love with the other one." And then you realize it is expressed in the film perfectly.

Okay. Let's move on to the second half of the scene. The rhythm of the scene cannot be played about one thing and another at the same time. "You – you are unique – a brilliant writer." Perhaps it needs to be spelled out. One argument, another argument, so that he realizes it is impossible to stop her.
DMITRIEVA–MASHA. It seems to me she humbles herself to evoke pity.
YAKOVLEVA–NINA. She tramples herself so he will not trample her.
EFROS. We need to return it to a million concrete things. Remember, we talked about *Molière*? It is the same there. Return to light the candle, etc.[32] And here – this is not emotions, this is the concreteness of their relations, which are large and long-standing.

The do an etude.

Everything is correct. You can get on your knees and crawl. But continue this concreteness. But for him is impossible to bear. He lifts her up, and she crawls again, he walks away, and then, "All right, take me away."

The last scene. "I forgot my cane" – this is probably spoken to someone outside. And here is what is interesting: Nina comes back in to inform him about her plans, and he does not know and thinks this is goodbye. He embraces her only to imprint her in his memory, but she is deaf and blind, "I have decided, I am going, we will meet again," she spells it all out. And then the oath of allegiance.

What could we come up with here to include some external feature? I am very sorry that in *My Poor Marat* we did not introduce something – a sound, a door, or lighting. I hate to end the act only with [psychological] realism.

5 January 1966[P]
Rehearsal hall
Act IV

EFROS. Let's think over the act once again.

The starting moment, of course, is the fact that two years have passed – and nothing much has changed.

I want this first scene between Masha and Medvedenko to be based on direct communication, even when it seems it is not present: "There are waves on the lake. Enormous."

How should we treat such lines as: "Let's go home, Masha . . . Masha, let's go! Our baby is probably hungry."?

What is she busy with here according to the action? I would like to avoid lyrical situations like: she looks out the window thoughtfully. Perhaps she says nothing special and everything is all right in an energetic tone. She leaves the room, he enters it. Then he wants to go out the same door she is entering: "How boring you've become."

So, he follows at her heels.

Efros shows this in sharp, gusty movements.

EFROS. But Medvedenko should not whine: "Masha, let's go." his is a reserved, constrained request, concealed. Do this quietly, privately whenever possible. Like a lame husband. Masha tries to avoid speaking with him.

Medvedenko leaves. Treplev, Polina Andreevna, and Masha remain.

POLINA ANDREEVNA *(looking in the manuscript)*. Nobody ever thought or even guessed you would become a real writer, Kostya. And yet here you are, thank God, and the magazines have even started to send you money. *(Passes her hand through his hair.)* And you've become handsome, too . . . Dear Kostya, you are a good boy, be nicer to my Mashenka!

MASHA *(making the bed)*. Leave him alone, mother.

Polina Andreevna *(to Treplev).* She is a nice girl.
Pause.
A woman does not ask for much, Kostya, except a tender look. I know that myself.

Here Polina Andreevna can make a sharp glance in hopes of connecting Masha with Treplev. She grasps Treplev by the hand, asks him, entreats him. Treplev leaves abruptly. It did not work.

And here Masha reveals her thinking to Polina Andreevna: "Whenever love gets into your heart, you've got to drive it out. They promised to transfer my husband to another district. And when we move there, I will forget everything . . . tear it out of my heart by the root." She seldom needs to speak the text, but walks around and dances cheerfully. Physically, she is dancing and moving, but psychologically, in conversation, she is tearing out the love from her heart. There should be a sharp characterization here. She almost starts fighting in reaction to Medvedenko and Polina Andreevna. Not one second should be done slowly, everything must be done abruptly, sharp characterization, even pushing Sorin's chair.

And what if everything is done with direct, close communication? An active life for everyone, even Sorin: "Where is my sister? If you called my sister, it means I am dangerously ill." And all of Dorn's lines should sound like obscene curses: "Oh, the moon sails across the night sky . . . " sounds like an abusive curse. Sorin's: "I want to give Kostya the plot for story. It should be called "The man who wanted to," and in the background of his mind is: doctors are guilty of everything. They – Dorn and Sorin – should be in a rage against each other. After all, it is a shocking thing: two years have passed and he still wants to live, two years have passed and he still does not give me any medicine. Both proceed not according to a so-called Chekhovian rhythm, but sharply, impulsively.

Medvedenko introduces his eternal subject again: some are destined to live badly and some to live well. "I have six at home now, and flour is up to two kopeks a pound."

From his ivory tower, he asks Dorn what is the most interesting city abroad.

MEDVEDENKO. Allow me to ask you, Doctor, what city abroad was the most pleasant to you?
DORN. Genoa.
TREPLEV. Why Genoa?
DORN. Wonderfully crowded streets there. When you leave the hotel in the evening, the entire street is alive with people. You move around in the crowd without any purpose, here and there, in a broken line, your life is linked together with everyone else's, you merge with it mentally, and you start to believe a single world soul is really possible like what Nina Zarechnaya performed in your play. By the way, where is she now? Where is she and how is she?

Further conversation about Nina follows. Unwillingly, Treplev starts to lead it. It is a sore point, but he gets farther into the conversation because he is talking about it for the first time, and while he has a contact with Dorn, he ignores the others. And everything goes on and on until this line: "How easy it is, Doctor, to be the philosopher on paper and how difficult it is in practice." There is a big pause, a moment of understanding. After this, Dorn abruptly parries Sorin when he says: "She was a charming girl," to which Dorn responds, "You old Casanova." He is sharp with Sorin because he is old himself.

Then Arkadina and Trigorin arrive. Roughly speaking, the scene is built for the meeting between Trigorin and Treplev. He apologizes politely for his behavior. They exchange a few words. And then the lotto game starts.

Masha has a line here: she wants Medvedenko to leave. He loudly declares: "I wouldn't have troubled anyone, but the baby . . ." Nobody reacts, and he silently leaves.

They meet and greet a little, and that's enough. They sit down for lotto. The main thing is to twist all this together. They play at the game, through which strong remarks erupt from time to time.

When Treplev is left alone, he has a monologue, a fight with himself, with bad forebodings.

I wonder how to finish the acts? All the endings are very difficult.

The first act comes to an end with a question: what should be done, what? I do not know.

The second with a dream. This is the bad ending.

The third with a kiss. This too is bad.

The fourth, "The fact of matter is that Konstantin Gavrilovich has shot himself."

A story about Edward Albee follows, about the ending of his play *Who's Afraid of Virginia Wolf?*[33]

The protagonist chastises his wife for betrayal because she spoke about the death of their child. The child is their dream. A disturbing action.

Is the fourth act clear?

In the beginning Masha wants to avoid Medvedenko.

Polina Andreevna wants to connect Masha and Treplev, it is now or never.

6 January 1966[P]
Rehearsal hall
Act IV

EFROS. The beginning. Here is what is important. Masha: to avoid communication with Medvedenko. Medvedenko: to detain her, to stop her. Let's perform without the text.

Masha and Medvedenko's scene.

MEDVEDENKO. Let's go home, Masha!
MASHA *(shakes her head).* I am going to stay here for the night.
MEDVEDENKO *(pleadingly).* Masha, let's go! Our baby is probably hungry.
MASHA. Nonsense. Matryona will feed him.

EFROS. I think this is correct. In their communication and dissociation. Only more intimately about the baby.

> Enter Treplev and Polina, Treplev brings pillows and a blanket, and Polina brings bedding. They place everything on the sofa, then Treplev goes to his table and sits.

MASHA. What is this for, Mama?
POLINA. Peter Nikolaevich asked for a place to be fixed up for him in Kostya's room.
MASHA. Here, let me . . . *(Makes the bed.)*

Here is what Polina needs to do in the pause: Medvedenko needs to leave so that Masha and Treplev will be together.

> They play the scene between Polina and Treplev.

EFROS. Truthful, but not sharp enough. It will be now or never. You need to find a path that expresses this. Now there was a long and wordy introduction. But you need to rush it. And it is impossible for him to listen to it. And sharply, immediately, he leaves. Masha's embarrassment and shame follows. And she needs to overcome it. [As if] it was nothing, nothing happened. Sharply, angularly. And the same reaction to the waltz. Treplev should enter like this: in his office, everyone is jostling and people are in the way. To enter or not to enter, he enters, sits down, and thinks about nothing.

> Dorn and Medvedenko roll in Sorin's chair.

SORIN. If you had to send for my sister, it means I am dangerously sick. *(Keeping silent for a while.)* That's the way the story goes. I am dangerously sick, and meanwhile they do not give any medicine.
DORN. And what would you like? Valerian drops? Baking soda? Quinine?

EFROS. Sorin – to find out why they sent for his sister and where she is now. To publicly accuse Dorn of dishonesty for caring badly for him, and Dorn – to criticize him for not understanding it is impossible to burden the earth indefinitely. Their temperamental dispute should be interrupted by pauses. Then they part and silently exit.

SMIRNITSKY–TREPLEV. Why do I return to my office? I am angry that people are getting in the way. And now they are having some conversation about Genoa.
EFROS. No, perhaps, they talk about Genoa, but really it is about Nina – it is awful, it is difficult to talk about this. You know what I thought? This is a tangle. Everyone wants to explore all the questions at the same time.

> They perform the scene. Efros reads the text again. Then they try the scene again, overlapping each other, stepping on each other's lines.

EFROS. Do not expend yourself on any one thing, just explore, some slight pauses.

> **MASHA** *(to her husband).* Haven't you gone yet?
> **MEDVEDENKO** *(feeling guilty).* Why blame me? When they will not give me a horse!

(To Dmitrieva–Masha.) You need to ask Medvedenko: "Are you still here?" as a super-event. They already kissed, and he did not leave.

> They perform the scene.

(To Vovsi–Sorin.) And your question is even more important. Where is my sister? After all, if they sent for her, it means I am at death's door. And look to the others for sympathy as well.

> They perform the scene.

(To Pelevin–Dorn.) It is very important he does not have anything, no money. This is not a complaint and not an irritation. It is a fact!
(To Dmitrieva–Masha) Behind all this was a whole day stuck with her husband. A whole day. It sits like a bone in her throat.
(To Vovsi–Sorin.) "Where is my sister?" and all the rest – this needs to be thought about. Pauses are necessary. Dorn needs to steel himself to grant him anything. And these pauses are necessary for Sorin. Ancient enemies – the doctor and the patient.
SOLOVYOV–SHAMRAEV. It is like they are fencing with foils, parry and then thrust.

> Efros plays Sorin.

(To Pelevin–Dorn.) Do not answer me, do not hurry. Gather yourself together and then answer.

> They begin, but Efros stops them.

EFROS. Play everything, but do it extremely sharply. I have – money – he places a finger on his breast pocket [his wallet], but I cannot get at it. They [his patients] take it all, shakes his finger.

> They try. Everyone shouts over each other higher and higher.

DMITRIEVA–MASHA. I do not understand why they all shout at each other, as if there were a fire.
EFROS. Really, no fire?
Now I will tell you, and you need to respond, to what I mean by that.

> The beginning is performed.

I think the primary condition of the characters is internal irritation, rather than the habitual Chekhovian mood. We could do it so, but then what about Sorin! After all, there is no lyricism in him. He is a self-confessed materialist: "Now I am going to describe a man who wanted to . . . " And he goes on to describe what he wanted to do with his life, but did not. And Dorn destroys him at once: "He wanted to become a state councilor, and he became one!"
SOLOVYOV–SHAMRAEV. So, everyone is convinced he is doing something important – it needs to be proved.
EFROS. Yes, yes! And to me it is very important they are not passive, they are fighters! One struggles with the doctor, another one struggles for youth, etc. There is unusual activity in all of them. This is essential. The other type of Chekhov is already well known – one person sings, another looks out the window, and everything in a lyrical mood. It seems to me we should move away from that and try another Chekhov: fighters and defenders of principles. "You have become too demanding! Things are good for you, you are a doctor, and you are a crook." – "Me, a crook? I have given my patients money out of my own pocket, and I do not even have a second pair of shoes." Certainly, they quarrel, but behind this is the impossibility of directing their energy somewhere in another direction. Therefore, every question is a question of biography, as before a court. It is despair expressed in an active form. It seems to them the limitations of their lives are found in their neighbors. Because they have spent their entire lives together. But if there were other neighbors, there would be a different life. In everyone's soul there needs to be the feeling of: today or never. I will say everything and I will change everything.

> They perform the scene.

EFROS *(to Vovsi–Sorin.)* Tighten up the text into rapid speech like a single thought.

(To Pelevin–Dorn.) In your line about money, do not get too caught up in the words. Here we need to change course all the time, even to humorize. Internal irritation, but external shifts and adjustments can change continuously. Therefore, we need huge pauses, during which you can readjust.

Let's continue.

This is very interesting. Treplev sits, listens, understands everything about them, and realizes: Picasso, with the modern world he made spread before him. "No, no, you do not upset me." It is even curious how awful it is, and that Treplev comprehends it. And then suddenly, unexpectedly, Medvedenko's question.

> **MEDVEDENKO**. Allow me to ask you, Doctor, what city abroad was most pleasant to you?
> **DORN**. Genoa.
> **TREPLEV**. Why Genoa?

And the conversation about Genoa has begun. It begins with irritation, and ends with a story about beauty, about the promised land, about the world soul. Here there is almost a feeling of complete communication among them. From this they remember Nina. I do not want to talk about Treplev and Nina, I want to talk about the horror of life. Therefore, he does so.

They perform the first scene.[34]

EFROS. *(To Pelevin–Dorn.)* Rush to Sorin [as if to scold], hold off for a moment, and then be silent again.

(To Vovsi–Sorin.) Laugh. This is a confirmation of your thoughts. So, this is a doctor! A doctor! Punish your soul.

(To Pelevin–Dorn.) Stop his complaining: "He wanted to . . . And then he became . . ."

(To Gaft/Treplev) The monologue should be divided into two parts. It is hard to talk about the child, about Trigorin, and then he needs to share, he wants to share.

> **DORN**. I was told she started to live some sort of peculiar life. What happened?
> **TREPLEV**. It is a long story, Doctor.
> **DORN**. You can make it shorter.
> **TREPLEV**. She ran away from home and took up with Trigorin. You know this already, right?
> . . . Now she is here, in the city, at the hotel. She is been there about five days. I've already gone to see her, and Marya Ilyinichna [Masha] has gone too, but she will not see anybody. Semyon Semyonovich [Medvedenko] is sure that he saw her yesterday after a dinner in a field nearby, about two versts from here.

MEDVEDENKO. Yes, I saw her. She was walking away from here, towards town. I greeted her and asked why hasn't come to visit us. She said that she would.
TREPLEV. She will not come.

(To Durov–Medvedenko.) Simplify everything. "Yes, she will come." Routinely, without a shadow of doubt. There is an eerie disconnection of events in this. It is a very interesting scene, and there is even meaning in it.

As soon as we start talking about Genoa, there is a hint about the possibility of human communication. But it does not happen. Genoa is a dream of human communication and contact.

6 January 1966[S]
Rehearsal hall
Rehearse Act IV

EFROS. Let's play the beginning of the fourth act without scripts. Masha's task is to avoid Medvedenko. Medvedenko's is to catch Masha somehow, to stop her. Polina's is to connect Trigorin and Masha.

> They perform according to the intentions of yesterday's plan. Masha leaves, Medvedenko behind, right after her.

EFROS. I think that's correct.
FADEEVA–ARKADINA. Yes, we felt how people are connected and not connected, and not to untie them.
EFROS. *(To Kuznetsova–Polina.)* You need to find the right moment, wait for the right moment. Ready for the moment when Medvedenko leaves.

> They try it.

(To Kuznetsova–Polina.) You were truthful, but not sharp enough, now or before. Now I will do it, or die trying. She should rush in sharply, recklessly. Unscrupulously. And you had a long preparation.

And then Treplev does not stay, but leaves the room.

Because he was embarrassed, Masha wants to drown her own embarrassment in dancing. Her scenes are sharper after this embarrassment: [as if] nothing happens, and nothing is necessary for her anymore. And Konstantin falls apart. You know how it goes?

> Efros demonstrates: sharply, abruptly, effectively, falling apart.

EFROS. Next. Medvedenko – complains about his money problems.
Sorin – blames the doctor for not treating him.

Dorn – blames Sorin for not understanding that every life has its limits.

Just conduct their dialogues temperamentally, with long pauses up to the big quarrel. And then Konstantin enters when they are quarreling. About Genoa he speaks readily, about Nina – no, not until you are carried away by the story about her. Let's play it.

You know what? Let's try this: they arrive, and everyone wants to explain his own questions, all at the same time. They get all tangled up.

Sorin – I am seriously sick, isn't it time to call my sister?

Dorn – I said that I do not have any money, etc.

Masha should ask Medvedenko why he hasn't left yet, like an event, a super-event. That's what she is here for.

And all this talk covers Sorin's question: "Where is my sister? If she was called, it means I am seriously ill, why not treat me?"

Keep all the sharpness, talk through big pauses.

After the scene.

EFROS. *(To Dmitrieva–Masha.)* Tonya, you should drop your voice on your reply, of course.

MASHA *(to her husband).* Haven't you gone yet?

MEDVEDENKO *(guiltily).* What do you mean? They will not give me a horse!

MASHA *(with a bitter disappointment, in a low voice).* I wish I never laid eyes on you!

There needs to be a buildup, all day he has been stuck in front of you. You already said goodbye once – and here he is again.

Now, the issues and disputes between Sorin and Dorn. This is not a quarrel, but a biography. Because this question has been asked a thousand times, it is particularly acute.

Let's play it again. I will play Sorin. Sorin is asking a typical patient's question, and in response to this Dorn begins his philosophy. Do not be afraid to be extremely furious. Let Medvedenko begin very sharply. And Dorn will answer him super-sharply.

Play the pauses, and accumulate evil in them for a response.

They perform the scene.

DMITRIEVA–MASHA. But why are they all rushing like there is a fire?

EFROS. No fire? I take this as the initial condition of the people here. As if it were an infinite, infinite condition.

> *Efros performs the beginning of the act, revealing the essence: the awkwardness, the absurdity of each one.*

What do I mean by this, what is the essence?

SOLOVIEV–SHAMRAEV. Two years have passed, and the tangle of nerves only grew. Nothing has changed.

EFROS. And you could say they are fighters. They all have incredible energy. Everyone is struggling. One against his health, another against everything that is old, against an old love, another against the reality of being a teacher. Of course, they argue, but why?

Against something else – the inability to exert their energy wisely. Therefore, each question is a question of his own biography. Just do not rush: Now I have turned up and will reply to you . . .

Despair expressed in an active way. They think the limitations of their lives are their neighbors. They think this is because they all have lived side by side, and from all their troubles.

They repeat the scene.

EFROS. Everyone should be deep in their own soul – it is now or never. Right now, I am going to resolve everything. After living together for one hundred and fifty, no, four hundred and eighty years. It is necessary to change the scenic adaptations all the time. The urge is there all the time, and the adaptations need to change all the time. Therefore, we need a huge pause, a long silence, in which you can find another adaptation, the [tone of the] responses may be different each time.

And Konstantin could observe it all: for God's sake, carry on, carry on. Picasso picks up the picture and places it before him. Now let's suppose it is delusional, crazy to go to Genoa, to go to Nina. And then we will sort this all out.

The conversation about Genoa began with irritation – that is, logically, and then coalesced into a conversation about Nina.

They try it again.

> **SORIN.** I always wanted to live in the city – and now I am finishing my life in the country, and so forth . . .
> **DORN.** He wanted to be an official state councilor – and he became one.
> **EFROS.** And you know that Dorn will rush at Sorin, and the others will restrain him.

(To Vovsi–Sorin.) Reprimand your soul, reprimand yourself.

(To Pelevin–Dorn.) Rush at him, and Sorin says with a laugh: "Look, look at him," – and retreats.

(To Smirnitsky–Treplev.) In the story of Nina – paint a terrible picture of her downfall.

There are two parts to Treplev's story. Initially, it is hard to talk about everything related to her child with Trigorin, and then after a long pause – in another key about her creative work.

They perform the scene.

A very interesting scene. It even makes sense. When people talk about Genoa, there is even the possibility of human rapprochement, contact. But the essence is that the grass is greener on the other side of the fence.

7 January 1966[P]
Rehearsal hall
Run-through of Act I

> Durov–Medvedenko speaks in a half-whisper. Efros interrupts him. He suggests that he should speak publicly, loudly. Really, it changes the scene. Earlier there was a private conversation with Masha, now a public conversation. Medvedenko is so confident in the correctness of his views that he can assert them, preach them loudly.

EFROS. *(To Durov/Medvedenko.)* "Why do you always wear black?" – You need to emphasize the sense of the question, i.e. not yellow, not red, but black.

(To Dmitrieva–Masha.) "All you do is philosophize . . . " Masha speaks to Medvedenko. She says this casually. The main thing for her is Treplev.

(To Vovsi–Sorin.) Your eyes are closed, you do not see Treplev. In fact, your entire text exists to draw out Treplev.

Therefore, you need to open your eyes, open your communication. And when you talk about yourself now, you are suffering. But this is not necessary. You should say everything for Treplev, and you want to shift his attention to yourself. And never leave off from communication with him.

(To Smirnitsky–Treplev.) While Sorin speaks, walk along the same line.

> They express intensity and persecution more physically.

To stop Sorin, you shift his attention to the stage: "Look, here is the curtain, then the first set of wings, and the second, and beyond that is empty space. No scenery."

Gaft had a good idea. Let's try this: when Treplev says: Look, here is the . . . " he means that it is a special theatre, i.e. without scenery, without furniture, only a platform, wings, and the moon.

When Sorin says, "Why is my sister in such a bad mood?" Treplev should stop hurrying. Up to this moment, he could hurry up, speak quickly, but not here. This is a very important moment for him. For the first time, he tells Sorin the most intimate things about his mother: she is bored, she is jealous, she is avaricious, she is against the play because she is not performing in it, but Zarechnaya is. Immediately, Treplev has bad feelings from yesterday evening. For half a year he did not see his mother, but now they have met, these feelings have emerged with new force. Except she knows he does not love the sort of theatre she plays in, her theatre. He talks about this sort of theatre accurately and distinctly, recalling what they do on stage "They eat, drink, wear costumes . . . "

And then: "Sometimes I simply feel selfish, like an ordinary mortal . . . " He tells everything all at once, as though it has been growing in him for a long time.

When the conversation turns to Trigorin, however, he waves away this unpleasant question at once.

The scene between Nina and Treplev. Everything is built on Nina's desire to escape from Treplev's caresses, from his embraces. When they talk about the performance, she speaks more willingly. For her this is a release from the love scene.

Nina asks about Trigorin, whether he is young. This question is unpleasant to Treplev. it is unpleasant because she asks about Trigorin as about another man. This question strikes him in the back, he sharply turns to answer her.

The scene between Dorn and Polina.

> **POLINA**. It is starting to get damp. Go back to the house and put on your galoshes.
> **DORN**. I feel hot.

(To Kuznetsova–Polina.) This time you threw yourself at him.

But you have a different relationship to him. For you the issue is that this boy, Dorn, went out into the rain without galoshes.

(To Pelevin–Dorn.) All of Dorn's lines should feel exhausted. "I am hot," "Do not say that youth is wasted," etc. In general, this scene is about someone who is overburdened. You are doing it incorrectly because you do not relate to her in any way. Here you should place emphasis on "I." "I am 55 years old."

> The scene with Shamraev, Arkadina, Trigorin, and others.

> **SHAMRAEV**. At the fair in Poltava in 1873 she played wonderfully. What a delight!

> Shamraev/Solovyov declares his artistic preferences in full force. All this sounds absolutely categorical; however, the others are indifferent.

EFROS. Vladimir Solovyov [Shamraev] does it correctly, and it turns out clichéd because nobody supports him, i.e. nobody actively argues with him. And this reveals the various tastes of Shamraev, Arkadina and Dorn.

(To Smirnitsky–Treplev.) When Arkadina says to you, "My dear son, when will it start?" – pause the offensive, "In a minute. I beg you to be patient." Arkadina: "My dear son, Thou turn'st mine eyes into my very soul. And there I see such black and grained spots as will not leave their tinct." She reminds Treplev, "We are expecting a representation from you no less than

the spirit of Shakespeare." He answers with the quote from *Hamlet* as well: "And why did you succumb to vice, seeking love in an abyss of crime?" the sense of his answer is, "I also know what you will answer to that, but we will not go into it."

> Picking up on the remark of the director, Smirnitsky answers Arkadina very well. His remark extinguishes her hidden irony.

TREPLEV. "Oh, you venerable old shadows who rush over this lake in the night, calm us, and let us dream of what will be in two-hundred-thousand years."

This needs to be said terribly prosaically, but friendly. These shadows are directly over you, you are asking time to create a miracle, let's dream what will be in two-hundred-thousand years.

> Smirnitsky did not provide a prosaic but a friendly tone.
> Efros suggests that he address it directly to him, and parries his intonation with the answer: "I am the shadow worker who will do this for you." The first time, when Smirnitsky said this too sharply and exactingly, Efros shouted at him, "What the hell are you shouting about?"
> The next time "Ask, then we will do it for you."
> The third time, "Ask better."
> Gradually, the actor achieves the necessary tone.

EFROS. During Nina's monologue, everything is a disgrace: noise, conversations, fussing around by the audience. This should not happen sharply and rapidly, but slowly and gradually.

Nina says, "Cold, cold, cold. Empty, empty, empty. Horrible, horrible, horrible." You need to say it without suffering, if only He had heard, if only He knew what He created on earth.

(To Yakovleva–Nina.) Without any relationship to the others. If only He could be reached by all these terrestrial affairs. She needs to be courageous. But this will happen only when there is no relationship to the others.

TREPLEV. So, let them show us nothing.

(To Smirnitsky–Treplev.) For yourselves "nothing" is really "nothing." But for Treplev, "nothing" is the world soul.

(To Kashirin–Jacob.) Enter and place yourself matter-of-factly.

On Arkadina's line, "The doctor has taken off his hat before the devil, the father of eternal matter." Treplev throws something [to the ground] and grows tired, tired, his legs are wobbly, the play is ended.

TREPLEV *(flaring up, in a loud voice)*. The play is over! Enough! Curtain!

When Nina withdraws to the wings, "I broke up the monopoly." He leaves crushed, everything is over, nothing is left, and let it be, he does not want to speak, "I would better go to bed."

ARKADINA. What is the matter with him?

(To Fadeeva–Arkadina.) She explodes. She does not need to argue logically. And when everything comes to an end, she simply rests. She smokes, she bristles. Impudently, she breaks into their conversation, she is not embarrassed.

DORN. "I believe the curtain can be closed now. It feels strange."

(To Pelevin–Dorn.) Muffle this remark awkwardly.

Nina's scene.

NINA. I should leave . . .
SORIN *(beseechingly)*. Stay, please!
NINA. I cannot, Peter Nikolaevich.

(To Yakovlev–Nina.) Say it after looking at Trigorin. Say it to him.

ARKADINA. Unfortunate girl, really.

(To Fadeeva–Arkadina.) Say it to him, to Trigorin. Cover up what happened. Nothing will destroy your relationship. Nothing has happened.

7 January 1966[5]
Rehearsal hall
Act I

EFROS. Let's quietly remember what is what.

They go on stage and try it out.

(To Durov–Medvedenko.) Lev! "Why do you always wear black?" – emphasis on black. We must start strongly. On Masha's question: "Will the play start soon?" He replies: "Yes" (common sense).

(To Dmitrieva–Masha.) Tonya! "All you do is philosophize . . . " – this is an afterthought, do not dwell on it.

(To Smirnitsky–Treplev.) Enter slowly. The first thing he notices is that Masha and Medvedenko do not belong here.

(To Vovsi–Sorin.) You are drawing him out, talking to him, it is not a monologue. You closed your eyes. But you need to communicate openly with Treplev, you need to get him to talk. You are suffering, but it is necessary to get him to talk. Super-open dialogue. Treplev should only move in the area around the platform stage. And move wider only when Medvedenko and Masha have left.

(To Kashirin–Jacob.) Leave promptly, then notice the conversation is not finished yet. Come back, and then leave again promptly.

(To Smirnitsky–Treplev.) Shift your uncle's attention from himself to the theatre, and then start talking his ears off. Put Jacob to use.

>Smirnitsky [Treplev] repeats the scene.

EFROS. Maybe try it like this? Is Valya Gaft here? He suggested a truthful thing: "Here is a theatre for you! Without scene shifts, with the moon instead of scenery!" It is a dispute specifically with another theatre.

>Smirnitsky tries it.

And then to yourself, "Where is Nina?"
(To Vovsi–Sorin.) Never for yourself – all for him. "This is the tragedy of my life" – in direct communication.

SORIN *(combing his beard).* The tragedy of my life. When I was young I looked as if I drank heavily, and so on. I have never loved a woman. *(Sitting down.)* Why is my sister in a bad mood?

There is no hurry. This is very important. Up to now, maybe, but here there can be no more mere talk. And no sort of exaggerations. For the first time, the most intimate thoughts are expressed. "She is jealous, he is avaricious." It is very important that you have a direct experience. Long ago he did not see this, but yesterday she arrived, and he saw her anew. A revelation: "She is superstitious." He has witnessed her naive fixations.

His relationship to theatre needs to be immediate. He talks particularly about all the high-priests of art: how they eat, wear fancy clothes. And then – how everything bothered him, made him tired, and about Maupassant's loss of nerve. And then he talks about his mother again – everything has not been said yet.

>They repeat the scene between Treplev and Dorn.
>Entrance of the stage audience
>Polina and Dorn enter.

POLINA. It is getting damp. Go back and put on your galoshes.
DORN. I feel hot.
EFROS. *(To Pelevin–Dorn.)* Your answers should be thorough. But behind them is: "It is over." I feel hot, "it is over." "Do not say that youth is ruined." – it is all over.

It is not necessary for Polina to raise a stink, you just need to summon him back home, so he does not catch a cold. I am asking you only one thing – to play a game: Who will prevail over whom? Will you or he back down?

You are doing it wrong. You should not relate to her in any way, but each remark needs to be concluded, since [now] they all point to "and."

> Efros plays for one and then the other. For Polina – do not listen to any refusals, she continues to assert her own attitude, her own right to care. And for Dorn – he categorically rejects her, whatever may be said. Then everyone goes to see the Treplev's play. Pelevin is defensive in the dispute about art, but he does not adopt a position of his own.
>
> Smirnitsky [Treplev] does everything point by point in response to Shakespeare. Shakespeare with the subtext: "I know you think of Shakespeare as the ideal and demand only that, but I have something different."

NINA. People, lions, eagles and partridges, horned deer, geese, spiders, silent fish living in the water, and those we cannot see eye – in short, all lives, all lives, all lives, having completed the sad circle, have faded . . .

EFROS. (*To Yakovleva–Nina.*) No need to say each word separately – "People, lions." What is necessary is – "Everything. Died away."

(*To Smirnitsky–Treplev.*) It is necessary to ask to hear the shadows actively, so we will see what is not there. I want to see what is not there. This is hypnosis (i.e., a strong-willed act). After all, they can destroy everything he planned to do. This feeling is both in his answer to his mother and in the remark of his uncle.

(*To Yakovleva/Nina.*) "Cold, cold, cold. Empty, empty, empty . . . " – she does not suffer. But reports the meaning of these words, conveys their essence.

> Konstantin extinguishes Arkadina's grand style. Efros turns to the lighting technician: "Oh, you venerable shadows" – he shouts hoarsely and wickedly.

EFROS. (*To Smirnitsky–Treplev.*) "Let's look at this nothing." For you – uncle, Arkadina, and everyone else – this [really] is nothing. But [for Treplev] this is – the kingdom of the world soul, which is the answer for everything. Here Durov [Medvedenko] slaps a mosquito.

KONSTANTIN (flaring up, loudly). The play is over! Enough! Close the curtain!

Konstantin is tired of fighting. Enough! A huge pause is needed to recover himself, his hands drop, he has no strength . . . "I forgot that this was for the elite." Completely without malice. Go to hell!!! I am tired and going to sleep now. I wanted to say something nasty, but I do not have the strength. "For me . . . I . . . " – he exits quietly, mechanically, melancholy, tired.

They go through the scene.

ARKADINA. What is wrong with him?
SORIN. Irina, you should not treat a young man's pride that way.
ARKADIN. What did I say to him?
SORIN. You hurt his feelings.

(*To Fadeeva–Arkadina.*) "What is wrong with him?" You ask this too specifically. But it is necessary to really wonder – "What is it?" And in both the scandal and the subsequent conversation it needs to be more illogical.

(*To Durov–Medvedenko.*) Loiter about during the arguing – light a cigarette, etc.

Fadeeva [Arkadina] begins to light up, holds out her cigarette, "Thank you," they give her a light, "I did not bring any with me" – and immediately there is characterization in this.

Lyricism, when sitting down next to Trigorin, is replaced with illogical text, thinking about something else, she needs to calm down. "Fifteen years ago, . . . they sang then . . . every night . . . "

The meeting of Nina and Trigorin.

ARKADINA. Here, let me introduce you: Boris Trigorin . . .
NINA. Oh, I am so happy . . . (*confused*). I always read you . . .
ARKADINA (*sitting next to her*). Do not be embarrassed, dear. He is a celebrity, but he has a simple soul. You see, he was embarrassed himself.

EFROS. (*To Fadeeva–Arkadina.*) Crash into the scene and compromise Trigorin. "He has a simple soul" – he was embarrassed, you are showcasing your closeness to him.

Everyone watches as Trigorin turns away. Everyone senses something has happened. And Dorn says – "The curtain should be closed." Everyone is delighted. The curtain is closed, and then they all sit down. An awkward pause. It runs into Shamraev's story about the church chorister.

8 January 1966[P]
Rehearsal hall
Rehearse Acts I and II

They play the ending of the first act.

DORN (*alone*). I do not know. Maybe I do not understand anything or have gone mad, but I liked the play. There is something in it. When the girl spoke

about loneliness and then when the devil's red eyes appeared, I got excited and my hands trembled. It was fresh, naïve . . . I think he is probably on his way here now. I want to say good things to him about the play.
TREPLEV *(enters)*. They have already gone. Nobody's here.

EFROS. *(To Smirnitsky–Treplev.)* You hurl your accusation that already everyone has left. The play failed, and already they all have dispersed. You do not see Dorn. But you are pursued by Masha, she looks for you all over the grounds. She can appear from any side. Therefore, Treplev looks around, as though escaping from pursuit.

(To Pelevin–Dorn.) When you approach Treplev, the thread of thinking about the play is necessary for what you say to him here. When he enters, you prepare for a while and then rush to him. Treplev does not understand what you are saying to him right away. But once he understands, Treplev rushes to him. But he hides his face. He afraid that Dorn will notice his sadness and tears, and so he pulls out a handkerchief. Dorn tries to calm him. His line – "A work of art needs a clear specific thought." – is not to teach him but to help him.

TREPLEV *(impatiently)*. Where is Zarechnaya?
DORN. She left for home.
TREPLEV *(in despair)*. What can I do? I want to see her . . . I have to see her . . . I will go . . .

Masha enters. Both hold Treplev by the hands.

EFROS. *(To Smirnitsky–Treplev.)* Do not escape. Be surprised that they are holding you by the hands: "Go away! Stop following me around!" Only after getting himself back under control does he approach Dorn and says, "Goodbye, Doctor. Thank you . . . "

Masha rushes to Dorn.

MASHA. Wait a moment.
DORN. What?
MASHA. I want to tell you something once more. I would like to talk . . .

(To Dmitrieva–Masha.) No need to demand much from him. Only a request for him to listen to you.

And the Doctor thinks, "They are all troubled, and they all want me to listen to them. They all ask for medicine, they are all nervous, they are all are troubled. But what can I do?"

Let's move on right away to the second act. Only remember who enters with whom. Arkadina enters with the thought, "Now I will prove to all of you, and to her, that I am the youngest. They want to take him away from me. It will not be so easy. I will fight for him. I am young, and I am still strong. She compares herself to Masha because she is close at hand. If it were someone else, she would speak to that one.

(To Fadeeva–Arkadina) You express your perfection directly with a saying: "I am constantly on the go . . . I have a rule: never look into the future."
DMITRIEVA–MASHA. Why does Masha talk about herself so frankly all the time? The action is hidden here, and I do not understand it
EFROS. Let's take a break and think about it.

After the break.

EFROS. I will try to explain it to you, and you can interrupt as much as you like if anything is not clear. It seems to me she is a very open-hearted and naïve person. Therefore, everything she tells Dorn in the first act comes directly from her soul.

When Arkadina hesitates about something, she comes in with full confidence in herself, with self-affirmation, she defends and asserts herself very much. But conversely, another person may not have this characteristic. She may have no faith in herself, no confidence, no desire or will to assert herself. What it is, I do not know, but [Masha] lives in each of these moments, which is all I can suggest.

Here in the second act I want her to have an active nature, not to represent a black dress and abstract melancholy. It should be interesting for her to be near Arkadina, so steadfast, so strong-willed. But Masha, "Why do I live as if I was born long ago, why?" She actively wants to learn. She needs to find out why she lives badly. With all her aspirations to live differently, strangely enough, she is cheerful. "Read from Treplev's play." It is interesting to her. Her aspiration is to understand, to understand so as not to live as others have lived. There is Chekhovian philosophy in her. She grieves and is unhappy, not because she is unhappy, but because she does not want to be unhappy. As soon as we play unhappiness, Chekhov comes to an end and nonsense begins.

Three persons enter, and each one has their own turn. Arkadina is engaged in self-affirmation against age. Masha asks herself a question. She asks Arkadina why she lives as she does, and she asks Dorn about his aspiration to put an end to the past, all accounts, with a life that has given her nothing, only this hateful love. Let's play the second act.

They try the act.

EFROS. *(To Fadeeva–Arkadina.)* I suggest you should act only in these circumstances: yesterday there was a meeting in which you were told you are a bad actress and never played any role decently.

And here, today, you are on an ego-trip, and you are engaged in this self-assertion about society, you assert yourself for everyone to hear, for everyone to know your love of life. Do not be interrupted, do not interrupt your communication, do not retire into yourself. Now, let's go please.

> Fadeeva [Arkadina] spins around, displaying her youthful appearance.

That's correct, spin around even more furiously, spin around ten times. And Dorn pulls you back to the book to continue to read, he was bothered by her antics. But Arkadina takes the book away. I will read, because I am better, I understand more subtly. The same self-assertion continues.

And when making comments on the book, "Well, maybe that's the way with the French, but we are nothing like that, no such scheming," you are affirming your own national superiority: these Frenchmen use cunning, but we are sincerer, more frank.

This is a desperate self-façade: "I am not ashamed of it."

> Nina's entrance. She rushes to Arkadina and embraces her.

The embrace is long, Arkadina does not reciprocate, Nina herself disengages.
"Where is Boris Alekseevich?" Arkadina arranges her small clique; we will talk about her family.

> Dorn's scene with Sorin.

The second act begins and it begins with great tension. They step on stage to do battle for themselves: one is a statement, another is a question, a third is a denial. Sorin too lives for the hope that Nina and Treplev can meet up today. Up to this point, everything goes well. Then a long pause.

Most important, the basic point from which you step on stage, is the fact that you arrive charged up, you are fighters who battle for their lives.

> **ARKADINA.** . . . Where is Boris Alekseevich?
> **NINA.** He is down at the bathhouse, fishing.
> **ARKADINA.** Does he ever get tired of it?

(To Fadeeva–Arkadina.) You are showing that he is yours. Nina just silently observes the difference between yesterday and this afternoon.

Sorin snores in his chair. Dorn says, "Good night," cuttingly, an entire century of hostility in this remark.

Everyone enters into some type of communications with each other, so close, so twisted that there is no way to get out.

Something strongly weaved together. One person's denial, another's statement, a third's question, and then all together. It is impossible to escape. Only one manages to do so – and he kills himself.

9 January 1966[P]
Rehearsal hall
Rehearse Act II

> They perform up to Sorin's line, "Send all my horses here at once!"

EFROS. Two impressions. First, what a dull play *The Seagull* is. What a bad writer Chekhov is.

The second impression I will keep to myself. The trouble is there is not even an attempt to go in the right direction. I see, in the evening nobody thought of the morning's rehearsal. Only Solovyov [Shamraev] tried.

FADEEVA–ARKADINA. You try it out in the evening, and it seems you understand, but in the morning, it is impossible.

EFROS. Let's start from the beginning. I will be interrupting you now.

> Fadeeva–Arkadina begins the second act. The director interrupts her.

The beginning of the second act also depends on the first act. If you begin just as you did in the first act, it will be ruined. But if you begin as I have prompted you *(he demonstrates)*, everything will connect with the first act. She begins with a purpose – to assert herself. Her purpose does not depend on what Dorn tells her, she does not doubt his answer, and it does not depend on how quickly Masha approaches her. The sharper this is, the more psychologically specific and livelier it will be, and the more it will connect strongly with the first act.

What we have now is approximately how they have always played *The Seagull*: up to Shamraev's entrance it is unclear what takes place, then Shamraev enters as a stereotype figure and a quarrel begins, but the reason for the quarrel is not clear. Because there was no prior aggravation, nerves were not strained to the limit. A run-of-the-mill, old-fashioned Chekhovian mess. Here we are fighting against that, but the same thing turns out. This is terrible. Give it another try.

(To Fadeeva–Arkadina.) Activity, impulsiveness, over all their heads, you admire yourself – this is the purpose of your entrance in the second act.

DORN *(sings quietly).* "Go and tell her, my flowers . . ."

You do not notice Dorn's sarcastic remark. If you hear it, you will become even more active, you will assert yourself not only for those on stage but also for any bystanders.

The main thing is not the logic of the words, but the accuracy of the internal message. The message should be aimed far away, towards distant opponents. As though you received some letters from Kharkov, where they doubt your youthful appearance. The adjustment should be such that they could hear it even there. But to do this, you do not need the words, but the force of an internal adjustment.

(To Dmitrieva–Masha.) Just as Arkadina is on self-display, so also Masha has absolutely the same openness with her questioning. She does not suffer, she asks. I am convinced this is a very interesting quality. Nina enters. This is good. Now I, Masha, will ask her what she valued from yesterday's play. It is a free and easy activity. It is terrible how from the outside we view this activity as tragic because she can accomplish nothing, paths to pleasure are unknown to her.

> **SORIN** *(in a caressing tone, as if speaking to a child).* Yes? Are we happy? Are we enjoying ourselves today when all is said and done? *(To his sister.)* We are happy! The father and stepmother have gone to Tver, and now we are free now for the whole day.
> **NINA** *(sits down near Arkadina and embraces her).* I am so happy! I belong to you now.

(To Vovsi–Sorin.) Sorin enters correctly, but then becomes disconnected. There is no need for this. You, Sorin, continue to live with what came before, until Arkadina waves off Nina. He should notice this.

(To Shirvindt–Trigorin.) Did they play correctly?

SHIRVINDT–TRIGORIN. No. At first it was correct, but then everything stopped.

EFROS. Let's play for others.

> As a result, everyone plays for others. Efros is Arkadina, Durov is Masha, Shirvindt is Dorn, Strunova is Nina,[35] Gaft is Sorin.
> The most interesting is Efros himself. He showed that each of Arkadina's remarks is generated by her desire to prove her superiority. Internally, this heat does not cool down even for a minute. It only accumulates. Immediately the nerve is found that binds the scene together. The others multiply this nerve until there is a huge outbreak.

EFROS. Ultimately, we should see an extremely vicious quarrel erupt. But we should see the lighted fuse from the very beginning. A real biographic quarrel erupts among them, not some fake imitation.

> Fadeeva–Arkadina goes on stage. Efros reminds her once again that the target is far away, not close. Efros: "Kolevatov should be able to hear you."

During the entre scene Efros reminds her: "Kolevatov. Kolevatov has left his office, he is gone off to Red Square."

NINA. What do you have there?
ARKADINA. Maupassant, "On the Water," darling.

(To Fadeeva–Arkadina.) Say it something like this: "It is a philosophy book, child." Not for children.

We are changing the scene where Sorin falls asleep. He does not snore, he falls off the bench. This situation is a terrible shame, because Sorin falls asleep while Nina is reading from Treplev's play, and falls asleep so publicly.

(To Vovsi–Sorin.) As a result, the subsequent skirmish between Dorn and Sorin becomes especially aggravated. Do not rush your answer to Dorn. Let it be a long pause, in which you store up the internal state you need.

(To Pelevin–Dorn.) Nonetheless, Dorn's remarks should be final, complete. Speaking about tobacco and drink, you do not teach him with these words, you wound him. And when Sorin answers Dorn, he denounces him as a fat–cat doctor who does not want to treat him.

SORIN. I would be happy to be treated, but the doctor here does not want to.
DORN. Treatment for a man of 60!
SORIN. Even at 60, I want to live.
DORN *(annoyed).* Aach! Well then, take valerian drops.
ARKADINA. I think he should go to a health spa somewhere. It would be good for him.
DORN. What? He might go, but then again, he might not.
ARKADINA. I do not understand.
DORN. There is nothing to understand. Everything is clear.

(To Vovsi–Sorin.) Go up to him, set your sights, and then tell him off.

Efros and Shirvindt play Dorn and Sorin, showing the essence of their conflict.

EFROS. Is there any difference between how it was done by you and by myself? This is a beautiful scene. It is the eternal dispute of the patient and the doctor.

Vovsi–Sorin and Pelevin–Dorn play the scene.

(To Pelevin–Dorn and Vovsi–Sorin.) Do not hold onto the text. Say all the words so as not to constrain their mutual antipathy. Dot all the i's. Then this [problem] should go away, but the sharpness will remain.

> ARKADINA. Ah, what can be more boring than this lovely rural boredom! Hot, silent, nobody does anything, everyone philosophizes . . . Well, it is pleasant to listen to you, friends, but . . . to sit in your own hotel room and study your role would be much better!
> NINA *(enthusiastically).* Yes, I understand you.

(To Yakovleva–Nina.) It should not be dreamy, but supportive, with a sense of understanding.

Shamraev's entrance. For Arkadina, he is one more person she needs to struggle with. Everyone is an opponent, she is surrounded by opponents. He does not calm her down. Everything grows into a grandiose scandal.

Now we will sit down for a minute and try to understand how it all ends with Sorin's extremely senseless remark, "Send all my horses here at once!" A further long pause. Nina should not get involved in this quarrel. After a long pause, her remark, "To refuse Irina Nikolaevna, the famous actress!" They cry, go fishing, play cards, become angry and laugh, just like everyone else, but for her this is a brutal experience.

Scene between Nina and Treplev.

> TREPLEV *(enters without a hat, carrying a gun, and with a dead seagull).* Are you alone?
> NINA. Alone.

(To Yakovleva–Nina.) Do not get involved in a conversation with him. The more rudeness there is in his text – "I will kill myself." – the more simply you speak.

(To Smirnitsky–Treplev.) To hit out at her, he needs to fix her with a look, an attitude, instead of words. To beat her to death for her treachery. She, like all women, does not forgive failure. You ask her, and you need to hit out at her. You are losing the simple idea, "I came to execute her." To execute her for all her behavior. It is in his personality to do this. Destroy her, be contemptuous of her, show this in all your behavior. Say this banal thing: "Women do not forgive failure." He too is subject to this banality: I am Gogol, and because of you I burned *The Inspector General* while you slept . . . [36] "There is the real talent." Pull her by the hand towards to Trigorin.

They repeat from the beginning of the act twice.

(To Yakovleva–Nina.) When Masha prevails upon you, go directly to the platform stage. And Sorin's snore is heard on the way. This disrupts everything. From this comes shame, from this comes a quarrel, it is all bad. Arkadina is ashamed of her brother's disgrace, and he feels ashamed, too. So, the quarrel begins and goes further and further. Nothing should calm you. But now Masha's departure calms you. And in fact, "She will go and have a couple of

drinks before lunch." And on the crest of this, Arkadina says, "Well, it is pleasant to listen to you, but it would be better to sit and study a role."

When Shamraev enters, it is a continuation of the scene, and not the beginning.

About Nina's monologue, "How strange to see a famous actress crying, and for such a trivial reason." Everything is great. It is possible to summarize everything generally, but it could also be examined more closely. With Nina's generalization, "They cry, go fishing, play cards, laugh, and become angry, like everyone else . . . " we need to tie up in a package everything that happened up to the peak of the quarrel.

As for Treplev, there is a thousand times more in him that he could speak about for a whole hour. But he will not speak for an hour, only a few minutes, and everything needs to be fitted in. This is her execution, her trial, you can attach this kind of weighty relationship to it. We do not know what Chekhov might have written further here. Maybe he killed her. In any case, he did not let her out of this iron vice. The point is that I will take this gun and kill myself before your eyes. That you know what I am hiding under my words and silent behavior. It feels like the lake has completely dried up. The nail of vanity is sucking my blood.

If she stopped and looked at his face for one minute, she would run away from him, because he is about to shoot himself.

> **TRIGORIN** *(writing in his notebook).* Takes tobacco and drinks vodka . . . Always wears black. She is loved by a teacher . . .
> **NINA**. Hello, Boris Alekseevich.

EFROS. Trigorin enters. There should be a step forward. A push towards her, "I thought I would not see you again. I have never written about young women, tell me about your life." You should be prepared for this sudden advance. Do you know how it should end? You should take a drum and beat it for five minutes – boom, boom, boom! That's what happens in this act.

Once again Efros himself performs the entire act, showing its continuous tension, increasing tension, and internal drama.

9 January 1966[5]
Act II

> They go back to the last rehearsal.

EFROS. Two impressions: first – what a horrible play *The Seagull* is, what a bad writer – you cannot understand what all the chatter is about. Some kind of suffering. So, in effect, it goes and falls flat.

I will keep silent about my second impression. The issue is not that it is good or bad, but that you do not try to put into force what is necessary.

> Scene between Arkadina and Masha.

ARKADINA *(to Masha).* Here, stand up.

Both stand.

Stand beside me. You are 22 years old, and I am almost twice that. Evgeny Sergeevich, which of us is younger looking?
DORN. You, of course.
ARKADINA. That is so . . . And why? Because I am working, I feel like I am constantly on the go, and you sit still in one place, you do not live . . . And I have a rule: Do not look into the future. I never think about old age or death. What will be, will be.
FADEEVA–ARKADINA. I feel that I do not understand something here.
EFROS. I do not know how to explain. Let me show you, and you tell the difference between what you do and what I suggest.

> Efros plays it very differently – vehemently displaying youthfulness.

"Why am I younger looking?" – This subject is the whole point. I am annoyed that I need to argue about it. Indeed, you are right. This conversation is not as important to Arkadina as the controversy was in the first act. By the way, her entrance can determine everything . . . But now everything in the first act is lost. The entire first act, since it appears that the second act does not relate to the first. Everything starts all over again. But if this act is an active link with what happened earlier, then the second act is immediately associated with the first.

Masha, too. Today, with unusual sharpness, she finally decided to assess why her life developed as it did. Now she wants to get an answer.

And Dorn – it is not just a desire to shut down, but vice versa – a struggle. And then there will be both transparency and perfect psychology.

Interestingly, we "fight" against the traditional Chekhov, and then slide into the same direction ourselves. An old-fashioned Chekhovian mess. In the first act Shamraev is always played so that when the quarrel starts in the second act he has already become a stereotypical figure. Everyone needs to understand that they live like everyone else, quarrel like everyone else, become angry like everyone else, and create quarrels like everyone else.

> They try it. Efros stops them.

EFROS. *(To Fadeeva–Arkadina.)* You are reprimanding Masha, but promptly, over everyone's heads, you need to argue with Trigorin. The logic of the words is not important, but the message in them. The words can be both effortless and illogical.

> They repeat the scene.

You are doing everything at close range, but it is as if he is [far away] in Kharkov . . .

They repeat the scene.

Again, you played the logic of the text, rather than the logic of the message.

> **DORN**. Well, nevertheless, I will continue. *(Takes a book.)* We stopped with the corn merchant and the rats . . .
> **ARKADINA**. And the rats. You read. *(He sits down.)* However, give it to me, I will read it. It is my turn. *(Takes the book and looks through it.)*
> **EFROS**. You stopped, but you should have continued. As if to say, Please, I can read about the French myself and I will explain everything to you.

> *Again, Efros illustrates, specifies all the lines . . .*

By the way, at the end of the run I thought Treplev might become pitiable. This means it touches one, it means something true emerges. The common fault is mournfulness, but it needs to be rougher, tougher. Controversy is controversial. There is nothing to be ashamed of. Things are not like they used to be. It should start with Lev [Durov–Medvedenko] in the first act: "Why do you always wear black?" But the fight has been planned, the outline is already there. We need to develop it.

When Arkadina says: "My son! You have turned my eyes into my very soul . . . " this is Shakespeare. This is a challenge, instead of the nonsense [she feels that] he is engaged in. Even more than in *Making a Film*, it is important to break through to the main thing, to blow it up at the top of the show. By the way, the first quarter of the first act yesterday the actors looked like a sendup. But it must be done so that these jerks do not laugh.

The external design and internal nerves need to be sharper. Then we will take it down a little. Lev Durov [Medvedenko] will have the initial task – to provide the right spirit.

10 January 1966[P]
Rehearsal hall
Rehearse Act III

> **MASHA**. I am telling you all this because you are a writer. You can use it if you want to. I can tell you honestly that if he had wounded himself seriously, I could not go on living for one minute. But all the same I am brave. I have faced up to things and made up my mind. I will tear this love out of my heart, pull it out by the roots.
> **TRIGORIN**. How will you do that?
> **MASHA**. I am going to get married. To Medvedenko.

> *Masha's first scene with Trigorin is played by Shirvindt and Ponomareva.[37] Trigorin guides the scene, offering his hand for a*

farewell. She keeps hold of it to continue their conversation. He talks absent-mindedly, but politely.

EFROS. It did not achieve what is necessary. But that it is not important [at this point], whether it is interesting or not. Try it again from the beginning.

(To Dmitrieva–Masha.) To thank him for his kindness. To pay him back for his kindness, you pay him back with such tenderness and such honesty.

Let's play. Do not rush. When you rush, neither you nor he will have time to adjust.

They repeat the scene.

(To Yakovleva–Nina.) Enter here as though you were on stage. So that Trigorin sees her. But be as quiet as possible. Appearing in one place, and in another. Look for points where you can connect with Trigorin. Strangely enough, Masha sees Nina. Yet her desire to thank Trigorin is so great that, although she notices Nina and Trigorin exchanging glances, she cannot stop. From somewhere in the garden Nina tries to signal him there is only four minutes left. Only four minutes in which you can talk together. But still Masha does not release him. Then the scene will be very intense. And you, Nina, irritate Trigorin even more. You appear, make a sign that there are three minutes, two, one and a half. Do you know what intensity this scene can be brought to? Nina reflexively runs from place to place, and this rhythm could be transferred to him. The scene reaches the level of psychological grotesque.

Masha leaves at last.

(To Dmitrieva–Masha.) Kiss him at the end.

Nina appears, running, this is a continuation of her reflexive running around.

Now this scene continues the rhythm. But it should also be different. We will do it so there will really be three characters on stage from the very beginning. Nina will appear and reappear all the time. They only have one and a half minutes left. But in these one and a half minutes they need to be more exhaustively precise. All the way up to the end, to talk, to pack everything into one and a half minutes.

The next scene: Sorin and Arkadina.

ARKADINA. Really, Petrusha, you should stay at home . . .
SORIN. After you leave, it will be hard to stay at home without you.
ARKADINA *(after a pause)*. Well, go on living here, do not be sad, do not catch a cold. Watch over my son. Protect him. Keep him on track.

(To Fadeeva–Arkadina.) The main thing is to concentrate on Trigorin, who just spoke with Nina, instead of on your brother's request for money. You are busy trying to figure out how to psychologically tear Trigorin away from Nina. And if this disturbs you, from this your shouts will also arise.

(To Vovsi–Sorin.) Sorin came to ask for money. But to ask her for money is an awful business; besides, she is already busy with something else, she is half-dressed and preparing to depart.

But there are some moments of relief in this scene. It is awful for him to ask her for money. And so, he falls into – I will not ask, I will not ask, I will not ask. Then – I will ask, I ask, I am humiliated, I ask. And she rejects you. He recovers and begins again. The entire scene is built on this: I will not ask and I ask, I will not ask and I ask. And on the last throw he faints.

But for her, the main thing is not whether she will agree, whether she is kind or avaricious, but the fact that they do not understand how she lives. From this comes her scream, "I have no money!" This is a departure from how this scene is usually played.

Arkadina's scene with Treplev.

A little inconsistency in the film of *Making a Movie* means nothing. Here one tiny deviation changes everything. Therefore, our reasoning needs to be three times as precise.

> **ARKADINA**. How he frightened me!
> **TREPLEV**. It is unhealthy for him to live in the country. He becomes sad. Now, Mother, if you suddenly showed a bit of generosity and lent him a thousand or fifteen-hundred rubles, he could live in the city a whole year.
> **ARKADINA**. I have no money. I am an actress, not a banker.

EFROS. What happens with Arkadina in this scene? Her emotional state is like after a funeral. She lies down and looks at the corner, at the wall. And Treplev should let us know it. He looks long and hard for a way to pull her out of this "funereal" condition. He searched for a long time and then he unfortunately finds: "Mother, give him some money." After the first misfire, he needs to find a second way. But if he is mistaken now it could be forever, and so he tries again: "Mother, change my bandage for me. You do it so well."

We need to see how she moves away from him during this. We need to see this process.

We can see how she forgets what she is doing while changing the bandage. And how he stands beside her and speaks gentle words. And in this conversation the hammer falls, "Well, why do you love this person?" There is no need for her to explode at once. She should try to suppress the fact that her son has awakened something in her from his remark. But he does not understand this. And then the explosion, the showdown.

11 January 1966[P]
Rehearsal hall
Run-through of Act I

EFROS. Some changes in Masha and Medvedenko's scene. He enters with a tirade prepared in advance, he is not even very interested in Masha's answers.

Everything is clear to him: from his point of view, she has no right to go around in black, to be unhappy, because she is well off.

(To Durov–Medvedenko.) When Medvedenko says that he receives only "indifference" from Masha, it is necessary to emphasize the reason, again from his point of view, – "Of course, who wants to marry a man who cannot even feed himself?"

(To Dmitrieva–Masha.) Everything that Masha speaks to Medvedenko: "Your love touches me, but I cannot love you in return. Have some tobacco." – all this is transitional. The main thing for her is Treplev and "the performance will begin soon."

The scene between Treplev and Sorin.

EFROS. *(To Smirnitsky–Treplev.)* When speaking about the theatre, let it be directed against amateurish theatre or against symbolist theatre, something hostile to you; speaking about your mother is all in one paragraph. Yesterday all this was brought together. The monologue, "Priests of sacred art" simply grew weak on the last words. And the final words of the monologue, ". . . I run away, just as Maupassant ran away from the Eiffel Tower." Say this while lying on the platform stage. Next, Sorin says "It is impossible to do without the theatre." Here, Treplev quickly jumps up. "What we need are new forms. We must have new forms, and if there are none, then we are better off with nothing . . . " He lies down again.

Then the conversation about his mother. "Usually actors and writers were her guests and they paid little attention to me. It seemed to me they only put up with me because I was her son, and that I was a nobody. I guessed their thoughts and suffered from the humiliation." Treplev jumps up again. This should be the impulse that raises him up and from which we deduce the core of the scene.

"I hear steps . . . Even the sound of her steps is beautiful." He almost whispers, but exhaustedly.

To Nina's question about Trigorin, "Is he young?" Treplev answers almost roughly: "Well, you will see for yourself."

Dorn's scene with Polina.

EFROS. Dorn enters first. Then Polina. Seeing her, he turns away, his back to her. For an instant she does the same, but then she turns back to him. "It is getting damp. Go back and put on your galoshes."

(To Kuznetsova–Polina.) She has only one desire in this remark: to return to him.

> **DORN** *(shrugging his shoulders).* What? There was a lot of good in my relationships with women. Mainly they loved the fact that I am an excellent

doctor. Ten or fifteen years ago, you remember, I was the only decent doctor in the entire district. I've always been an honest person."

(To Pelevin–Dorn.) Offend her with each word, each remark, wound her, get her off your back. "I was always an honest person." This is delivered against her too: get away from me, leave me alone.

A change in the entrances for Solovyov–Shamraev and Fadeeva–Arkadina. They continue the conversation, but they enter from different sides of the stage. This is both indirect communication and disconnection.

NINA. People, lions, eagles and partridges, horned deer, geese, spiders . . .

EFROS. *(To Yakovleva–Nina.)* Nina's monologue from the play: she tells Him what is happening on earth. There is a pause before the monologue. Her face looks upward.

(To Smirnitsky–Treplev.) When your audience gets restless, go after them with a croquet mallet, like an overseer. Use the mallet to go around and calm them down. Ask like a threat. Complete obstinacy.

After Arkadina's remark, "The doctor took off his hat before the devil, the father of eternal matter." Treplev noisily throws the croquet mallet on the ground and wearily goes onto the platform stage. "That's enough . . . To me . . . I . . ."

Only a very long pause. Do not be afraid of a long pause.

> Nina and Trigorin's first meeting.
> Trigorin approaches and helps Nina from the stage, moves towards the right wings, and Arkadina jumps on the stage, to Nina's place, and says all her lines from there.

EFROS. But the contact between Nina and Trigorin has been noticed. A pause. Dorn's remark, "I believe we can close the curtain now. Otherwise, it feels strange." A pause. Shamraev's story about the church chorister. A ridiculous story, but it is such an awkward moment that nobody laughs.

Nina leaves. Everyone actively tries to detain her, they rise, Sorin takes her by the hand. She stands near Trigorin and says, "It is impossible!" only to him.

(To Pelevin–Dorn.) "I do not know, perhaps I understand nothing or have gone mad, but I liked he play." This should be a living, moving monologue–reflection.

Ending. Masha remains alone with her question.

In general, it was roughly what we spoke about. The common fault is that it is terribly timid. But we are planning a fight. We need to start more roughly, more frankly.

When Arkadina says, "My son, you have turned my eyes into my soul . . . " Play Shakespeare, nothing less. The external portrayal and external daring needs to be sharper. Then we will accept it.

15 January 1966[S]
Act II

> Efros suggests new staging. When Arkadina reads Maupassant, they will sit geometrically this:
>
> **ARKADINA**
> **DORN   MASHA**
>
> On the text, Trigorin enters and checks the croquet balls.
>   It is an awkward [position] but there is something to it. Everyone immediately becomes nervous, the essence of Arkadina [her control] is revealed more precisely.
>   The next scene. Efros plays Nina: Arkadina says, "'On the Water,' darling. it is uninteresting and not even true."
>   Nina looks back at Masha.

EFROS. Dorn and Sorin sit at different ends of the stage, and from Dorn's remark, "Good night," the eternal hatred of the doctor and the patient flashes again.

(To Pelevin–Dorn.) You need to speak your text more meaningfully now, explaining that if a person smokes, it will be bad for his health, etc. But that is not what is important. What is important is overpowering each other.

> **SORIN** *(laughs).* It is all right for you to argue. You've had your day, but what about me? I served in the Department of Justice for 28 years, but haven't really lived yet, haven't experienced anything really, but it is obvious that I want to go on living very much. You've had your fill of life and consequently have a liking for philosophy, I want to live and consequently I drink sherry at dinner and I smoke cigars. That's all there is to it.
> **DORN.** You need to be serious about life, but to ask to be treated after you are 60 years old, to regret there was little enjoyment in your youth, excuse me, that's a joke.
> **MASHA** *(rises).* It's time for lunch, I should go. *(She walks out lazily, with an unhurried gait.)* My foot's asleep . . . *(She exits.)*
> **DORN.** She'll go and have a couple of glasses of vodka before lunch.
> **SORIN.** The poor thing has no personal happiness.
> **DORN.** Nonsense, your excellency.
> **SORIN.** You argue like a person who's had a full life.
> **ARKADINA.** Ah, what could be more boring than this lovely rural boredom!

(To Fadeeva–Arkadina.) On the line, "What could be more boring than this lovely rural boredom!" you need to literally howl.

And before that, a real quarrel regarding Masha, who went to drink a glass of vodka.

Shamraev's entrance.

SHAMRAEV. Here they all are. Good afternoon! *(Kisses Arkadina's hand, then Nina's.)* Very glad to see you in good health. *(To Arkadina.)* My wife says you are going to go to the city today together with him. Is this true?
ARKADINA. Yes, we intend to.
SHAMRAEV. Hmm . . . That's wonderful, but how are you going to get there, dear lady? We're hauling rye today; all the workers are busy. And what about horses, allow me to ask you about the horses?

With Shamraev's entrance, his failure to provide horses continues this line [of action], bringing it to the end. It is not enough to have to listen to these idiotic scenes, but now we also have harnesses and horses – and immediately the anticipated quarrel erupts. Sorin blows up too and leads everything up to the point of absurdity: "I'm sick of it all. We must send for all the horses now!" And we need to go back to understand: how did they get to this?

Vovsi–Sorin does this accurately and looks back at everyone with a triumphant air.

(To Yakovleva–Nina.) Nina should move to the forefront and solemnly give the flowers to Dorn. He accepts the flowers and thanks her, already knowing this will create a quarrel.

Nina is alone. How strange that a great actress cries . . . – these are big thoughts about the world!

(To Kuznetsova–Polina.) Return to Dorn, and without hiding it, tear up the flowers in front of Nina.

Scene: Nina and Treplev.
Then Trigorin and Nina.

EFROS. Let's think up a lot, and then we will cut. We need to find a key, as in *Making a Movie*. [Where the character] drags out a bench, fusses, then "Sit down everyone," a long pause, "Well – what shall we begin with?"[38] We need to begin with energy at once, straight away.

They perform . . .

To let out the idea of compulsion, we need to work. More, and more, and more . . .

(To Shirvindt–Trigorin.) Sasha! This is magnificent text: you need to speak it slowly.

NINA. Your life is beautiful!
TRIGORIN. What is especially good about it? *(Looks at his watch.)* I should go and write now. Excuse me, I don't have the time . . . *(Laughs.)* You've

stepped on my favorite corn, as the saying goes, and here I am starting to worry and becoming a little angry. However, let's talk. Let's talk about my wonderful, beautiful life . . . Well – how should we begin? . . .

TRIGORIN. Yes. I am happy when I'm writing. And I like to read proofs, too, but . . . after it is published, I cannot stand it, and I see already that it's not just a mistake but that it should not have been written at all, and I am annoyed and worthless in my soul . . . *(Laughing.)* And the public reads it, and they say, "Yes, it is lovely, talented . . . Lovely, but not as good as Tolstoy," or: "A subtle thing, but Turgenev's *Fathers and Sons* is better." And to my dying day everything will be lovely and talented, lovely and talented, no more. And when I die, people I knew will pass by my grave and say, "Here lies Trigorin. He was a good writer, but not as good as Turgenev."

EFROS. He is speaking to her about what is most important to him. He is afraid of the public, his readers, hates literature and theatre. And he has a tragedy of misunderstanding too. And a tragic ending. "Here lies Trigorin, he was a remarkable writer, but Turgenev was better." Such words on his gravestone – how horrible!

NINA. For happiness like that, being a writer or an actress, I would endure the hatred of relatives, poverty, disappointment, I would live in an attic and would eat only rye bread, I would suffer from discontent from consciousness of my own imperfections, but I would demand fame . . . real, resounding fame . . . (Covers her face with her hands.) My head is spinning . . . Phew! . . .
TRIGORIN. It's very nice here! *(Seeing the seagull.)* But what is this?
NINA. A seagull. Konstantin Gavrilich killed it.
TRIGORIN. A beautiful bird. I don't feel like leaving, really. Please see if you can persuade Irina Nikolaevna to stay. *(He writes in his notebook.)*
NINA. What are you writing?
TRIGORIN. Oh, only some notes . . . A subject crossed my mind . . . *(Pocketing his notebook.)* The plot for a short story. A young girl has lived her whole life on the shores of a lake, a girl like you. She loves the lake like a seagull, and she is as happy free as a seagull. But a person happens to come by, saw her, and from nothing else to do, ruins her, just like this seagull.

EFROS. "What success? I hate myself as a writer" – this is a *confession*.

(To Yakovleva–Irina.) On the line, "It would be such happiness to be a writer," swear allegiance to him and demand fidelity in exchange.

And then Trigorin tells her everything that will happen. "On the lake there lived a seagull," this is a prediction of her destiny.

> They run the act.
> Efros stops them almost at once.

(To Dmitrieva–Masha.) Tonechka! That's incorrect. You are worried, but you need to know why you do not want to live.

(To Fadeeva–Arkadina.) You do not need to break up your lines into the first, the second, and the third. First 1, then 2, then 3! The first two lines penetrate the third line about your son. What is the matter with my son? What did I say to him? Why does he talk to me like that?

(To Smirnitsky–Treplev.) He actively desires to get through to Nina so that she understands why he wants to execute her. But she does not want to understand.

(To Shirvindt–Trigorin.) Trigorin is bad, because he is unintelligible. Sasha! This is a remarkable monologue, but it does not make any sense. How can you make the play text organic? Sasha. Think about it.

> **TRIGORIN.** Hello. Circumstances have suddenly changed, so apparently, we are leaving today. We are hardly likely to meet again. And it is a pity, I do not often meet young girls, young and interesting, I have already forgotten and cannot remember clearly what it feels like to be 18 or 19, and consequently the young women in my stories are ordinary and false. I would like to be in your place for an hour or two to learn how you think and what you are like.

From the very beginning, even though it is quick, nevertheless it is understood. "She wears black and drinks vodka." This works. "Hello" to Nina – there should be a moment of assessment and a careful reaction to an 18-year-old girl – this is a hook. He does not know how to hold her fast. He needs to say something, but you do not know how, you do not know how to talk about yourself.

And about the fact that this life is not good at all. "What is so good about it? – really! "Our obsessive, painful thoughts. I *need to* write. It is a wild sort of life. Even now, I have to leave." And then he decides to remain and talk about his soul, about the horror of his life up to the end. "Catching each phrase for my literary warehouse, and there is no rest for me either in the afternoon or at night." This should be: "She fell in love with him for his sufferings . . ."[39] After all, the words are mindful of Poprishchin, Gogol's madman.[40] That's a fact.

And to return to his "best" younger years is even more awful. She: "But what about inspiration, doesn't that bring you joy?" He: "Only when I *write*." And then, listen, what a roll call: "I love the water, the sky. But I am also a citizen. I need to write about people and about their torments. Everything keeps going forward, but I keep falling behind, and I am always catching up, always hurrying."

There something big between them now that he has said everything. And she has said everything too. Here is my house, my step-mother, my father. I would give everything for the happiness of being a writer and for the glory. Then right here Arkadina says, "We are staying . . ."

So, what is going on in this scene? The main thing is to understand whom we are playing. When I spoke about this character before in Perm,[41] I said our innovation is not that this is a person we dislike. Whether he is bad, whether he is good, but that we are him and he is us. Everyone should write as he can and as he wants to, as Treplev, as Trigorin, as someone else.

Trigorin is not a pleasure-lover, he is like Arbuzov, like us. He is in you, in your creativity. Consequently, Arkadina orders them about. And in the scene with Nina, he needs to confess, he needs to talk with someone. And he begins all this, he spreads before Nina all his insane and long-felt torments.

Scene between Nina and Treplev.

This scene is not alien to what is necessary, and from up close it seems this is what is needed. But from far away it is not so obvious, it is not audible, it is unclear. You need to enlarge and intensify in this direction.

(To Smirnitsky–Treplev.) Like someone who has not slept for seven days, pondered, brow furrowed, he is exhausted – either I will kill her, or myself

Efros performs.

Take your time so you can think. How to put into words what she has done to you. These words need to be found.

(To Pelevin–Dorn and Vovsi–Sorin.) Your scene is not specific enough. Nothing works for you, and you simply start to shout. I am convinced this is correct, but it needs to begin to live.

Dorn's life has passed senselessly. He has nothing except this woman whom he hates. As for money, he does not have a kopek. And all this nonsense because of what? Because of patients. His internal desire should be for vengeance against them, these patients, for everything, to take it all out on the patients, but as soon as this is not lived [organically], as soon as it becomes externalized, it results in a quarrel, and only that.

The patient's life has passed equally meaninglessly, and he sees the reason for this only in the doctor. Once this happens, the scene will become very interesting.

And here Arkadina interposes. She is an actress, excitable nerves, but everything should be less tragic, lighter: "You are friends and comrades, but in the end, none of this matters to me. I can leave too."

Let's sort through this. When I say at one point that I do not see you experiencing. As I visualize it, it is quite light, dynamic, and the result I would like to see is a mess from which there is no escape. They do not worry, they act. Only it is necessary to do this subtly. Then there will be a mess from which there is no escape. Martyrs come one after another – Treplev, Trigorin. But not in the sense of a martyr's soul, but in the sense of action.

If it is strained, it will be like a power drill – a drill that needs oil. But we need to drill subtly, like a corkscrew. And it is a strain because they are not able to think, to consider, and create exactly what is needed for the situation.

Imagine this: up to Treplev's entrance there is a big room with a set of doors. And everyone enters, leaves, questions. Everyone moves, moves with an imperceptibly smooth increase building up to a quarrel. But this is done imperceptibly, lightly. But we are performing it like tanks. The target is not in our crosshairs. You are beating it over the head with a log, but you need to insert a needle directly into the eye. For the rest of the month I want to hammer everything together roughly. But while you work, remember what you need in the second act.

PELEVIN–DORN. It troubles me all the time, because I do not want to become a murderer.

EFROS. It seems to me this is not likely. But you need to do everything precisely. The issue is not in the absence of kindness, but that you are 60 years old, and there is nothing left, and the patients are to blame for this. It can be played knowing nothing more, since everything is strung on this rod. I have a hand grenade, and I step on the stage with it.

> Efros plays the line of hatred with such force and accuracy that his adaptations emphasize only the essence: it is affectionate, ironic, frankly rough, etc.

EFROS. This is remarkable, now I understood what I did not understand for a long time. All of them go mad from their terrifying lives.[42] One has a mania that they will not cure him. Another, revenge. Trigorin needs to confess so that somebody understands how unfortunate writers are. But in all this straining, there should be some sort of lightness.
KANEVSKY–SHAMRAEV. I did not understand what happens to Masha here. As you said earlier, she occupies a very precise place, but it is unclear now. Everything is separated in pieces.
EFROS. Masha tries to find out everything, why she would not like to live, and then she loses interest since there is no one left to ask, she has asked everyone, and goes off to drink vodka.
KANEVSKY–SHAMRAEV. And what does Medvedenko do in this act?
EFROS. Medvedenko has his own note. It is like a triangle in an orchestra, which has only one ding for the entire symphony, and here is his ding. "You need to quit smoking." And it is all in this act. But in the following act his part is huge.

I think we will have a rest from this act and begin the act from the very beginning. Only remember what you should do, check how precisely it will sound in this symphony. For example, Dorn: imagine that you have a trumpet part and you should play precisely so much, how much is necessary, and only those notes that are necessary.

20 January 1966[5]
Rehearsal hall
End of Act IV

> The actual stage setting is under construction. A large table, lots of chairs. Lots of extra things. The table is round. Trigorin sits in a chair near the door.
> Shamraev brings in an effigy of a seagull, which he carries throughout the entire scene.
> Everyone plays lotto.
> A shot. Arkadina jumps up. Dorn calms her and goes to find out what happened. Everyone is motionless. Only Trigorin rises and slowly goes to the proscenium at the other end, closer to the door, and stops. Dorn enters, on the way he explains about

the burst flask and sits down. Arkadina finally calms down and immediately sits down too. Gradually everyone calms down, except Trigorin. He stands. Masha calls out numbers.

Efros asks Arkadina to sing.

Dorn rises and silently approaches Trigorin. It is a long game. Who will report the death of Treplev to Arkadina? Trigorin backs away and leaves the stage.

They try this.

ARKADINA. Put the red wine and beer for Boris Alekseevich here, on the table. We will play and drink. Let's sit down, gentlemen.
POLINA ANDREEVNA *(To Jacob)*. Now bring the tea as well. *(Lights the candles, sits down at the card-table.)*
SHAMRAEV *(He leads Trigorin to the sideboard)*. Here is the thing I spoke to you about recently . . . *(Gets an effigy of a seagull from the sideboard.)* Your order.
TRIGORIN *(looking at the seagull)*. I do not remember! *(Thinking.)* I do not remember!
To the right offstage, a shot, they all shudder.
ARKADINA. *(frightened)* What was that?
DORN. Nothing. It is probably something in my medicine cabinet. Do not worry. *(Goes to the right door, comes back in half-minute.)* Just as I thought. The bottle of ether burst. *(Sings.)* "I stand before you, fascinated again . . . "

EFROS. *(To Solovyov–Shamraev.)* Enter with the seagull immediately on the text, on the general conversation, and before everyone has sat down, paid attention, and then quietly settled down . . .

The samovar needs to be placed by Jacob a little before the shot. The shot, and everyone stiffens at once. Then, after Dorn's remark, Jacob picks it up and leaves.

They repeat the scene.

EFROS. *(To Pelevin–Dorn.)* Enter so that everyone believes about the bottle of ether. Even sing "I stand before you, fascinated again . . . " And immediately sit down to play lotto.

I can offer Shamraev another option with the seagull: do not approach Trigorin, but announce this surprise from far away, counting on its effect.

Dorn comes in, sits down and plays lotto with everyone for a long time. So long that Trigorin comes back to his place, although he does not sit down in a chair, but stands at the table to play. From across the table, Dorn tells him about the article: "Three months ago an article was published . . . " beckoning him.

ARKADINA *(sitting back down at the table)*. Phew! I was frightened. It reminded me of . . . *(Covers her face with her hands.)* Everything went blank before my eyes . . .

(To Fadeeva–Arkadina.) Say the line, "Ah . . . it reminded me . . . " thoughtlessly, since, after all, she believes nothing has happened, and that's a great relief, then immediately back to the game.

> They try to perform all this as Efros suggested – Dorn calls Trigorin to himself. On the first line about Trigorin's article, everyone understands and behaves like they are drawn by a magnet. But Dorn behaves perfectly the same as he does about the article, when he says that Treplev was shot.
> Efros suggests that Dorn should sit down in a rocking chair and tremble after that. And further suggests that Trigorin should to go all more slowly and stand with his back to the audience. A long pause . . . Arkadina sings.
> The entire portrayal is very disturbing. A feeling that either something has occurred, or is inevitably approaching.

EFROS. And now let's do this: Trigorin turns, although he is not distressed, but looks for help, realizes nothing yet, and goes to Arkadina. But then he cannot, turns back, and sits down in a chair. The game of lotto proceeds. Then Masha notices something is wrong with him, rises, then notices Sorin, Polina, and Shamraev. Arkadina starts singing alone, and notices nothing.

(To Larionov–Trigorin.) You do not need to be aware of Dorn's remarks, but go to her. What? What? What?! And address the "What" to Arkadina."

Everyone else should notice that something happened. First Masha, and then Trigorin. Then everyone looks at Arkadina.

> Break.
> After the break, they move on to the end of the third act. The departure. The scene proceeds without remarks.

21 January 1966[5]
Act I

> Somewhere a horn and the sound of croquet mallets and balls are heard. After that, Masha and Medvedenko's entrance.

EFROS. *(To Dmitrieva–Masha.)* Tonya! A good thing came out there: the pride of her misfortune. The dispute needs to be larger.

> They try it once again.

EFROS. Medvedenko does not complain either. He is proud that he does not wear mourning in such circumstances. For him, spiritual torment is nonsense when there is nothing to eat.

Masha asks a question about the performance – rejecting all his primitive talk. She lives for spirituality alone.

His "Yes." blocks all her spirituality.

And her "nonsense" applies to everything, everything, to all his "philosophy." Go to him with a cigarette for a peace offering more openly.

DUROV–MEDVEDENKO. Do I understand where she rushes off to when Treplev leaves? Do I tolerate this?

DMITRIEVA–MASHA. I do not understand: "All you do is philosophize." Is this a continuation of the dispute?

EFROS. Yes, but you need to say it so it is clearly the last remark in the dispute. For you, it is boring to talk with him. You say it now so that he will change the subject.

They repeat the scene.

EFROS. *(To Dmitrieva–Masha.)* Tonechka! Go slowly and try to be kind to him. I do not love you, but I am so afflicted that I cannot help you with anything. Smoke, and everything will pass: "Do unto others . . ." But then you blow up and say "That's enough! All you do is philosophize . . ." To get away from him, you move aside and then bluntly gesture for him to go away.

(To Vovsi–Sorin.) First, everything you say to Treplev is softer, quieter, gentler. You want to draw him out, but now you are so nervous he will shoot himself even before the fourth act. You do not see it, but it must be seen to understand what is happening to him. Do not hurry. Do not be afraid of pauses. And in the pauses, observe how he reacts, what his facial expression is. Only after that, can you speak to him compassionately. De-energize, without nervousness, quietly. Sit still and slouchy, and take your time before you call to Masha, consider why Treplev offended the woman who loves him.

> **TREPLEV** *(listens)*. I hear steps . . . *(Embraces his uncle.)* I cannot live without her . . . Even the sound of her steps is beautiful . . . I am insanely happy. *(Quickly meets Nina half-way, who is entering.)* Magician, my dream . . .

(To Smirnitsky–Treplev.) Valya! "Magician, my dream." This is playful. Then Sorin leaves.

(To Yakovleva–Nina.) Olechka! The continuity of life is there now, but the scene with Treplev starts as if it was a new beginning, and the entire past is thrown out. You need to continue everything with the same rhythm of impatience and excitement as before. Treplev and Jacob's scene should not interrupt this.

> **TREPLEV.** Take your places, everyone. It is time. Is the moon rising?
> **JACOB.** Right on time.
> **TREPLEV.** Do you have the alcohol? And the sulfur? When the red eyes appear, we need to smell the sulfur.

This is not an ordinary statement either. It is the beginning of the hostilities. Treplev gives his final orders. Jacob replies to them all: "Yes, sir." Then disappears backstage.

(*To Yakovleva–Nina.*) Olechka! There is less movement in the following scene. Only a hint of movement, so it feels like something serious.

(*To Smirnitsky–Treplev.*) Valya! She plunged a knife into you before the performance when she said, "There are no living persons in your play." After all, you have spoken to her a thousand times about this. What living persons? That is the same old routine! And then suddenly she says this. But for her it really is awful to perform this work before Trigorin, since she considers him remarkable.

Now, the performance as a whole. I ask you to make everything subtler and more tentative. With tentative expression, it is as if the audience is not listening, so the author entreats them to be quieter.

(*To Smirnitsky–Treplev.*) Valya! Fling it at your mother more sharply when she chimes in with Shakespeare. You need to ask the ancient shadows to calm everyone, but when your uncle inserts his idiotic remark, "In two hundred thousand years there will be nothing," hold for a pause (My God!), and then collect your strength and simply say to him, "Well, let them dream anything, then."

> **TREPLEV.** Ladies and gentlemen, we are beginning! I ask your attention! (*Pause.*) I will begin. (*Taps with a stick and speaks loudly.*) Oh, venerable shadows of old, who soar over this lake at night, calm us, and let us dream of what it will be like in two hundred thousand years!

One more thing. When you ask the shadows for help now, it is like you are having a conversation about a potato. But it needs to be about life, about the history of life. About Hiroshima, but not about the divine. And you need to be very precise to get the audience's attention.

> Efros demonstrates: everything that is happening to Nina and the fact that she should appear less emotionally wounded. And only one hand movement – a plea for silence. And he continues, almost enclosing Nina with his body.
>
> Smirnitsky tries. His reaction to his uncle's remark is very accurate.

EFROS (*To Fadeeva–Arkadina.*) You are saying "no escape" incorrectly. This is an important phrase. It means that Shakespeare will not rescue Treplev if his play is not worthy of Shakespeare.

Nina's remarks, "It is cold. It is empty" are clear to everyone, and consequently they start to listen, but then their interest vanishes – abracadabra – and appears again at the third paragraph: "I am lonely. I open my lips to speak once in a hundred years . . . "

And then they lose interest again and for the rest of the time, remaining in place, but not listening, internally at work all the time.

(To Durov–Medvedenko.) Lev, when you decide that it is totally ludicrous, get up and go, occasionally glancing back.

(To Smirnitsky–Treplev.) Valya! You immediately realize it was pointless to address them. Turn your face away here and stand indifferently and without emotion.

(To Durov–Medvedenko.) Lev, for Medvedenko this play is heaven knows what, and you shake your head. This, for heaven's sake, is what the theatre has come to: neither scenery, nor sense. Only some kind of rubbish. You listen to the text like a teacher and identify each phrase: spirit separated from matter.

> Break.
> They play the first scene.

EFROS. *(To Dmitrieva–Masha.)* Tonya! Your remarks in the conversation with Medvedenko are not thrown away, they need to contain serious content – "I am not guilty for not loving you, I treat you kindly."

> They attempt the beginning of the scene with Treplev and Sorin before the performance.

EFROS. *(To Smirnitsky–Treplev.)* Valya! You should play as if you had angina, a temperature of 38, and are dreaming nonsense. And have been this way for two days.

> They try once again.

24 January 1966[5]
Rehearsal hall
Act II

> **ARKADINA** *(To Masha).* Stand up.
> *Both rise.*
> Let's stand next to each other. You are 22 years old, and I am almost twice your age. Evgeny Sergeevich, who looks younger?

EFROS. *(To Fadeeva–Arkadina.)* You forgot everything that happened in the first act and starting all over again. For you everything is good and you are stubborn about it. You need to take almost no notice of what happens here and exist in another set of facts, another situation. You should argue with Trigorin, who is somewhere nearby. But try catch yourself in time to say a bunch of nasty things to him.

They try it.

This scene is a transition point for you – the main thing will be when Trigorin arrives.

(To Dmitrieva–Masha.) And you pose a question with your strong opposition to something important. About life and the fact that you do not want to live. Without pathos, but with conviction.

They repeat the scene.

EFROS. Good, but Arkadina is even more indifferent to what is going on here. And do not get too involved in the dialogue with Dorn. He is in a furious state, he wanted to take his mind off things by reading, and you took the book away.

Everyone makes an attempt.

Try to understand! Everyone lives by himself.

Three persons, and all of them live with their own mixed feelings, thoughts. The rhythm of the second act is amazing, the first act began with what? "I am unhappy!"

They make an attempt.

EFROS. *(To Fadeeva–Arkadina.)* You already enter later, carrying something. Out of shape.

And Masha, speak the text as a direct opposition to the fact that Arkadina is young in spirit. "It feels like I am dragging my life behind me like and endless train." And that's that.

And Dorn – I hate them all, I despise their conversation. Let's read. It is better than listening to this idle talk.

Efros demonstrates.
They repeat the scene.

EFROS. *(To Fadeeva–Arkadina.)* You need to read with the implication: I understand more subtly and better than all of you. I understand even more than Maupassant.

They try the scene. Fadeeva expresses the exact notes of irritation when reading Maupassant.
Nina and Sorin's entrance.
Efros achieved a simple human phrase from Vovsi–Sorin – "She is beautiful today."

EFROS. *(To Fadeeva–Arkadina.)* You have one shortcoming – It is static. You say, "This is uninteresting" – It is static and frozen, and then a new unit, and everything is closed.

But it should be open and dynamic: one, two, three. "This is uninteresting, and what is matter with my son?"

FADEEVA–ARKADINA. But I thought closure was necessary here.

EFROS. No, extreme openness is necessary for everyone throughout the whole performance. As I have been saying to all of you: my dears, do not play complexity, play primitiveness – one tells, another asks, the third answers.

(To Pelevin–Dorn.) Do not live with the others. Your only object of attention is Sorin.

It is interesting when all of you play like that.

It shows in the convulsive tension of the body, which is cast backward.

I am pushing you against each other and I want open, free communication. Then the distinctive commotion that is necessary will be produced.

> They repeat the scene.

(To Pelevin–Dorn.) Incorrect. Again, you are starting a new act, but it should be drawn from the first act. You should leave the dressing room with such a charge of destructive force that it splashes out in all the stage situations. Rush into Arkadina and Masha's dialogue. But not to destroy. She will destroy everything.

Do it all over again! I look and I think: what is happening? And I do not understand.

They sit around and talk. But I should understand the undercurrents of this scene. Here Chekhov shows one at war with another who thinks his time is over; a second has a furious desire to learn about herself, the world, and those who are happy, to learn how; a third, to destroy.

Let's do this!

(To Shirvindt–Trigorin and Larionov–Trigorin.) Sasha, Seva, go over here. I will play Arkadina, Sasha will play Dorn, Seva will play Masha. And the rest of you watch. Now I will explain once again.

Sasha, enter with one desire: to destroy. And Seva, as soon as I start, immediately put your question to me. Sasha, you are not as direct. It is sickening to listen to them. I do not want to, listen I cannot do it. I am leaving.

> An etude with unbelievable transformations. Efros as Arkadina, then Masha, then Dorn – and everything is consistent.

EFROS. No matter how wrongly we may have shown it, it is more accurate than what you have been doing. Consider what was correct here, and try once again.

> They make an attempt.

EFROS. *(To Dmitrieva–Masha.)* Tonechka! It is very important that you adjust to Nina's arrival immediately, so your thought about Treplev's poetry arises at once. This is interesting. Then, passing over all the rest, she lives with him now: a person arrived, and I will ask her now. Now you are living with something else, and the text of the poem comes second. You have two interests in this scene.

DMITRIEVA–MASHA. But we decided differently. We decided that I oppose her.

EFROS. But for what reason?

> Break.
> After the break. Efros talks to everyone separately and explains over again.
> They try the scene once more.

EFROS. *(To Fadeeva–Arkadina.)* Let's speak all the subtext about Trigorin aloud – that he is a bastard and a rascal.
And Masha, react as if it is the text of the play.

> They play the etude. Fadeeva: "And me, like an idiot, yesterday I even went to bed without my face cream, and today my eyes are sleepy, and he has gone off fishing without saying a word. And I need to wait for him," etc. And Masha interjects: "And I have a feeling . . . " And Dorn, "Let's read" (it is better to read, than talk to them).

This is it, this is what is needed. Now at last there is that notorious Chekhovian implication which defines everything, instead of the text the characters speak.

> They try once again using the text of the play and go further.
> The scene with Sorin and Dorn.

ARKADINA. You are not being treated at all, and it is not right, dear.
SORIN. I would be glad to be treated, but the doctor here does not want to do it.
DORN. Treatment for a 60-year-old man!
SORIN. Even at 60 you still want to live.
DORN *(annoyed)*. Oh! Well, then take some valerian drops.
ARKADINA. I think he should go to a health resort somewhere. It would be good for him.
DORN. He can go or he can stay. Whatever.
ARKADINA. Try to understand that!
DORN. There is nothing to understand. It is all very clear.
  Pause.
MEDVEDENKO. Peter Nikolaevich should give up smoking.
SORIN. Nonsense.

> **DORN**. It is not nonsense. Wine and tobacco dehumanize you. After a cigar or a glass of vodka you are not Peter Nikolaevich anymore, but Peter Nikolaevich plus someone else, your own personality is distorted, and you even treat yourself as a third party, as "he."

EFROS. It is like this. Two people have hated each other for a long time. They sit down for a chat and a light skirmish begins. "Why are you silent? Speak up, if you are not a coward." – "Me, a coward? Ha! I will tell you something. You . . . " etc. Yet it is necessary for them to speak almost without looking at each other. A shot, and then a look, like a kick in the teeth.

(To Pelevin–Dorn.) The proof of the harmfulness of tobacco and vodka can be done even more ridiculously.

> **ARKADINA**. My God, what can be worse than this country boredom. It would be so good to sit in a hotel room now and study a role.

EFROS. *(To Fadeeva–Arkadina.)* It should be a severe, rigid confirmation of this thesis. After all, it is so clear – the desire to escape from this quagmire. That was good. It should be done like that. Now it is much more precise. Something is happening.

(To Solovyov–Shamraev.) "Here they all are." This is already a concealed quarrel. "Now I will give it to them . . . "

(To Fadeeva–Arkadina.) Elena Alekseevna, do not communicate with him after the first question. "Here we go . . . My God, here he is!" Turn away at once.

> They attempt the scene.

> **NINA**. It is so strange: a great writer goes fishing . . . just like everyone else . . .

EFROS. *(To Yakovleva–Nina.)* Olechka! It should be like this. The answer is in the question itself. From one, from the second, from the third, comes the same answer: "Like everyone else." You say the first part casually. And then make a fresh start: "I think . . . "

> They repeat the scene.

EFROS. No, it feels like all this was from ancient history. The rhythm was lost right away. This, and this, and this. Everything with pauses. But you need to rush promptly into her reflections about these very important things. And then she will have accurate reactions.

> The scene between Nina and Treplev.

> **TREPLEV** *(enters without a hat, with a gun, and with a dead seagull)*. Are you alone here?
> **NINA**. Yes, I am alone

Treplev places a seagull at her feet.
What does this mean?
TREPLEV. I had the heartlessness to kill a seagull today. I place it at your feet.
NINA. What is wrong with you? *(Picks up the seagull and looks at it.)*
TREPLEV *(after a pause).* Soon I will kill myself in the same way.

EFROS. *(To Yakovleva–Nina.)* "Am I obliged to you for something? Is there something we have agreed about?" This should be roughly and boorishly frank. And Treplev should respond to this rudeness as though he were turned inside out, the whole truth: I understand the full degree of her meanness, and I will show it. Because that is what is happening with me.

(To Smirnitsky–Treplev.) Valechka! Do it again, make some nonsense, swing your hands, run around. Let it be nonsense. Then we will clean it up afterwards.

They try the scene.

Efros suggests that Nina should speak to Treplev over her a shoulder. Everything becomes truer.

They go through the act from the beginning.

EFROS. *(To Fadeeva–Arkadina.)* Imagine Trigorin says terrible things to her: "Madam, if you wish to be pleasant to me, then at least rinse the cold cream off your face in the morning."

(To Dmitrieva–Masha.) Tonya! You are doing it more accurately now, but you need to emphasize "I do not want to live."

(To Pelevin–Dorn.) While Arkadina is running roughshod over everyone, you have a growing feeling of miserableness. With each word, it becomes more unbearable to listen to her, to listen to this nonsense. And the words are the same for the umpteenth time.

(To Dmitrieva–Masha.) Tonechka! Be sure to emphasize "I do not want to live." This will be a shock for you at first, but it will immediately become clear to you how to continue. From here on it will be easy to say more actively: "Sure, I know, it is necessary to cheer up." But it is still important: she too is sick of it all, "Talk, talk, you do not live, but how can anyone?"

Sorin and Nina's scene.

SORIN *(in a caressing tone, as if speaking to a child).* Yes? Are we happy? Are we cheerful today after all? *(To his sister.)* We are happy! Father and stepmother have gone to Tver, and now we're free for the whole three days.

EFROS. *(To Vovsi–Sorin.)* You need to cheer up a two-year child, but you are cheering up yourselves.

ARKADINA. I am deeply worried in my soul. Tell me, what is matter with my son? Why is he so sad and depressed? He spends whole days at the lake, and I almost never see him.

EFROS. *(To Fadeeva–Arkadina.)* This is incorrect because it does not follow from the previous episode. It should be like this. She is living two days in hell. She is feverish. And her questions are feverish. But, besides this her questions also exclude Nina from the conversation.

After Dorn's quarrel with Sorin, Arkadina needs to begin to yell: "Oh, this country boredom ... " Do not let down, but take it to the limit.

(To Yakovleva–Nina.) And you, Olechka, should read Arkadina's monologue and fasten it all into your own remarks, so that they are on top.

And Sorin, the whole text about the city is encased in huge melancholy for city life.

They try the scene up to Nina's and Treplev's episode.

TREPLEV *(enters without a hat, with a gun, and with a dead seagull).* Are you alone here?
NINA. Yes, I'm alone.

EFROS. That is not correct. The question should be one of prohibiting: "I will not allow you to talk to me like that, to address me like that."

(To Smirnitsky–Treplev.) Valya! You are in a hurry and do not gather anything together. You have no place to save up any force for an explosion. Let's have some pauses. Your hatred is accumulated in them. Valya! Is it clear?
SMIRNITSKY–TREPLEV. It is clear. But the scene was explained differently before.
EFROS. No, just the same. Only you lost it, and now we need to bring it back to the level it needs to reach. This is a living scene. He came to tell her what she had brought him to. And it is necessary to put her into each phrase. Her life is very important to him. And he lets fly with devil knows what.

They go through the scene once more.

27 January 1966[5]
Rehearsal hall
Act II

The end of Nina and Treplev's scene, and Trigorin's entrance.[43]

Change Trigorin's entrance. In Trigorin's previous rehearsal he entered completely absorbed in his notebook, and then he noticed Nina and immediately seized her and started to tell her everything about himself.

> Now: "Hello!" is said immediately upon his entrance, but he does not interrupt his "creative process" and he does not react to her until she says: "And I would like to be in your place."

EFROS. From here, his question "Why?" [response to her statement that she would "like to be in (his) place for a while"] begins with all the sharpness of his previous line. He is no longer passive about this question, and he "gets worked up" because he is afraid she will also ask: "What are you writing?" But his first "Why?" is different. He is surprised because he cannot imagine what could be so interesting about his life. He thought she would say: to see if he was happy, for example. But when she talks about "fame," his immediate and specific reaction is that it is women's nonsense. To him it is uninteresting.

YAKOVLEVA. I cannot do this if he is indifferent. How can I go to him and collect his thoughts point by point?

EFROS. But why point by point? You should have one big thought for the whole event: to break into this wonderful, unusual world of his. This is a longing for his world, an unusual world. And his indifference – well! After all, the fact that Hemingway does not respond, this is not so important. Her feeling from this does not become less. If you have no other options, try that.

> They go through the scene, and Efros stops them.

EFROS. *(To Yakovleva–Nina.)* Olechka! At first it was good, but then you started to convince him outright. But that is not necessary. Break into the dream, into the longing.

(To Larionov–Trigorin.) Seva! You do worry, you explain, get angry, be surprised! Less temperament and more meaning: "You talk about fame, but for me it is like candy, which I do not eat." These needs to be sharper: "That's what it is for me."

This is not a beautiful, elegant phrase, as you have done, and it is not an opportunity to show temperament.

He plays sharply and almost indignantly: "What the hell, what nonsense. Wow, is that what you think, how does it feel to be famous?"

Seva, say you need to leave in the same way – he is angry and it is better for him to leave. And then – "You got me excited, and I cannot work anymore." And there is irritation here, too: "Well, now I have to talk."

> TRIGORIN. What is good about it? *(Looks at his watch.)* I should go and write now. Excuse me, I have no time . . . *(Laughs.)* You hit my sort spot, as they say, and now I am starting to worry a little and become angry. However, let's talk. Let's talk about my wonderful, bright life . . . Well, where should we begin?

EFROS. "Let's talk about my wonderful life." Do not begin like it was the start of a new scene. Begin like it was the middle. A continuation of the same. And for all the rest – not experience, not reflection, and not judgment, but a concrete desire to destroy her illusion, to explain to her there is no happiness is what she was just talking about. All the time – destroying her illusion. It is a simple event. Here, watch.

> He plays with terrible bluntness: "Happiness? In what?! Where is the happiness? It is a nightmare!!! Everything, everything I write."

Only do not complain, but explain simple things.

> Nina and Trigorin go through the scene.

EFROS. "Here lies Trigorin. He was a good writer, but not as good as Turgenev." – this is simple, like someone else's epitaph. In a cemetery. Seriously. "A good writer. But Turgenev is better."

(To Yakovleva–Nina.) Olya! And you do not give a damn. You need to snap him out of this mood immediately – "You are crazy."

(To Larionov–Trigorin.) And for you, Seva – there is a new event: I do not love myself as a writer."

And now the entire second act from the beginning. Only I ask you, everything lighter. Like a light intoxication. The scandals flash by in an instant.

> They begin the second act.

EFROS. Stop! *(To Fadeeva–Arkadina.)* Elena Alekseevna! What was that last line?
FADEEVA. "To sit in your own hotel room and study your role – is far better."
EFROS. "Is far better" – do not hesitate.

(To Yakovleva–Nina.) Olya! And you are by no means standing apart. You are with her, and this line "better" – is like a continuation of her unit.

And, Sorin, join in, do not break away.

[Regarding] Elena Alekseevna, in the beginning – play nothing, it is all about herself.

> Remarks after the second act.

SHIRVINDT–TRIGORIN. Trigorin, in my opinion, should not be so impressive at the beginning. Maybe they prevent him from writing, or something.
SAIFULLIN.[44] Seva brought me to tears in the second part of his monologue. It was terrible for him.
EFROS. It seems to me generally it was there, although some reactions are still inexact. Now I will try to explain one thing. Yesterday I spoke about the second act at the Actors' Union and it was interesting to everyone. Now you need to understand, despite what I said there, today you were worse. Arkadina comes to this village once a year. And she has a complicated son, then there

is Trigorin. Then she is overwhelmed by thoughts – my female life has come to an end. And I am desperate, without theatrical exaggeration – because I am fighting for my female destiny.

In the pathos and greatness of the second act – this rather tragic moment occurs, but now it occurs awkwardly and falsely, as though Arkadina is being played as a bad woman. But she is – Hamlet. And if this is true: "My God, how tired I am" – this should tear something from my soul – there is such melancholy.

And the same for Sorin – there, in the city, are telephones, life . . . but here is only a communal flat.[45]

A lot of things seem truthful now.

(To Pelevin–Dorn.) Alexander Aleksandrovich, you grasp things more accurately than anyone now. Though awkwardly in that monologue with Sorin.

(To Dmitrieva–Masha.) Tonya! You are there, too. But in the first act – everything they say – is a discovery. Broad contrasts of the most various things. Masha has "Mourning, I am unhappy" – an active, almost proud statement. And the second act cannot begin any less so. It is necessary to talk about melancholy, to continue the fight. But in her melancholy – she is proud, proud.

And Arkadina cannot play the event timidly, the event about Trigorin. They are talking about the ruined lives of people who furiously, persistently want to be happy.

Nina is quite accurate too, but it needs to point more towards callousness. Suddenly you have learned you are in a family of syphilitics [so to speak]. And you not only learned, but saw that they understood that you know. And these are not surprises, but simply knowledge. Steel-hearted, without surprise, without sympathy – I want to know that Arkadina suffers, and having learned, I understood that I want this life, the glory. So much so that my head begins to spin. Here it needs to be almost like Brecht in its cruelty.

The beginning I would leave the same, but in the melancholy, there needs to be less compassion, and more work. And in conversation with Nina, Trigorin immediately needs to protest – "I am happy?!" Chekhov is a tremendous writer. To avoid the philosophizing of three "melancholics," a rigid framework is necessary. Everyone says that Chekhov is atmosphere, but I think there is meaning. And if we approach *The Seagull* from this point of view, the second act is the limit of the characters' patience.

Masha has an active nature. Bear in mind that Treplev is miserable, and do not speak of him casually. And then the action is active – "read from his play" – Overcome.

Treplev should not complain, because that is like Trigorin. He needs to be tougher.

29 January 1966[5]
Rehearsal hall
Act IV

> At the beginning of rehearsal, they clear up the structure of the act.

TREPLEV *(sits down to write, looks over what has already been written).* I talked a lot about new forms, but now I feel myself slipping little by little into routine as well. *(Reads.)* "The poster on the fence said . . . The pale face framed with dark hair . . . " Said, framed . . . it is dull. *(Exits.)*

EFROS. To Smirnitsky–Treplev – all the questions are important – a martyr is inquisitive. And the monologue after everyone has gone to supper is almost senseless. He rushes about, cannot write, he wants to be released from a foreboding, a worry.

Nina and Treplev's meeting.

NINA *(looks intently into his face).* Let me look at you. *(Looking around.)* It is warm, comfortable . . . There used to be a drawing room here. Have I changed very much?
TREPLEV. Yes . . . you have grown thin, and your eyes have become larger. Nina, somehow, it is strange that I am seeing you here. Why didn't you let me come to you?

EFROS. *(To Yakovleva–Nina.)* Stop. "Let me look at you." – And then sharply at the objects in the room: "Warm, comfortable. Have I changed very much?" Stop the flow of questions, because really you have changed very much: "Yes, you've grown thin, and your eyes have become larger." This is rather cruel. And suddenly he feels how fantastic it is that she is in this room again, and from this comes his question: "Why didn't you let me come to you?"

Olya! And the full text about "warm, comfortable," "it says in Turgenev" – it is like a sling that winds up and winds up, and then the stone flies – the last line at his forehead.

And then do not suffer, but deride this old fool Turgenev, about whom God only knows what has been written.

And the following event – again not suffering, but since it is easier to cry now, you begin to cry for the first time in two years, it is a relief.

"So, you have become a writer! You are a writer, I am an actress . . ." Take him by the hand, seeing him as a writer. "You and I are trapped in the same circle."

(To Smirnitsky–Treplev.) "Nina! I tore up your photographs" – this is a last attempt to return everything. Use more energy.

I think this is interesting, please, begin. But after that there is a huge pause, which accurately reveals your passivity. I [Treplev] am like an engine, but you are extremely passive and cannot get involved.

They perform up to Nina's monologue.

NINA. Why do you say you kissed the ground I walked on? I should be killed. *(She leans on the table.)* I am so tired! To have to rest . . . Rest! *(Lifts her head.)* I am a seagull . . . That is not right. I am an actress. Yes!

EFROS. *(To Yakovleva–Nina.)* Please, without reference to the [stuffed] "seagull." There is no need to color the word so that it becomes trite. She is simply stating and explaining why: you shot a seagull, a plot for a short story. He came and shot. And all the preceding is without suffering, without blaming Trigorin and disputing with him. He demanded one thing and another, etc. That has become part of me now – "I am like that. I have understood it, I believe it."

And Treplev should understand and consider that he has nothing – neither belief nor understanding. Let's go through the fourth act once again.

Run-through of the fourth act.

EFROS. *(To Dmitrieva–Masha.)* Tonya! The waltz and the happiness come about because you can forget everything when Semyon [Medvedenko] is transferred to another district. A fantasy.

The absurdity of the dramas of Dorn and Sorin, Masha, Medvedenko, the horses, Trigorin's arrival. The long meeting, the exchange of greetings with everyone. Masha was very much delighted, and she is happy that she learned, is ready to tell everything, and that he [Medvedenko] has already left. Trigorin's meeting with Treplev is the same as with everyone else, everything is fine, he tells a few stories, asks how he [Treplev] is getting along.

1 February 1966[S]
Act I

EFROS. *(To Dmitrieva–Masha.)* Tonechka! "That's just the way it is." and "I cannot love you in return" – this is a single whole, instead of love she offers a cigarette and kindness because there is nothing more. And when he refuses the kindness – make a face at him, at his philosophy. Everything without pauses, as a single whole.

And then, without taking your eyes from Treplev, very gently, as he waves nervously to Medvedenko.

(To Smirnitsky–Treplev.) Valya! Jacob must be answered more precisely, authoritatively, and then it is necessary to know precisely what you want to say, showing the theatre. You need to know precisely what to argue with. And the text [about the platform stage] is not factual, since there are neither first nor second stage wings. In general, there is nothing. This is [Treplev's aesthetic] principle. After that, you need to return very vigorously to the entreaty about Zarechnaya's arrival.

TREPLEV. If Zarechnaya is late, of course, the whole effect will be wasted.

This line is directed at the person who manages Zarechnaya's arrival.

Valya! About the theatre – sneer on each word. Do not let it slide. "Here is the stage, here is the curtain – but there is nothing there. There is only a space, but you talk as if it exists."

Valya! And when you started talking about your mother – immediately it felt lead-footed. Physically he was tired, but ethically everything lives actively.

The first time he decided to speak to his uncle about his mother, he understood this only yesterday: this is a terrible discovery, not a moment of internal passivity. Through terrible pain we must tell the most unbearable things to another person, and behind these words – "She wants to live, to love" – there needs to be one thought: an old woman is trying to look younger. Destroy her in the estimation of your uncle, smash her and the theatre she loves.

Treplev and Nina's scene.

TREPLEV. Do you have the alcohol? And the sulfur? When the red eyes appear, there needs to be the smell of sulfur. *(To Nina.)* Go now. Everything is ready. Are you nervous?

EFROS. From the line "Are you nervous?" a very business-like conversation begins: each of his lines has a feeling of other requirements not yet transformed into art. This is active, they address this now for the first time, when the decisive moment arrives.

They proceed further.

FADEEVA–ARKADINA. I feel a falseness in how I face him, such a big pause, and then immediately I say, "What is the matter with him?"
EFROS. Certainly, because you stand and simply wait to be surprised. But you need to be amazed at every word. Why does he take offense? His mother is a great actress, she makes some remarks – well, what of that? You have mastered the event, already know everything, and present each line logically.

Trigorin's meeting with Nina.

NINA *(leaving the platform stage)*. Obviously, it will not continue, and I can leave. Hello! *(Kisses Arkadina and Polina.)*
SORIN. Bravo! Bravo!
ARKADINA. Bravo! Bravo! We were delighted. With your looks and your wonderful voice, it is a sin for you to stay here in the country. You have talent. Do you hear? You must go on the stage!
NINA. Oh, it is my dream! *(Sighing.)* But it will never happen.
ARKADINA. Who knows! Here, let me introduce you. This is Boris Alekseevich Trigorin.

Arkadina needs to insert herself into the conversation vulgarly, emphasizing their intimacy.

Trigorin – answer Nina's question about the performance – that you understood nothing – professionally. The subtext is that it is a curious form of theatre, and I do not understand it yet. And then about the lake and fishing after a second pause – a transition.

(To Yakovleva–Nina.) Olya! Start to protest against fishing earlier, in the middle of the line – after all, the pleasures of creativity are available to him.

DORN. I believe the curtain can be opened now, otherwise it is a little strange.
SHAMRAEV *(loudly)*. Jacob, my man, the curtain!

Dorn and Shamraev should immediately hurry to smooth down the awkwardness of the small pauses, instead of emphasizing them.
Treplev should speak decisively: I think the present theatre is dull. I love my mother. I'm a petty bourgeois from Kiev . . .
The first act from the beginning once again.

> Run-through.
> After the run-through of the first act.

EFROS. I think it is almost right: some are already comfortable with it, others are still not there. What is interesting? What meaning needs to be developed? That all this is modern and eternal. For example, "O, venerable shadows! Let's see what will be. There will be nothing. Let's see this nothing." It needs to be bolder, brighter. More restlessness during Nina's monologue.

We all love Chekhov, and when we watch we noticeably feel there is no other like him, so much sincerity, and he says what all of us care about today.

> Run-through of the second act.[46]

EFROS. *(To Shirvindt–Trigorin.)* Trigorin's monologue. "Here lies Trigorin. He was a good writer . . . – read it like an inscription on a gravestone.
SHIRVINDT–TRIGORIN. Aha. Like poetry. Here lies Trigorin. He was a good writer.
EFROS. And then immediately prose – "but Turgenev was better."

> Shirvindt tries. It turns out perfectly.
> Efros talks quietly to Shirvindt.

EFROS. Let's move on to the third act! *(To Shirvindt–Trigorin.)* Sasha! Sit down from impatience, instead of calming down. Masha's walk has changed – make it smaller, tinier.

> He checks his notebook.

Another period of work has begun – you need to live, not to safeguard your nerves, not to simulate. Quarrels needs to be quarrelsome, so that the words are not just literature. At this point, it is no longer necessary [to be so] technical. It is less good, but sincerer. Why can't you grasp what I'm saying? The problem is that it seems to be impossible for you to overlook anything. For example – "I love writers." Pause. Then wait, and that makes one unit, and the next one is equally slow.

> Run-through of the entire performance.
> The beginning of the second act is changed. Fadeeva–Arkadina has removed the sharpness from the argument with Trigorin.

EFROS. *(To Fadeeva–Arkadina.)* You have to be worried – from the questions: "Where is Boris? Where is my son? What is matter with all of them, have they gone crazy?" But you ask the questions quietly.

(To Dmitrieva–Masha.) Tonya, please speak the lines about his unhappy soul as something self-evident and significant.

DMITRIEVA–MASHA. To me this interferes in some way with my move to Nina before my request to read from the play.

> **MASHA.** He is sick at heart. *(To Nina, shyly.)* I beg you, read from his play!
> **NINA** *(shrugging her shoulders).* You want me to? It is so uninteresting!
> **MASHA** *(restraining her delight).* When he reads something, his eyes burn and his face turns pale. He has a fine, sad voice, and he has the manners of a poet.

EFROS. Why? After all, it is interesting to you, although to Arkadina it is already uninteresting. Speak as if a new, a different performance will begin now – and it is something unusual, spiritual. This tone continues up to the line, and then you just need to return to tone of the line.

> Scenes between Treplev and Nina, Nina and Trigorin.
> Trigorin's entrance now takes place earlier, Treplev's last remarks now take place in the presence of Trigorin.

> **NINA.** You are overworked, and you have no time or desire to be conscious of your own importance.

EFROS. Nina does not teach him. This is wrong. She understands what he said, she examines herself. She does not think that she knows more, she wants to understand. She waits for him, full of intuition and interest.

> They try again.
> Treplev's entrance is changed. He became less hurried. Efros explains something to Yakovleva [Nina] and Smirnitsky [Treplev].

> **TREPLEV.** I had the meanness to kill this seagull today. I place it at your feet.
> **NINA.** What is the matter with you? *(Picks up the seagull and looks at it.)*

EFROS. *(To Smirnitsky–Treplev.)* Why did you change what we planned? What are you entering with, where did such passivity come from? [You are thinking] I will not notice it, I will overlook it, and so it will remain. You should enter with such a load of pain that it overflows, from the time when you wandered around and thought about her treachery, about change, and how to arrive and pour all this out, to say it to her directly. He pauses only because he chokes, and not because he is playing melancholy and grief.

(*To Yakovleva–Nina.*) Olya, you should keep going from your previous monologue "like everyone else." At this point you can understand that wonderful world you dream of getting into.

> They repeat up to Trigorin's monologue about happiness once again. Efros stops them.

EFROS. Here, let's try it.

(*To Yakovleva–Nina.*) Olya! "And I would like to be in your place." This is not right. You are simply saying that it is quite good. But it should be fantastic – to break in, to break through there, into his world, from this lake. It is very active.

> Efros plays for both characters, exacerbating the severity of the conflict beyond belief.

Trigorin's text about happiness is a cry from the heart: "I'm happy? Is that it!!! What happiness?!! It is torture!"

(*To Yakovleva–Nina.*) This is interesting, Olya, on your line in the second act it should be: here is Nina – "I'm happy," and then is the splash of cold water – "This is Maupassant, darling." The inhabitant of heaven has insisted on a distance, and everything is a wound, a wound up to the monologue – the understanding – "Like everyone else." And there it is even worse: Treplev with the seagull, and then suddenly Trigorin. And at this point there is such longing for another, for his life.

(*To Smirnitsky–Treplev.*) We calmed down this scene – we wanted to return it to the meaning, but now, if we do not to feel full scale of it all, the degree of what she did to him – nothing will result. She made him the murderer. "I had the meanness to kill." You realized how mean mankind can be, and this tragic knowledge needs to be expressed and spoken about.

> They go through it once again. Efros stops them.

EFROS. (*To Smirnitsky–Treplev.*) Valya, when you see her reaction to Trigorin – it is just as horrible for you as if she were beaming with pleasure. "I will not disturb you anymore." – this is not politeness and it is not contempt. It is intolerable. All of you can go to hell, live in this terrible, inconstant world, but I cannot.

(*To Shirvindt–Trigorin.*) Sasha! For you it is very important that the conversation with Nina is laid over your already tragic feeling of life. At this point you need to leave – it is horrible. I can learn nothing about you, and I will not write. Everything is like a leapfrog jumping around everywhere, driven, but there are still questions. And he feels all this quite differently. Today you understood it very sharply. From this point on you must address her with complete frankness. A confession that pulls everything together and transfers it to another plane. There is a new relationship.

> They perform it once again.

EFROS. *(To Smirnitsky–Treplev.)* Stop, Valya! It is already better.

But you must feel even more sharply that the best of women immediately betrayed him as soon as his performance failed.

(To Yakovleva–Nina.) Olya, you need to connect your entire life to the conversation with Trigorin.

12 February 1966[5]
Run-through[47]

> Remarks about the run-through.
> Act I

EFROS. *(To Smirnitsky–Treplev.)* In the beginning, Valya, you entered mechanically, without changing the rhythm, and you mishandled the monologue very badly, in a whisper, but these are thoughts that just came to you now.

(To Vovsi–Sorin.) You are singing too much, it is only necessary to begin, that's all.

(To Kuznetsova–Polina.) You need to drag the doctor back.

(To Yakovleva–Nina.) The monologue was nervous in the first act.

Dorn attacks with a hammer, Sorin attacks with a stick, but their weapons are identical.

(To Durov–Medvedenko.) Talk about the church chorister's salary right away, without a break.

(To Pelevin–Dorn.) Move away from the conversation with Masha right away – you know she will complain.

> Act II

(To Dmitrieva–Masha) Well, read; well, we will make something – good. But the quarrel is bad. You are sitting in the text, but you must be less logical. This is irascibility, and not logical justification.

(To Vovsi–Sorin.) "Of course, it is better in the city" – is late, step on each other's lines progressively more.

(To Smirnitsky–Treplev.) Treplev needs to enter more promptly on: "Are you alone here?"

(To Shirvindt–Trigorin.) Since Trigorin enters promptly, there is no need to write on the wall.[48] In the beginning there is no communication, no elementary truth in the conversation. Sasha, you are playing panic, purely external excitement. External temperament.

(To Yakovleva–Nina.) You must physically go to him, not away from him, and for one purpose: "All the same, I still envy you and want to be an actress."
(To Shirvindt–Trigorin.) Trigorin needs to converse and think at the same time. The third and fourth acts were better before.

[Repeat] Act II

(To Fadeeva–Arkadina.) "You can stay" – is cunning, but not permission.
(To Yakovleva–Nina.) Olya, exit earlier at the end of the scene with Trigorin.
(To Durov–Medvedenko.) [Referring to the earlier run-through.] Lev, in the beginning in the fourth act, "The weather is awful" – is spoken actively. Without a moment's pause.
Let's try the second act again.

They repeat the scenes with Nina, Treplev and Trigorin.

EFROS. *(To Shirvindt–Trigorin.)* Sasha, everything you say has a straightforward character, since you say what is directly written in the text. He must be in direct communication, but thinking of something else – like he is sitting on a nail.

14 February 1966[S]
Run-through of the entire performance[49]

Minor notes after the run-through

EFROS. Dorn rises earlier, before Treplev's line ". . . let them portray nothing."
Konstantin stands in the corner when Dorn praises the performance. He is driven into the corner, mindful of one question: "Where is Nina?" On Masha's entrance, he is sharp – "Leave me alone! Do not follow me."

They run through the second act.

EFROS. *(To Fadeeva–Arkadina.)* Arkadina on the swing. Then she "stands beside someone younger-looking? Why [do I look so young]?" Everything needs to be more accurate.
(To Yakovleva–Nina.) Nina! "Like everyone else" – Now she condemns, and we need to understand. Nina's blocking – she holds Trigorin's hands – for a long time.
(To Larionov/Trigorin). Develop the subject of the story about the seagull much more.

17 February 1966[P]
Run-through

Discussion of the run-through

EFROS. I have a strange feeling – I did not like the run. I began to analyze, to sort through my impressions – and I concluded that almost all the significant errors were found in two places. The beginning and end of the second act, they should be clarified, but in terms of results and structure, everything else is correct. But besides accuracy, we are still waiting for more acting discoveries, waiting for someone to feel the scene and put across something special. Now there is a fairly accurate compliance with the rules, but no surprises, no discoveries. In the first run, everyone was still groping and much was still obscure, but there also needs to be something unexpected here. I am worried it was too emotional.

Everyone probably needs to dig in more deeply, search for special paths for the present moment, not repeating dead portrayals.

Everything is correct, but at this point the spectator is not yet experiencing it because we are too mechanical. This is in general. Now some specific comments.

(To Dmitrieva–Masha.) The scene is good, but the mechanical quality is still there: "All you do is philosophize." You are teaching a person [Medvedenko] whom you obviously dislike, but I'm convinced this can be subtler and deeper. I think this can be the result of a big moral and philosophical debate that stretches across centuries, not simply a nervous rejection. And physically – she should probably turn around and speak with full voice and full gesture *(demonstrating)*, no messing around.

(To Vovsi–Sorin.) You enter – and immediately: theatrical, mechanical. It should be softer, quieter, more graceful, more tender. This is my nephew, I am his uncle, things are bad for him. Therefore, tenderness. Ask questions about his mother more unpredictably than the scene was played.

(To Smirnitsky–Treplev.) Valya, the monologue about your mother. You are rushing and fussing around. I cannot find other words for it – I think it is important that these discoveries took place only yesterday. Therefore, frankness. Otherwise the scene collapses.

The episode with Sorin singing [from *The Two Grenadiers*]. It is bad. This is a lyrical, affectionate joke about two tender lovers. You should sing precisely as much as you need to exit, and then immediately look back.

(To Smirnitsky–Treplev.) "Is the sulfur ready?" Like preparing for war. More actively – "it is necessary to write . . . " – this is a conviction.

All the entrances are too hasty.

"My son! You . . . " – this is not a fine phrase, it is a reminder of greatness. About Shakespeare. About genuine art.

"Close the curtain." No pause after this, you can pause after: "I . . . I . . . "

(To Fadeeva–Arkadina.) Elena Alekseevna! The quarrel is better, but it should be without feeling. Like smoke. Lightly and without a break.

Make all the pauses shorter in the scene with Nina and Trigorin, Dorn and Shamraev. Otherwise it is unintelligent, and emphasizes the awkwardness.

(To Shirvindt–Trigorin.) Do not start everything in a vacuum.

The beginning of the scene with Treplev and Dorn – softer and more truthful.

(To Smirnitsky–Treplev.) Valya, when it drags, it pulls together only at the end. But the act is good.

The second act – I think my mistake is that everything is hidden, and this blocked your customary confidence.

(To Vovsi–Sorin.) Do everything ten times slower. By the way, yesterday evening I was listening to [Managing Director] Kolevatov's speech and thought: he does not understand anything. I support something quite different. But I went anyway – and it lapsed into politics.

(To Dmitrieva–Masha.) Tonya! Let's try the scene [about Treplev's] poetic manner differently. It is as if Arkadina pushes your request aside.

DMITRIEVA–MASHA. I think this remark is very difficult to direct to Nina. Since she is so opposed.

EFROS. I understand, but I do not know what else to consider here, since the beginning – melancholy – is already understood by me, the spectator. And if this line turns out to be [further] melancholy – it is awful. Masha needs to put an end to this. Press her so that everything changes, so that this melancholy, this gloominess, comes to an end. And when it is refused and it does not happen – then I will have a very clear idea of Masha's line.

You have fabulous material, and you cannot [possibly] do badly in the role. You make it quieter and less surprising, and this is good as far as it goes. I did not interfere with you, or interrupt you, but my thoughts are not being read. I would like her to be a woman who does not want to obey. If she is crushed after the first act, then there is no place to go after that. But I want her to "Move to another region," from first act to last. All this has broken down. Even a remark like – "I will call him [Treplev]" – was without anguish, without sadness, willingly. Nina arrives – the people there want to tell jokes, they are bored. Then a story teller arrives – she needs to move closer to him. And in the fourth act sadness involuntarily emerges, even in the scenes with her husband. But it needs to be different from that, since only in this burning desire to break out will the beautiful, gentle, sad, and traditional Masha go away.

Dorn, in the quarrel with Sorin, you play it about the valerian drops, since you want to live in the text, but it is necessary to flare up. What always happens when one person punches and yells at another? It is not literary. It is all about something else, and the actual text is not important, one thing needs to build on another – Arkadina howls, Sorin yells about the telephone.

He demonstrates.

I cannot find the words now for your adaptations, colors. When we rehearsed this, I thought about how well the second act was planned. In the beginning, there were three of you who lived their individual energies. Three lives, each with their own energy.

He demonstrates.

Sharply. Everyone lives on their own. This needs to be preserved. I sit, and I walk, and I read – everything in opposition, internal conflict.

(To Smirnitsky–Treplev.) Valya, the scene with Nina: you enter and in a few seconds, something happens. And then everything goes wrong. Every thought needs to be terribly conscious, and he is on the defensive from this. And the action – I came to you [Nina] to understand what I discovered, and now I will go and shoot myself. I need you to know what you did.

Trigorin's arrival – this is also a sequel, an awareness of all that is happening. The second time, save the second plan with Trigorin. In the finale – change the entrances and exits.

(To Yakovleva–Nina.) Olya, be violent with each other, let it fly and create a big, almost hooligan-like scene – [their relationship] is finished.

(To Smirnitsky–Treplev.) Valya, in the first scene – Nina's arrival – pour out tender kisses. Two things are important – do not force any adaptations, do not make it lyrical, sad. Make it cutting, intense, sharp.

Did I tell you about yesterday? I came home, took off my coat, and suddenly I heard some conversation in the kitchen. What was it? The television. [Mikhail] Kozakov and [Oleg] Tabakov in a scene from [Ivan Goncharov's novella] "An Ordinary Story." They spoke quietly but pointedly, with such communication in their dialogue that all the fine nuances were expressed.

> They rehearse the second act before the beginning of the scene between Trigorin and Nina.
> Director's remarks.

EFROS. *(To Dmitrieva–Masha.)* Tonya, collide [with Nina] even more rudely when you ask her to read from the play.

(To Vovsi–Sorin.) The text is haphazard, without pauses. After the "horses" [incident], sit down excitedly, not tragically.

(To Yakovleva–Nina.) Olya! "What does this mean?" Her reaction to the seagull is immediate, direct.

(To Shirvindt–Trigorin.) Sasha, do everything slowly and without vanity, so I can understand.

> They run the second act again.
> Director's remarks.

EFROS. Sorin enters separately from Nina, then he takes her hand.

(To Dmitrieva–Masha.) Tonya, do not be afraid to start crying, blow up the situation and the reading, the "my leg has gone to sleep" – anything, but blow it up.

In Sorin's dreams about [life in] the city – like a motorcycle racer who has had to live in a village for ten years and says everything in terms of movement – the whole scene is louder, more active, even shouted.

(To Yakovleva–Nina and Smirnitsky–Treplev.) Olya and Valya – vulgar quarreling up to the start of the music, then stop and say this important thing: "Soon I will kill myself in the same way." Be victorious, transcend yourself.

(To Trigorin–Shirvindt.) Even slower, gather your thoughts for each unit.

Now it is a little bit closer to what we need. I think it is incredibly important they are all frantically clinging to life, to joy.

(To Sorin/Vovsi.) "We are happy."

(To Dmitrieva–Masha.) Masha. Everything is truthful, but it is even more active, as soon as I see how she shatters [the atmosphere of] melancholy – things get interesting.

(To Pelevin–Dorn.) Retain energetic destruction in everything: "People are boring."

(To Kuznetsova–Polina.) Polina. Sharper! Now, this minute you want to have him. Everything unusually active.

(To Smirnitsky–Treplev.) Enter quickly – and then immediately "Are you alone?"

(To everyone.) Play it again.

They run the second act.
Director's remarks.

(To Dmitrieva–Masha.) Tonya, it is almost there, but the beginning – "I feel like I was born a hundred years ago" – needs to be played as an objection. And then very strongly interrupt with – "I know it is all nonsense." And "My leg has gone to sleep" is frankly shouted.

Everyone lives by any means necessary, clings to any joy.

Scene Trigorin–Nina.

(To Shirvindt–Trigorin.) Sasha, with complete peace of mind – internal dynamics. Fishing rod – whistling – they reveal something about this character.

(To Yakovleva–Nina.) Imagine there is a motorcycle race. It is wonderful. But the motorcycle racer suddenly says it is awful, it is a nightmare. Not great. At first, she does not even listen to him, she speaks so ecstatically about how fascinating it was. And when she finally hears what he said – she rushes to dissuade him – "You are just tired."

SHIRVINDT–TRIGORIN. Isn't this boring – our two-hour conversation with Nina?

EFROS. It seems to me the development must be put together very precisely. Where is this development? He begins by saying he does not even want to talk about it, but she nudges him towards his memories – "Well, what is so good about it when two of us just broke our necks in the [motorcycle] race?" And he begins to remember, and climbs even further into these memories, and he cannot stop thinking about it and getting excited, though outwardly I try to control myself.

But something begins to emerge. For Trigorin the desire to live is also very important, come what may. Hence internally – do not give up. He is still a man, still chained by the present, turned inside out, because it really hurts. But in the fourth act he is no longer tormented by anything. He has surrendered. He no longer complains and does not grieve. But we will deal with this in later rehearsals.

17 February 1966[5]
Rehearsal hall
Run-through

EFROS. It is a strange feeling: on one hand, I did not like the last run, I even tried to write down all the scenes I did not like, but I concluded that almost everything was right, we must look for the beginning and end of the second act, everything else is right, but nevertheless I was not satisfied with the overall impression of the run. What is the issue then? Probably it is that in addition to the truthfulness of sense and truthfulness of pictorial representation, I'm still waiting for more acting revelations. Waiting especially for the actors to concentrate so that something surprising happens. But there were no acting surprises. It was the first run, and the seams started to show. The main thing is that what we already mastered and accomplished properly did not collapse. The impression from the run today was quite good, but the special quality necessary for people to empathize with us did not emerge, because we are too technical.

Individual comments.

(To Dmitrieva–Masha.) The first scene is good, but it has a mechanical quality. Masha: "All you do is philosophize" – there is opposition to the person with whom she is speaking. I think it is smaller than it could be. This is part of a philosophical debate, not just nerves. This is the conclusion of a match that goes on between them for many days, perhaps many centuries.

The adjustment is small, but it can change the meaning considerably.

In terms of physical changes, she says her line with full gesture and full speech.

Efros demonstrates.

She wants to stop the melancholy and intolerance of this life. She replaces it with a great desire for something else.

You have a lot of wonderful information with which you will find it hard to mess up the role. It will be good whatever happens. But you have a smoothed out the role, deprived it of unexpected drama. How do I imagine the second act? This is a woman who does not want to obey. If she is already trampled down in the first act, then what is there to play? But if you imagine she does not agree, then everything is different. Then she is constantly disagreeing, seeking, struggling, desiring.

The second act – once Nina has arrived – is very important for you. There are certain people who like it when you tell anecdotes, they are entertained, but if you do not tell anecdotes, if you are a poet, let alone a woman poet, then everything is different. You rebuild, you adjust to her. But when everything turns bad – "my foot is asleep." This nuance is very important. This provides an opportunity to move away from the gentle, traditional interpretation of Masha.

(*To Vovsi–Sorin.*) The quarrel with Dorn here should be lighter, more keyed up, easier. The quarrel should not be about the meaning of the spoken words, but because he had just fallen asleep, because life in general is lived badly. The quarrel is not about specific, private matter. Then it would not be Chekhovian. Maybe Gorky or Ostrovsky, but not Chekhov. Not his nervous, human organization.

I want to say something. I cannot find the words. Just as you sometimes do not find the adaptations.

An important nuance has disappeared from the second act. I thought how good we had planned a second act: three people enter – and each has his own aggressive inner life.

Nothing of that is in the second act now. It is necessary to change it. It should start quietly, one sitting, one standing, the third entering – and through this their entire inner existence would be viewed.

Treplev's scene in the second act went badly. He entered like a disheveled rooster. This seems to be good. But it is only enough for two minutes. The point is not to put pressure on Nina. Nothing would come of it. He has something else in mind: I am embarrassed to say I have only the same words to say. But there are moments of super-openness. The action – "I want you to know what I experienced, what I discovered." And the transition to Trigorin, "You are blushing, and he has hardly come near you."

In general, two important things.

First, do not soften the representation. Do not do it simply quietly, simply delicately. Make it sharp, harsh, nervous.

Second, do not fade out in the pauses. Sharp, sharp, sharp, even though everything has been lived gently.

Get hold of yourself, and play the second act quietly, with meaning. I would like it if he would get to some of these things I have mentioned.

> They play the second act up to the meeting of Nina and Trigorin.

EFROS. It is necessary to aggravate the inner life, the internal line of everyone. Aggravation and confrontation. The characters need to assault each other on the lines.

Masha – be even more insistent, "vulgar."

Dorn – say good night more sharply.

Nina – immediately react to the seagull.

> After the run.

EFROS. *(To Dmitrieva–Masha.)* Use plenty of force to exclaim: "I beg you, read from his play!"

(To Fadeeva–Arkadina.) "Oh, what can be more boring than this lovely country boredom! – As though you are a motorcycle racer and been sitting for ten years in a country village.

(To Yakovleva–Nina.) Play the ending until I stop you. it is possible to be more temperamental there.

I beg you, get hold of yourselves. Forcibly do everything I ask of you. As if you are motorcycle racing. Everyone needs to get to the lead.

They repeat it once more.

EFROS. When the characters start to explode, I understand what is going on. They're all clinging terribly at every opportunity to live. Therefore, Sorin says: "We are happy." He is shouting a slogan. And the same for everyone.

(To Kuznetsova–Polina.) You only have two minutes for a quiet conversation, so Dorn needs take you to himself right at this moment. All the links of one chain are here. Once again, I ask you to overwhelm him.

(To Larionov–Trigorin and Shirvindt–Trigorin.) Do not start the role as though it were of some importance. What is needed is simply a conversation about the play, about the lake, where there is a lot of fish.

(To Pelevin–Dorn.) Do not unintelligently emphasize the pauses during the meeting of Nina and Trigorin. With the tearful guy – Treplev – be natural, softer, gentler: the main thing is not that Nina left, but what I told you about the play. In the finale, you and Masha need to drag Treplev into the forefront, and if you hesitate to do this – the scene evaporates. This is the first act. Still, for all that, it is good.

They play the second act.

EFROS. *(To Fadeeva–Arkadina.)* Instead of being deeply hidden – that is, what occurred yesterday – Arkadina needs to routinely recover her optimism, her feminine charm, but all her troubles manage to break through in five minutes.

(To Vovsi–Sorin.) The first scene is good, but it goes directly to the subject of the theatre. Something does not feel home-like here. It needs to be subtler, gentler. A moment of singing – a gentle joke about love.

(To Smirnitsky–Treplev.) The monologue about his mother – it is difficult for me to find new words about it. More passionate about the fact that he needs to endure it. He only just discovered it and learned it yesterday. It burned him. Just yesterday he learned it, and now he perceives it very nakedly.

(To Fadeeva–Arkadina.) "My son . . ." – this should not be trivial. This is an ironic joke on a special scale. We are waiting for your art as though it were Shakespeare's. The quarrel, her temper are as light smoke, like the tips of a flame. Do not press.

(To Vovsi–Sorin.) In the second act, do everything more slowly, more quietly.

(To Dmitrieva–Masha.) This damn situation – "she reads poetry" is very artificial. Let's try another way: read the poetry – suddenly. At this point for me a second and badly understood boredom appears. I already grabbed at melancholy at the beginning, and I cannot play it anymore. And now she backtracks to this boredom. Let's try to be vulgar up to the end – so that I understand how much it is disgusting or how much it is acceptable. Try to break this empty talk of melancholy, and when this does not take place, you become uninterested and leave. You are saying that when he reads – that is fine. You have asked for this poetry – but then Sorin is heard snoring, and to you Dorn's remarks sound deafening and evil. So, "Good night."

18 February 1966[P]
Run-through of the performance

EFROS. The second act went well today.

The beginning of the third act is not enough of what is needed.

(To Dmitrieva–Masha.) Today you played it super-frankly. But this over-frankness is only half of what is needed.

Treplev's scene with his mother was bad. Everything was unconnected. An unconnected caress, unconnected dispute. But actually, one arises from the other. Now, you finish one and the other begins. Where can you go from that? Here, everything connects, all the pauses are filled with tremendous explosive force.

(To Fadeeva–Arkadina.) Today the third act scene with Trigorin was well done. In fact, I think it is your best scene. There was real dramatic structure in it. But you have deprived her of one lovely color – feminine wiles. When he stays with you, you deliberately missed the line "Now he is mine."

FADEEVA. I really do not want to say it. After all these efforts, he does not need me anymore.

EFROS. You do not need him, but she needs him.

> Again, a dispute that ended with words: "Generally, if you want, do it your own way, but I do not advise it."
> Run the fourth act.

EFROS. In the story about Genoa, everything is combined into one passion. Here the theme is to escape. They are merely making a big quarrel, and now they throw in Genoa, where there is a lot of color, a lot of sun.

Pelevin [Dorn] plays great, however it is not real life, but a picture. Simply a single lovely picture. But this is a very important locale, and it is no accident that that after this he is talking about Nina. And then how should this conversation proceed?

(To Dmitrieva–Masha.) You should perceive the [importance of the] meeting between Trigorin and Treplev, and your husband being here is just an excuse for you. You should break through this pretext, and live differently.

Medvedenko does not enter with line about "the baby." It is a scene of wild brutality. Medvedenko does not understand, since he himself lives in this brutality. But the line should bring everything outside.

(To everyone.) There is no need to play lotto as they did the nineteenth century. Quietly sitting around. They cling desperately to this game.

Trigorin's line – "If I lived in a manor house by a lake . . . " is a cry of the soul.

Treplev was anemic in the scene with Nina. When he suddenly grabbed for the wall, that was a unique temperamental moment.

Laughter.

Comrades, you are all very pleased with yourselves. But I ask you to listen to me. I worked for ten years at the Central Children's Theatre and for ten years I had heard about my work: it is all so lovely, lovely cute directing, but when will you choose a real career path? I think this is a breakthrough for everyone associated with that sort of anguish and pain.

Next. Treplev has not found his place [either]: "You have found your path . . . " and "I have no faith and I do not know what my calling is."

What does it mean to play one's greatest weakness? It means to be very confident that you have died. Here this does not happen.

19 February 1966[P]
Run-through[50]

Comments after the run

EFROS. Today's rehearsal was better than yesterday's, some made several steps forward, and I will talk about that later. And in today's run there was much of yesterday's, when a nice comfortable outline settled in. And when you breathe, when you put in human content – then there is genuine art.

Pelevin [Dorn] played very well, everything is there. Dmitrieva: the silence is good, "youth, youth" is good. Treplev with Nina, Nina with Trigorin – the meaning is starting to emerge.

Once again, I want to say – breathe, then the essence comes through, and then you begin to understand what it is like when the actor comes into his own. But only within a correctly prepared plan. The beginning is good, both Lev [Durov–Medvedenko] and Tonya [Dmitrieva–Masha], but Tonya can still be more active, even flying into a rage.

(To Vovsi–Sorin.) The scene with Treplev – everything is lost. The performance and the response to it need to be clarified.

(To Fadeeva–Arkadina.) First, Arkadina's arrival at the performance. No need to back away from the dispute about art. Second, you are starting to play a bad

woman. But you do not know this, you do not know what you are boorish. You are kind, do not imagine that you have offended.

(To Dmitrieva–Masha.) Tonya, "youth" is good, but then there is a stoppage in the text. But I want her to let go and cry about love.

I liked Trigorin's scene with Nina, despite the costs. The fishing rod follows organically and discloses his nature, but not the scarf, it is a bit too much . . .

(To Dmitrieva–Masha.) Tonya, in the third act she should be super-frank, he is a good man, tell him everything, that you drink and that the teacher is a fool.

(To Larionov–Trigorin.) Seva! "Why push" – this phrase expresses your entire role. This is vanity, which hurts [him] all the time. And then after the scene with Arkadina – "I am spineless, I am submissive" – is also a continuation of all that is intolerable [in himself].

The beginning of the fourth act. The third act ends with Nina standing for a long time. Pause. Tonya, *(To Dmitrieva–Masha.)* start the fourth act louder and more alarming. You need to continue the third act.

Look, what is the difference between good acting and representing. Here Pelevin [Dorn] was playing great in the first act, but in the Genoa [episode] he started to let himself down and just expressed what was already done. Like everything else, but not quite. No anguish, no terrible feeling of a failed dream. A subject that escaped [expression]. The scene is amazing. Longing for an extraordinary happy life, and then he asks about Nina, linking this with Treplev's performance.

Then Treplev: "I can't talk about it – I can't, I can't, I can't." And you calmly and slowly speak, everyone listens, everything is quiet and boring – a hundred pauses. The scene should grow, and grow, and then Trigorin slowly exits.

(To Dmitrieva–Masha.) Tonya! You should have a keen sense of the meeting between Trigorin and Treplev, in order to defuse [the subject of] her husband and horses.

(To Durov–Medvedenko.) Lev, about the baby in the final act – this is not the issue in itself, it needs to be thrown in their faces. Sharply! And then the brutality is revealed. Indeed, he does not even notice it himself, he sits down.

The game of lotto – this is not an antiquated game. Masha – Right now I . . . , #33, everything has gone to hell, I will leave, I will forget, #10, #20 . . . And everyone plays to console themselves, to kill the pain, the anguish.

He demonstrates.

Treplev at the window. He is not comforted. And in the scene with Nina – everything sharper, faster. Disturb yourself, at least outwardly, then you will get used to it.

I probably need to curse so something gets off the ground a little. I remember at CCT it offended me when we were told that my work was is lovely, organic, lovely directing. We always wanted to go for more sharpness. The path, probably, is all alone – requires human courage.

19 February 1966[S]
Rehearsal

EFROS. "The show will start soon" – Masha says this is to stop Medvedenko's philosophizing.

Today rehearsal was better than yesterday. Especially in the first part, some things broke through. Yesterday it was in the second half. You have adapted to the interpretation, it seems comfortable for you, and you think this is already the result. But the result appears when you break through this interpretation to some creative power. Was today good? Start with Durov [Medvedenko], "Why are you always in black?" This was just the strong push needed here. Dorn [Pelevin] was excellent. Dmitrieva [Masha] – a very good piece of action in the finale of the first act: "Youth, youth." All the scenes were beautiful where Masha is silent, when she speaks, this is 85 percent of what is needed. When it will be 100 percent it will be will beautiful. Today Smirnitsky [Treplev] tried to do in the second act what I talked about yesterday.

This was an overview. Now more about the shortcomings.

The conversation between Treplev and Sorin was bad. "Tears in her eyes" – Sorin's line about Nina was bad. The song is false.

The first entrance of Arkadina today was bad. It seems like she just doesn't know anything. The dispute about art did not come across.

"What is wrong with him?" – You are beginning to play a bad woman again. You come to the show as an enemy. It is not that. She has no idea that she is boorish. "What is wrong with him?" – With confidence in her charm, with a cry.

Trigorin played the first scene incorrectly. He does not react to the performance angrily and maliciously, but with a smirk.

20 February 1966[P]
Run-through of the performance

EFROS. The general impression is weakness. Weakness of temperament, sharpness. Smooth, calm. Too little departure from tradition. Tradition holds you back. Quarrels are half-hearted, explanations at quarter strength.

How can we do the next run to set ourselves the task: more desperate? The best places are those where there is a desperate sharpness, rather than smoothness. For example, in the fourth act, Masha when she meets her mother: "Yes, it is all nonsense, I will leave here, and all this will be forgotten."

Not enough open force of despair. If this does not take place, we will remain at half way, and nobody will understand us. This is the main thing.

There are no [showy] theatrical moments, and they are not needed. Everything depends on their radical sharpness. I understand this may be difficult now, but now you have no desire to try to do everything at full strength. And you know what my requirement is when I'm watching – the requirement of continuously playing to the limit. I know you are afraid to be false, and consequently you do everything in a quiet voice. By not being false, I think, we don't find anything. We need to go all out for this performance. Now we are going to rehearse the second act.

Rehearsal of the second act.

(To Shirvindt–Trigorin.) The scene with Nina needs to be played Shakespearean. Grand declarations of love. Not complacent. Not calmed down. Do not rush. Be detached from her, draw away.

During the scene Efros always shouts at Shirvindt "bigger and louder, do not die, come on."

(To Yakovleva–Nina.) "I'm sorry, I refuse to understand you" – rush to him, challenge him.

(To Shirvindt–Trigorin.) Argue with her internally and externally. It helps her to argue with you. "My name," – say this as an example of your painful life. Do not back off for a second.

Suddenly he sees the seagull. Timidly, he asks: "What is that?" And immediately the subject flashes through his mind. Now, speak about this with hatred. This glimpse of a new subject already gives him no peace.

Now we have the right to end the second act the way we planned.

Nina long, long after the departure of Trigorin, desperately circling around the stage with a fishing rod, which Gregory left behind. She is whistling it over her head.

Notes after running the second act.

EFROS. You cannot even imagine what can be squeezed out of this play of Chekhov's. After all, we all have a lot of experience. Will we really remain only a quarter of the way there again?

Now Tonya *(Dmitrieva–Masha)* is furious at me for performing the scene as it can only be dreamed of. That is what we all must do. But after her scene Arkadina's lines normally became insignificant, but now she needs to do everything differently to block Masha. And a real crazy Chekhov begins.

The entire life of the director during rehearsals, too, is a "real crazy Chekhov."

But this is the second act. How should the third, the fourth be played?

The third act now boils down to small things. It should begin with Masha. She tells Trigorin that he could describe her whole life. It is a scene that reflects life.

The fourth act – the ending. Masha states something terrible has happened, and you are forced to cash in your chips.

(To Smirnitsky–Treplev.) In the scene with Nina, you need to make a physical assessment [of her], all the rest is banalities.

(To Shirvindt–Trigorin.) This [run-through] was something like what you need now. It should be a cry from the heart of a writer.

Still, the main thing is that everything is naked up to the end, bring everything to the utmost point of collision.

I have staged a lot of performances, but in only one of them – *Making a Film* – and only in the second act of that play, have I reached the desired temperament.

It is a state of temperament when the whole body goes into it. This is indispensable. This is a point, a degree of temperament, when lying stops. It is simply not possible.

The first act needs to be played a thousand times more passionately, hotly. The kind of life we have been through at today's rehearsal: nerves, tears, dramas. Chekhov is the essence of life, and moreover, not just for one era, but maybe for all time.

21 February 1966[P]
Run-through

After the run-through

EFROS. Some kind of give-back is starting to show, so everything is becoming somewhat better. Now everything has come up to half of what we need. The following runs should be used to reach the limit. Treplev started well, but in the third act he began to turn sour.

At the end of the first act Dorn talks about things he himself suffered, – "write about what is important and eternal." In the final conversation with Masha, Dorn should prevent her from speaking, thereby helping her [emotionally].

"Papa, give him a horse!" – Masha's line in the fourth act breaks the mood. It should be loud.

Much was played correctly today. More rapidly. This depends on Masha. It is there now, of course, it is there. But believe me, even the best is only seventy percent of what is necessary.

Notes

1 Hereafter [P] indicates Nellie Plyatskovska's records and [S] indicates those of Inez Sidorina. In cases where both of them shared one rehearsal day, Plyatskovska's are printed first, followed by Sidorina's.
2 The cast list is given according to the program of play.
3 Here and throughout, Chekhov's text is more or less my own translation from A. P. Chekhov, *P'yesi: Kniga dlya chtyeniya s kommyentariyet na angliyskom yazikye* (Moskva: Russki Yazik, 1989) 36–77.
4 Actor Gennadi Saifulin, a Lenkom Theatre actor, was not a cast member and was probably present as an observer. Efros's unique rehearsal style frequently attracted theatre professionals and students as observers, a practice he allowed and even encouraged. For which rationale see Efros, *Craft of Rehearsal* 114–115.
5 Acts I and II were performed without an intermission; similary, Acts III and IV.

6 At this point in rehearsals the actors were introduced to Efros's use of Active Analysis, which they doubtless heard about but never encountered personally in rehearsals with other directors.
7 Reference is to Treplev's observation about Nina in their crucial Act IV scene.
8 Reference is to Vladimir Nemirovich–Dancheknko's newly interpreted production of *Three Sisters* at MAT in 1940.
9 See n. 7.
10 Efros's reference is to the opening shots of Andrey Tarkovsky's 1975 film *Zerkalo* (Mirror). Efros deeply admired Tarkhovsky' work.
11 Space in Soviet communal apartments was based on an predetermined number of 9 square meters per family member. One hundred square meters would be approximately 32 feet × 32 feet, the size of the stage floor to which Efros is alluding, or about 4 times the size of a typical Soviet communal apartment.
12 See n. 7.
13 Valentin Gaft rehearses Treplev.
14 Pavel Semyonich Chadin, an obscure, perhaps fictional, provincial actor.
15 Leading characters from Alexander Griboyedov's 1861 satirical comedy *Woe from Wit*, compulsory reading in Soviet schools. An idealistic young man seeks the affection of a cool and evasive young woman.
16 See n. 14.
17 Rasplyuev: reference to a character from two of Alexander Sukhovo–Kobylin's satirical plays, *Krechinsky's Wedding* and *The Death of Tarelkin*.
18 Mikhailovich Sadovsky (1818–1872), Russian actor of the Maly Theatre, widely admired for his performances in the plays of Ostrovksy.
19 Gaft rehearses Treplev.
20 The second plan is Vladimir Nemirovich–Danchenko's term denoting all the spoken and unspoken connections of a character to the thematic essence of the play. See "seed."
21 The seed is Vladimir Nemirovich–Danchenko's term for the concentrated thematic essence of the play. See "second plan."
22 The reference is to Eugene Ionesco's absurdist play (1959), to which audiences and critics initially reacted with puzzled skepticism, just as the stage audience does in *The Seagull*.
23 1965 Soviet comedy-drama feature film directed by Elem Klimov for Mosfilm. Screenplay by Alexander Volodin, several of whose plays Efros directed.
24 Gaft rehearses Treplev.
25 "To pour out all the bile and frustration." ("izlit vsyu zhelch i razocharovanie"). Familiar line from Griboyedov's classic play, *Woe from Wit*, whose leading character, Chatsky, is a youthful idealist.
26 Quotation from "Unfinished" (1928–1930), the notebooks of Soviet-Russian author, Vladimir Mayakovsky.
27 1959 film by French New Wave director François Truffault. A misunderstood adolescent in Paris struggles with his parents and teachers due to his rebellious nature.
28 Efros is not quite correct here. Maria Knebel, who introduced him to etudes and Active Analysis, addresses this misconception specifically in her formative essay, "Active Analyis of the Play and the Role." See Thomas, *Active Analysis*, 127–128.
29 A combination of Stanislavsky and Brecht, so to speak. For which see James Thomas, "Anatoly Efros's Principles of Acting and Directing," Amy Skinner, *Russian Theatre in Practice* (London: Bloomsbury, 2018).
30 This special correspondence between play and performer is one of the unique outcomes of Active Analysis.
31 See n. 29.

166 Rehearsal records of Efros's production

32 In Bulgakov's play, *Molière*, a character returns to the stage ostensibly to light a candle, but actually to interfere with an upcoming event.
33 Not unlike *The Seagull*, Albee's 1962 play is, indeed, about the destruction of innocence. A film adaptation of the play was released in 1966, directed by Mike Nichols and starring Elizabeth Taylor and Richard Burton.
34 Gaft plays Treplev.
35 Lenkom company actress Margarita Strunova, probably an observer here.
36 Russian author Nikolai Gogol is famously said to have burned the second half of his novel, *Dead Souls*.
37 Lenkom actress Lyumilla Ponomareva, cast as the second actress for the role of Arkadina.
38 Reference to a scene from *Making a Movie*.
39 Reference to Othello's speech about Desdemona before the Venetian Senate.
40 Poprishchin is a government clerk who descends into insanity in Gogol's monodrama, *Diary of a Madman* (1835).
41 Birgit Beumers, "Performing Culture: Theatre," in Catriona Kelly and David Shepherd, eds, *Russian Cultural Studies* (Oxford: Oxford University Press, 1998) 104.
42 Here is a valuable example of Active Analysis at work. By means of an etude, Efros has analyzed an event psycho-phyically, "on his feet," and thereby gained a fresh insight into the event and the play as a whole.
43 Vsevelod Larionov rehearses Trigorin.
44 Gennadi Saifulin, a member of the Lenkom Theatre acting company, probably present as an observer.
45 See n. 8.
46 Alexander Shirvindt plays Trigorin.
47 Alexander Shirvindt plays Trigorin.
48 Shirvindt–Trigorin had been writing on the fence here, in reference to Alexander Volodin's habit of writing on whatever was near at hand so as not to lose the thought.
49 Vsevelod Larionov rehearses Trigorin.
50 Vsevelod Larionov is playing Trigorin.

Epilogue

"How quickly time passes!"[1]

[The following extract is taken from *Teatr* 2 (1967).]

The Seagull is a wonderful play. It is a pity we have not yet been able to put it on properly. But maybe it is one of those plays that needs to be put on lots of times, gradually coming closer to the goal.

However, Stanislavsky and Nemirovich-Danchenko put it on only once each – and once is the point. There is nothing more to be done. But we will try again in a few years. Yet, when our *Seagull* is praised, I attribute it to our special situation and the goodwill towards us. And, if we can speak frankly, the ability to be attentive to other people's creative ideas.

And when they criticize us, I see this as entirely common sense. Indeed, Chekhov's plays are so rich, so diverse, and our performance is so unequivocal.

Any sane person, of course, must remain dissatisfied with our production of *The Seagull*.

Sometimes, however – and here I'm afraid of being mistaken – this common sense has a trace of Arkadina in it. While watching her son's play, she asks: "That sulfur smell. Is it really necessary?" Or speaking about Treplev: "No, there are no new forms, there is simply a bad temper." She knows what a weak character is from her own experience, but what is a new form? It is best for her to say, "This is something decadent!" That is the point. This common sense is particularly impressive, of course, when it does not concern our performance – because I already admitted it was not successful – and most of *The Seagull* or some of its characters: Treplev, say, or Trigorin.

One of our critics, for example, said that Konstantin is a "poor seeker of new forms, allegedly haunted by his environment.[2] Have you noticed this amazing word – "allegedly"? Not really hounded, but allegedly . . . if not – the guy is doing God knows what, got a false idea from God knows whom, and his friends spread a rumor that environment is everything. Actually, he simply has a bad disposition. And he shot himself because he was disappointed in his search for new forms of art, just as it is written there. A contemporary person, as it turns out, can argue with Treplev almost as Arkadina does!

("Truth is stranger than fiction!") But in matters of social consciousness and writing, Trigorin has something of value to say. And Arkadina can rely on him. In those issues there is something solid, substantial, but in Treplev – no. He is too high-strung, and you cannot understand that monologue either: "People, lions, eagles and partridges," and in the end – that shot in the head, "allegedly" a victim of the environment.

This viewpoint also claims to be Chekhovian, and indeed, why should it not be? After all, Chekhov the writer is not really all that simple. He is a rather difficult writer. And if you want to see the collapse of empty new forms in this play, you will probably be able to see it. Moreover, you will still be able to teach a lesson to modern young people. That, one could say, is what causes the collapse of unnecessary searches in art. But, since Chekhov is a complex and controversial writer, nevertheless I take a different position, and I will prove that Chekhov's sympathy lies on the side of Treplev, not Arkadina or even Trigorin. This concept suddenly seemed to me even very courageous, again there are people who think differently. I even thought that because Chekhov was Chekhov, he was attracted to Treplev, without looking at any complex reasonings.

It is not Chekhov, possibly that is why it is not Chekhov, that impulsively attracts them to Arkadina's point of view. Arkadina as well as they themselves have only one curse for Treplev – decadent. They "shoot them down" right and left as soon as they see before themselves a flimsy and weightless character, a figure made unstable because of his continuous searching. And when a young theatre produces a new completely successful experiment, they are right there.

"The sulfur smells, is it really necessary?"

"Yes, it is a special effect!"

Wise veterans – they make derisive jokes. They fret that someone wants to push them away from their usual point of view; he [Treplev] wants, in the words of Arkadina, to teach them how to write and how to act. However, if they were not taught and not forced to be angry, art would gradually turn into a swamp. This seems to be the eternal conflict between the petty bourgeoisie Arkadina, who welcomes "art that is comprehensible and useful for domestic purposes" and the "unsuccessful new forms" of Treplev. Unfortunately, the "new forms" have been so "successful" that only a few years pass until the next shot – and a new Arkadina already sits astride a new art, and through such efforts, art again becomes "comprehensible and useful for domestic purposes." And once again, there are [those] Treplevs.

However, this is a very primitively drawn literary scenario. It contains just a drop of truth, but a drop just the same.

So, Konstantin is allegedly badgered by his environment. Perhaps we ought to just leave it be, but this is somehow impossible.

In fact, it is really not so surprising in our time, when you can read so many books!

At the same time, this sacramental "allegedly" is also said to give a kick in the arse to today's so-called search for new forms. Let them know! Except the boomerang flies back.

What village is this where Treplev would have to live without ever leaving!? What is this lack of money? Never mind going abroad, he cannot even go to his home town. There is even an old man, Sorin, whose "brain is pasted to his skull." And maybe Konstantin is some poet, like Alexander Blok. Who knows?

And the old jacket he is ashamed to appear in among the celebrities around his mother?! The continual feeling of being a petit bourgeois from Kiev? And do these celebrities take over the leading places in art? Yes, and all their art, their theatre, which you want to run away from, "like Maupassant ran from the Eiffel Tower, which crushed his brain with its vulgarity." A theatre that shows "how people eat, drink, walk, wear costumes, a theatre of trite pictures and vulgar phrases from which they try to extract tiny comfortable morals for easy consumption . . . comprehensible . . ."

But what can be done if the Eiffel Tower does not seem vulgar and Treplev's environment is not capable of strangling?

"Denmark is a prison," says Hamlet after "allegedly" encountering the ghost of his father.

"Denmark is not a prison," say Guildenstern and Rosencrantz.

In contrast to Treplev, Trigorin seems to have a certain, so to speak, citizenly basis. You cannot make light of his civic and literary thinking! That is a remark one critic aimed at Treplev. We need to get a better grasp of Trigorin to understand him better.

I used to think Trigorin was very simple. Not socially conscious, but simply a sybarite. He and Arkadina are two boots of a pair or so it seemed to me at first. But in the process, I began to doubt Trigorin. His monologue about his own life – suffering! He is not a slave to routine and not a sybarite. Here is a tired, exhausted literary workman who dreams only of the time when he can be released from his gloomy thoughts. He is known for his sense of duty as a writer and citizen, but he fears this duty and feels like a fox exhausted by wolves. He is exhausted overstrained, weak, and contradictory. This was the Trigorin I saw.

I am afraid he really is like this, then for support – horror of horrors! – there is only Arkadina alone. Maybe I am wrong – Trigorin is possibly different, but in fact this still must be proved. And then at times some critics believe that the printed word – not the spoken word – does not need proof. This is a big mistake. And for the printed word to seem at least convincing, in our time anyhow, at least some elementary proof is needed.

But we will try to understand better why it is so difficult today for a young, rather strong theatre to put on Chekhov, as far as modern plays are concerned.

You have probably noticed that Chekhov is rarely produced [in Russia at the time of this writing] and almost never a success. In England, Shakespeare is rearranged all the time, from right to left and left to right, in modern dress and Shakespearean costume, with a "modernist aroma," and with beautiful old-fashioned ideas.

Sometimes it seems that the English actor gets new Shakespearean roles just as easily as our beautiful actor Nikolai Plotnikov of the Vakhtangov Theatre plays yet another collective farm manager.

Shakespeare's plays are regarded by the British as familiar and comfortable modern plays, only perhaps more beautiful than all the rest.

When the English actors or directors take Shakespeare in their hands, they know what to do with it.

For us, nearly twenty years pass from *Seagull* to *Seagull*, and when at last the young actor takes on the role of Treplev, then he holds it as a brilliant globe that he was given only to hold, cautioning that if he breaks it he will not be able to pay it off for the rest of his life. You can imagine how confident and brave that actor feels.

We wanted something very different, and this different path was not so easy, but we simply wanted to address Chekhov without fear. We decided to take him and fill him with modern ideas, not hesitate to employ our modern style, to try and convey through Chekhov everything we would like to convey, no more, no less.

However, here is what is strange. To remain oneself in art is also extremely difficult. We wanted to give up the stereotype, forget the traditional interpretation, and talk and express ourselves, but remain within three-quarters of the textbook reading. All the time we involuntarily kept this scale in mind without actually demanding it, striking some balance – is it Chekhov, or is it too soft for Chekhov, or too rough for Chekhov? Neither one extreme nor the other – neither Chekhov not fully open, nor Chekhov not fully expressed.

Oh, how we would like to put on *The Seagull* again and make our brains and hands work more consistently and safely! And riskier! I began by saying that I decided to build a wooden wall on stage, and at the beginning two people noisily playing croquet in front of this wall. Balls smacking powerfully against the wall. This would begin *The Seagull*, one of the sharpest plays expressing the tragic incompatibility of human desires, ideas, and characters. But then I shifted to a quiet and listless game of croquet, sustaining only a quarter of the heat and rhythm that the play assumed in performance. But croquet balls, you say, how could this be translated into the same path of the dialogue? Take, for example, the first conversation of Medvedenko and Masha.

As you may recall, the play begins with this. Who does not know how it should be played! She is dressed in black, sniffing tobacco, he is in a teacher's uniform jacket, a small Chekhovian man, funny in his amazing ordinariness and earthiness.

Both are strolling prior to the beginning of Treplev's performance. He wants to talk about love – he cares for her. She languishes and waits for the performance. They enter on stage from one side, maybe hand in hand or something like it. And then they turn and walk back. They stroll. No violation of everyday and ordinary psychological truth. She sniffs tobacco a couple of times, exactly when it is required by the stage directions. Although I've only seen *The Seagull* once, it seemed to me they always play it like this.

Meanwhile, something different is wanted, a new perspective, a sharpening, a new psychological twist that revives everything and starts to be seen anew.

"New forms," says Konstantin, "and if not, it is better not to have anything."

Of course, it is possible to see empty creative formlessness behind the words "new form," but you would probably agree this is too easy to say – a primitive opinion. Even Konstantin means something more substantial by it. Anyway, new forms are required, dammit!

Medvedenko cares for Masha – this is true. Nevertheless, he seems to be proposing a fundamental dispute about whether a man may be unhappy for spiritual or moral reasons.

He understands that accidents can happen from lack of money, because you need to buy tea and sugar, but why anyone having money can walk around in mourning, he does not understand.

It needed to be almost Brechtian to lay bare the semantic side of this dispute.

"Why do you always wear black?!" Medvedenko should ask this as a sort of challenge, offering a dispute, suggesting a certain debate, a theme, requiring almost a public resolution. Maybe someday every scene of *The Seagull* will return to its classic, domestic, psychological bed, but I am sure that today, now, to put on *The Seagull* in what is called the "classical" manner is impossible. Today it is necessary to break through the stereotyped shell, which imposes a coating of boredom on the entire play for the modern person: "Oh . . . *The Seagull!* We have read it. We know it."

It was difficult to find a new solution for each scene, not something invented, but drawn from our blood. All this is extremely complicated, of course. However, it is a free, uninhibited attitude to the classics, today's scale, private and nervous, is just one side of the coin. The second side is what is objectively there.

Quite a long time ago (as I already mentioned above) I saw *The Seagull* at one of our theatres. Konstantin – a middle-aged man (the actor was not young) – appeared to be melancholy in the scene with the gun after he killed the seagull. And the fact that he was no longer young, and his melancholy, and this gun, and the seagull – for me everything was a sham. And the properties were clichés and nothing there spoke literally to the mind and heart. At that time, I was the same age as Treplev, and I imagined that my girlfriend had just betrayed me as Nina did to Treplev. Me, an unknown, unlucky person, she traded for a writer with a name. Also, he is not very young. And here I am wandering around in the woods waiting for a meeting with her. She arrived half an hour ago. I saw how she stood and watched while he is fishing. She hung around there, near all these celebrities. But finally, she was left alone. I quickly went to meet her. What do I want from her?

I want her to know at least what she did to me!

I want her to know the emotional state of a man who had awakened, and it seemed to him the lake had suddenly dried up!

I want her to learn there is a nail in my head! Let her know what she has done! I killed a seagull today, but someday in the same way I will kill myself! There is nothing worse than betrayal. I want to take revenge at least to show my wounds! No, I would not be in a melancholy emotional state. I would not hold an elegant seagull in my hands! I would not able to speak – my heart would be pounding so. And occasionally some images of the wounds would escape from my breast. "Women do not forgive failure!" I would like to cover her with my wounds! I would like to leave her torn to pieces from my own suffering.

Having said all that, I would run through the woods, and spin around to shoot upwards, sideways, and fall down crying.

I would have shot myself from this terrible nervous shock.

Although I said earlier that representing each scene in and of itself and not as a cliché is rather difficult, yet it would still be much easier than it would subsequently be to perform. Not only because it requires a huge stage temperament, but also – particularly important – huge inner poetry. Without this, all these "innovative solutions" would become simply a vulgar quarrel.

We learned how to play a modern play, but to play *The Seagull*, you need at least to be able to say the following sentence: "I feel as if a nail had been driven into my brain, damn it along with my self-esteem, which sucks my lifeblood, sucks it like a snake."

It is not that hard to say in today's vulgar, fragmented, nervous style, but it is hellishly difficult to articulate sweepingly, broadly, expressively, poetically – but without losing the life of today's reaction. To do this, you need to stop being just a boy from the street, who is well aware of the songs of popular singers, but still needs to be like the poet Alexander Blok.

But can one be like Blok if you were not born him? We often live thoughtlessly. Suppose a wave of Modern Art has swept over us, and by this time we are bathing in it, while in the meantime the days go by and very few people notice how it could be time for something completely different, unknown. And I think: how can one become a Blok? Maybe by continually thinking about what we need to become?

What does it mean to play Trigorin? The actors playing this role for us are so smart and clever that they grasp the semantic solution of the role at the first rehearsal. But Trigorin still fails. Because even Trigorin, a man whom we are far from idealizing, is higher in terms of his thoughts than we, the actors intending to recreate him. Even he is more a poet than we often are, even he has more thoughts about life and art than is often the case with us.

A single, modern outline of a character is not enough here. It needs baggage, an addition to one's own "jargon" level, and then you need to spend many days thinking and brooding. In *Making a Film*, we grabbed almost any costume off the hanger and stepped on stage. That would be truthful for today's experience. But our Trigorin wears a beard: what should it be like? But there is not enough time – and so, everything from the beard up to and including the delivery of the monologue remains at the level of approximation.

Not only Blok, but even Trigorin cannot be achieved in one rehearsal period. It is necessary to be them all the time. A street guy, who perfectly understands popular music still needs to grow. After Hamlet, he can return to the new popular songs. They will not be harmed. All this seems to me a very serious problem.

Perhaps after twenty years we will return to *The Seagull*, matured and wise.

It was years ago when I saw *The Seagull*, I was the same age as the "prop shop" Treplev, and twenty years from now I will already be sixty.

Time passes so quickly! You barely have time to master one thing, and around the corner already looms a completely new helplessness.

An employee of the Ministry of Culture once daydreamed to me. He was sitting among a few people I know. Everyone looked sternly, and he even shook his head: "Why is it, Anatoly, that you still have not put on any of Shakespeare plays? And you only touched Chekhov for the first time. And you have been speaking about Bulgakov's *Molière* for ten years now.

"*Romeo and Juliet* has started rehearsing at the Central Children's Theatre, and the end is not in sight.

"And look at how much gray hair you already have!

"Meanwhile, the prominent Czech director Otomar Krejča has recently staged *Romeo and Juliet*, twice staged *The Seagull*, once in Brussels, and the second at home, in Prague. Then – *Three Sisters* and *Cat on the Rails* by his contemporary, the writer Joseph Topol. Now, that is productivity!

"What is the reason for your meagre record?"

This employee spoke like God himself. I could not believe my ears. [In other words,] nowadays [the Thaw era] we can no longer live in the old way. We will no longer be able to indulge in creative inertia.

And my mind worked furiously. I imagined that long ago I could have directed *Don Quixote* like Gogol's "Diary of a Madman."

Oh, what a performance that would be!

The well-known children's fairy-tale image, known since we were five years old, would give way to that of a tragedy.

Then I switched to *Three Sisters*. I imagined a great interpretation of this performance. Isn't it strange that coming up with a scenic design for a famous classical play is twenty-five percent of success? Do you remember that someone once said a proper distribution of roles is seventy-five percent of success? Well, the scenic design is worth twenty percent – twenty-five. Perhaps that would be enough. Then there is this new, non-MAT, plan I had for Tuzenbach when I heard Nikolai Khmelev's iron intonations.[3]

"Irina, I did not have any coffee today, please tell them to get it ready for me." It was always amazing, and before this I had never thought that Tuzenbach could be played any differently.

A famous contemporary writer said that death takes everyone, but before that it finds the best, the purest, the most beautiful. This is probably true for Tuzenbach. The first to leave are the kindest, most cheerful, most full of life. He says himself that he is happy. He has accepted the sun and the rain, walking without any purpose, the snow, and flying birds. He was as ugly and just as ridiculous as [the figure of poet] Wilhelm Kuchelbecker. He has agreed with Irina to work at the brick factory, and now the possibility of being killed in a duel seems to him a betrayal of the woman he loved.

"Irina, I did not have any coffee today . . ." – he is leaving, he tells Irina that he cannot fail her, and so he will be sure to come back.

I had an actor who at that time was not limited just to playing roles. He played the harpsichord, and I also saw his King Louis XIV dancing during intermissions. He was in our play by Bulgakov.[4] At one time, this play was not accepted at MAT, but now we have progressed a great deal regarding the staging of similar [politically aware] plays.

However, I did not mean to give preference to the classics. Plays were written by [contemporary writers] Vasily Aksenov and Edvard Radzinsky, and both were [allowed to be] produced in an instant.

And I felt so good about it! So far, I have counted sixty new ideas for plays.

Notes

1 *Teatr* 2 (1967): n.p.
2 Yuri Zybkov, *Izvestia*, "Contemporary and Classic," 1 August 1966.
3 Reference is to Nemirovich-Danchenko's 1940 revival of *Three Sisters*.
4 Bulgakov's play *Molière* ran for a seven performances at MAT in 1936, but was quickly banned because of its thinly veiled criticism of Stalin and the Communist Party.

Images

Figure 1 Act I Setting

Figure 2 Act I Treplev–Valentin Smirnitsky

Figure 3 Act I Nina–Olga Yakovleva

Figure 4 Act I Treplev–Valentin Smirnitsky, Sorin–Alexander Vovsi

Figure 5 Act I Nina–Olga Yakovleva, Treplev–Valentin Smirnitsky

Images 179

Figure 6 Act I (L–R) Nina–Olga Yakovleva, Masha–Antonina Dmitrieva, Sorin–Alexander Vovsi, Shamraev–Vladimir Solovyov, Dorn–Alexander Pelevin, Trigorin–Alexander Shirvindt, Treplev–Valentin Smirnitsky, Arkadina–Elena Fadeeva

Figure 7 Act I (L–R) Mevedenko–Lev Durov, Sorin–Alexander Vovsi, Shamraev–Vladimir Solovyov, Dorn–Alexander Pelevin, Trigorin–Alexander Shirvindt

Figure 8 Act I (L–R) Arkadina–Elenda Fadeeva, Nina–Olga Yakovleva, Trigorin–Alexander Shirvindt, Shamraev–Vladimir Solovyov, Dorn–Alexander Pelevin, Medvedenko–Lev Durov

Figure 9 Act I Nina–Olga Yakovleva, Sorin–Alexander Vovsi

Images 181

Figure 10 Act II Arkadina–Elena Fadeeva, Treplev–Valentin Smirnitsky

Figure 11 Act II Arkadina–Elena Fadeeva, Masha–Antonina Dmitrieva

Images 183

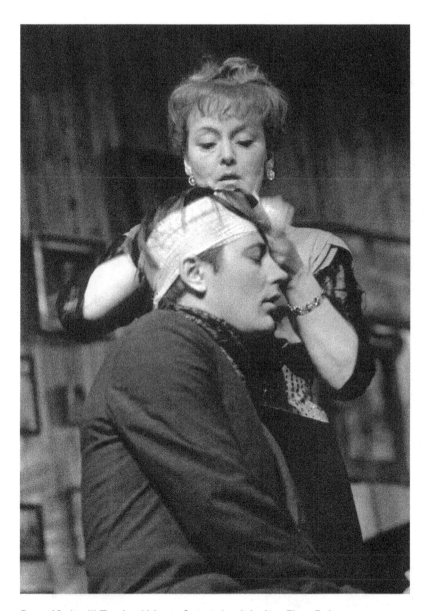

Figure 12 Act III Treplev–Valentin Smirnitsky, Arkadina–Elena Fadeeva

Figure 13 Act III Treplev–Valentin Smirnitsky, Arkadina–Elena Fadeeva

Images 185

Figure 14 Act I Dorn–Alexander Pelevin, Masha–Antonina Dmitrieva

Figure 15 Act III Masha–Antonina Dmitrieva

Images 187

Figure 16 Act III Setting

Figure 17 Act IV Shamraev–Vladimir Solovyov, Arkadina–Elena Fadeeva

Figure 18 Act IV Masha–Antonina Dmitrieva

Figure 19 Act III Dorn–Alexander Pelevin, Polina–Zoya Kuznetsova

Figure 20 Act I Arkadina–Elena Fadeeva, Trigorin–Valentin Shirvindt

Figure 21 Act IV Trigorin–Valentin Shirvindt

190 Images

Figure 22 Act IV Sorin–Alexander Vovsi, Masha–Antonina Dmitrieva

Figure 23 Act IV Masha–Antonina Dmitrieva, Medvedenko–Lev Durov, Treplev–Valentin Smirnitsky

Images 191

Figure 24 Act IV Treplev–Valentin Smirnitsky, Nina–Olga Yakovleva

Figure 25 Act IV Treplev–Valentin Smirnitsky, Nina–Olga Yakovleva

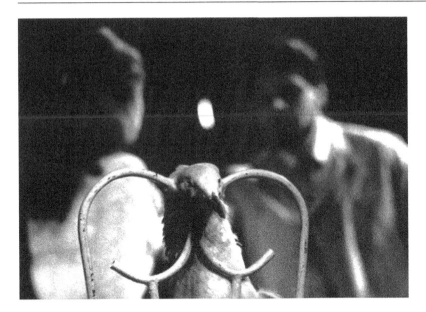

Figure 26 Act II Nina–Olga Yakovleva, Trigorin–Alexander Shirvindt

Glossary

Active Analysis An innovative rehearsal methodology developed by Konstantin Stanislavsky in his later years. The essence of this method is that in the early stages of preparation the play is not rehearsed intellectually at the table as usual, but after a certain preliminary analysis it is analyzed in terms of "events" by means of etudes (sketches) using improvised text. These etudes serve as stepping stones that lead the actor to creative assimilation of the author's text as the principal means of stage expressiveness. Active Analysis is still very much an embryonic methodology in English-speaking theatre teaching and practice. See James Thomas, *A Director's Guide to Stanislavsky's Active Analysis* (London: Bloomsbury 2016).

adaptations (adaptatsii) Term used by Stanislavsky "to designate the ingenuity, both mental and physical, people use to adjust their behavior and so influence other people, their object." For which see Stanislavski, *An Actor's Work* 258–272.

Adventures of a Dentist, The 1965 Soviet comedy/drama feature film directed by Elem Klimov for Mosfilm. Screenplay by Alexander Volodin.

Aksyonov, Vasily (1932–2009). Soviet–Russian author and playwright of contemporary life.

Alexandrinsky Theatre (Petersburg) (est. 1756). It was here that *The Seagull* was first performed, albeit unsuccessfully.

All-Union (USSR) Radio The Moscow-based radio broadcasting organization of the USSR from 1924 to 1989.

All-Union (USSR) Theatre Society (est. 1977). Originally the Actors' Benefit Society, now the Theatre Union of the Russian Federation. Founded for the development of theatre and performing arts in Russia in all its forms with an emphasis on special assistance to regions that are geographically remote from Russian and European cultural centers.

Alyoshin, Samuel (1913–2008) Polish–Russian author and playwright, wrote about the moral issues confronting modern society.

An Ordinary Story 1847 novella by Russian author Ivan Goncharov (1812–1891). Stage adaptation by Viktor Rozov (1966) produced at the Sovremennik Theatre, starring Oleg Tabakov and Mikhail Kozakov.

Arbuzov, Alexei (1908–1986). Soviet playwright whose works depicted the spiritual development of young people in the long run. Plays directed by Efros: *My Poor Marat* (Lenkom Theatre, 1965), *The Happy Days of an Unhappy Man* (Malaya Bronnaya Theatre, 1969), *Tales of the Old Arbat* (Malaya Bronnaya Theatre, 1970), *Marat, Lika, and Leonidik* (Central Television, 1972), *Tanya* (Central Television, 1972).

Appointment, The Play by Alexander Volodin, produced at the Sovremennik Theatre in 1963. Adapted for film in 1980.

Babochkin, Boris (1904–1975). Soviet–Russian actor and director of theatre and film, and influential teacher. Artistic Director of the Bolshoi Drama Theatre (BDT) in St. Petersburg (1936–1940).

Bakhrushin Theatre Museum (est. 1894) Founded by philanthropist and theatre enthusiast Alexei Bakhrushin. Originally built to house his private collection of theatre memorabilia, today the archival center of theatre history in Russia.

Bolshoi Dramatic Theatre (BDT), St. Petersburg (est. 1933). Considered one of the finest theatres in Russia. From 1956–1989, led by legendary director Georgii Tovstonogov. (Not to be confused with the Moscow's Bolshoi Theatre.)

Belinsky, Vassarion (1811–1848) Russian literary critic, often identified as the "father" of the Russian radical intelligentsia.

bent wire (izognutaya provoloka) "When we look at a medical cardiogram and we see a straight line without any change in direction, it means there is no life. A change in direction indicates life. It is the same in our profession. I shall act, perhaps, worse or better, but all the time I should read the design. *Everything must be as clear as a bent piece of wire*" (Efros, *Joy of Rehearsal* 45).

Bersenev, Ivan (1889–1951) Soviet actor, director and teacher. The Moscow Art Theatre (1922–1936), Moscow Art Theatre First Studio and Moscow Art Theatre II (1924–1938), Lenkom Theatre (Artistic Director 1938–1951).

Blok, Alexander (1880–1921). Symbolist poet and playwright, considered one of Russia's finest poets. In 1978, Efros directed Blok's play, *The Stranger*, for All-Union Radio.

Brezhnev, Leonid (1906–1982). General Secretary of the Communist Party of the USSR (1964–1982).

Bulgakov, Mikhail (1891–1921) Russian playwright and novelist. Author of *Molière, or The Cabal of Hypocrites*, directed by Efros at the Lenkom Theatre in 1967. Widely known for his novel, *The Master and Margarita*.

Central Children's Theatre (CCT) (est. 1936) Official state theatre for children and youth, where Efros directed from 1954–1964. Now the Russian Academic Youth Theatre (RAMT). Maria Knebel was Artistic Director there from 1950–1960 and 1966–1968.

Chekhov, Michael (1891–1955). Legendary Russian–American actor, personal student of Stanislavsky and originator of the Michael Chekhov acting technique.

communal apartment (kommunalnaya kvartira) Apartments in which several families shared one original apartment, which was divided with a family assigned one room each for living, dining and sleeping, while everyone shared one wash room, one bathroom and one kitchen. Space in Soviet communal apartments was based on a predetermined number of 9 square meters (≈100 square feet) per family member.

contact without communication (obshchenie bez obshcheniya) Catchphrase Nemirovich-Danchenko used to describe his understanding of the unique interpersonal communication among the characters in Chekhov's play.

continuous communication (nyepryerivnoye obshshyeniye) Catchphrase Stanislavsky used to describe his understanding of the unique interpersonal communication among the characters in Chekhov's play.

decontamination (dezaktivatsii) Soviet neologism for the elimination of anti-Soviet content.

De Filippo, Eduardo (1900–1984). Italian actor, playwright, screenwriter, author and poet. In 1958, Efros directed Filippo's play, *Nobody*, at the Sovremennik Theatre.

dalectical materialism Philosophical approach to reality derived from the teachings of Karl Marx and Friedrich Engels, that understands matter as the only subject of change and, furthermore, the constant product of internal contradictions inherent in all events, ideas and socio-political movements.

Dmitrieva, Antonina (1929–1999). Russian stage and film actress. With Efros at the Central Children's Theatre (1954–1964), Lenkom Theatre (1964–1967) and Malaya Bronnaya Theatre (1967–1984). Roles for Efros at the Lenkom: Inga (*Making a Movie*, by Edward Radzinsky, 1965); Elsa (*To Each His Own* by Samuel Alyoshin (1965); Masha (*The Seagull*, 1966); Nyura *(On the Wedding Day* by Viktor Rozov (1964).

Durov, Lev (1931–2015) Famous Soviet–Russian stage and film actor. With Efros at the Central Children's Theatre (1954–1964), Lenkom Theatre 1964–1967 and Malaya Bronnaya Theatre (1967–1984). Roles with Efros at the Lenkom: Jura (*Making a Film* by Edward Radzinsky, 1965), Funny Citizen (*104 Pages about Love* by Edward Radzinsky (1964), Semyon Semyonovich Medvedenko (*The Seagull*, 1966).

Ehrenberg, Ilya (1891–1967) Soviet writer, journalist, translator, and cultural figure. Author of *Ottepel* (The Thaw, 1954).

event (sobitiye) In Russian theatre, the word term event has a particular meaning, referring to an incident that changes things, that would not normally happen, that alters a character's psychology, thereby infecting the audience's psychology as well. "Man bites dog" would be an an event in the sense considered here. Thinking "eventfully" is Stanislavsky's way of approaching plays for production. See Thomas, *Script Analysis* 2–7.

Fadeeva, Elena   (1914–1999). Lenkom Theatre (1938–1999). Roles for Efros at the Lenkom: Irina Nikolaevna Arkadina (*The Seagull*, 1966) and Madeleine Bejart (*Molière*, 1967).

Fellini, Federico   (1920–1993) Italian film director and screenwriter. One of the most celebrated and distinctive post World War II filmmakers.

Gaft, Valentin   (b. 1935) Russain stage and film actor. Roles for Efros at the Lenkom: Grigorenko (*Judicial Chronicle*, 1966), Yevdokimov (*104 Pages about Love*, 1966), Konstantin Gavrilovich Treplev (*The Seagull*, 1966). With Efros at the Malaya Bronnaya Theatre, 1967–1984.

Gorky, Maxim   (1868–1936) Soviet–Russian writer, a founder of Socialist Realism, political activist. Author of *The Lower Depths* and many other plays, novels and stories. Original dedicatee of MAT; since 1987, dedicatee of break-away MAT.

Gorshkova, Nina   (b. 1934). Russian actor. Roles for Efros at the Lenkom Theatre: Maid (*The Seagull*, 1966).

Goshev, Dmitry   (1935–1980). Lenkom Theatre (1958–1980). Roles for Efros at the Lenkom Theatre: Cook (*The Seagull*, 1966).

Kamerny (Chamber) Theatre   Founded in Moscow in 1914 by the Russian director Aleksander Tairov. Closed by Stalin's order in 1949.

Kanevsky, Leonid   (b. 1939). Actor in Russian and Israeli theatre and film. Roles for Efros at the Lenkom Theatre: Ilya Afanasyevich Shamrayev (*The Seagull*, 1966), Trumpeter (*Making a Movie*, 1966). With Efros at the Malaya Bronnaya (1967–1984).

Kashirin, Nikolai   (1941–2005). Stage and film actor. Roles for Efros at the Lenkom Theatre: Jacob (*The Seagull*, 1966).

Khmelev, Nikolai   (1901–1945) Legendary Russian actor and preeminent member of the Moscow Art Theatre. Acclaimed, among other roles, for his performance of Tuzenbach in Nemirovich-Danchenko's 1940 version of *Three Sisters*.

Khrushchev, Nikita   (1894–1971) First Secretary of the Communist Party of the Soviet Union (1953–1954). Established a more open form of Communism in the USSR, publicized Stalin's crimes, provoked the Cuban missile crisis, and oversaw the building of the Berlin Wall.

Knebel, Maria   (1898–1985). Russian actor, director and teacher. Trained with Stanislavsky, Nemirovich-Danchenko, and Michael Chekhov, with a specific focus on Stanislavski's technique of Active Analysis. Efros was deeply influenced by her teaching.

Kolevatov, Anatoly   (1920–1997). Managing director of the Lenkom Theatre while Efros was there. In Soviet times, managing directors were political appointments.

Kozakov, Mikhail   (b. 1934). Soviet–Russian and Israeli actor and director of theatre, film and television. Role for Efros at the Sovremennik Theatre: Vincenzo (*Nobody* by Eduardo De Filippo, 1959). With Efros at the Malaya Bronnaya Theatre (1973–1979).
Krejča, Otomar   (1921–2009). Czech theatre director and dissident.
Kuchelbecker, Wilhelm   (1797–1846). Russian Romantic poet and political radical, known for the inchoate nature of his writings.
Kuznetsova, Zoya   (1920–1990) Lenkom Theatre (≈1950–1970). Role for Efros at the Lenkom: Polina Andreevna (*The Seagull*, 1966).
Kvasha, Igor   (1933–2012). Soviet–Russian theatre and film actor. One of the founding members of the Sovremennik Theatre.
La Strada **(The Road)**   1954 film directed by Federico Fellini.
Lalevich, Vladimir   (1918–1990) Russian scenic designer, generally worked in partnership with technical director Nikolai Sosunov.
life of the human spirit (zhizn chyelovyechyeskovo dookha)   Basic principle of Stanislavsky's System, denoting psychosomatic communication among actor–characters, not only when speaking but also in the silences. Stanislavsky's System does not fabricate the life of the human spirit, but prepares for it, disposes towards it and looks for it indirect ways.
Look Back in Anger   1956 play by John Osborne, directed by Tony Richardson and starring Kenneth Haigh, Alan Bates and Mary Ure. Toured to Moscow in 1957. Filmed in 1959 starring Richard Burton, Claire Bloom and Mary Ure and directed by Tony Richardson. Produced at the Sovremennik Theatre in 1965, with Igor Kvasha as Jimmy Porter.
Lunacharsky State Institute for Theatre Arts (GITIS)   (Est. 1878). The largest and oldest theatre conservatory in Russia. Originally the Shostakovich Music School, then the Musical-Dramatic School of the Moscow Philharmonic Society, from 1934–1991 [during Efros's time] the Lunacharsky State Institute for Theatre Arts (GITIS), now the Russian Academy of Theatre Arts (RATI).
Lyubimov, Yuri   (1917–2014) Soviet–Russian stage actor and director. Artistic Director of the famous Taganka Theatre from 1964–1984, 1989–2011.
Making a Film   Play by Edvard Radzinsky concerning Soviet censorship of the arts, directed by Efros at the Lenkom Theatre in 1965.
Malaya Bronnaya Theatre   Originally the State Jewish Theatre led by the celebrated Yiddish Actor, Solomon Mikhoels, from 1921–1948. Marc Chagall painted his famous murals for this theatre. From 1967–1984, Efros directed some of his most noteworthy performances here.
Maly Theatre   (est. 1806) Literally the Small Theatre, as opposed to the Bolshoi or Large Theatre located across the street in Moscow's Theatre Square. The leading Russian theatre of the nineteenth century and the

original venue for over 50 premieres of Alexander Ostrovsky's plays, hence designated "The House of Ostrovsky."

Maretskaya, Vera (1906–1978). Famous Russian film actress and one of the faces of Soviet propaganda films. Student and later wife of Yuri Zavadsky.

Mayakovsky, Vladimir (1928–1930) Leading poet of the Russian Revolution and early Soviet era.

Markov, Pavel (1897–1980). Theatre critic and literary manager of the Moscow Art Theatre from 1925–1949.

Meyerhold, Vsevelod (1874–1940) Legendary Soviet–Russian theatre and film director, the first auteur director, whose distinctive style played a leading role in the development of the modern theatre. Imprisoned, tortured and assassinated by Stalin's order in 1940.

Mikhoels, Solomon (1890–1948) Legendary Soviet–Jewish actor and Artistic Director of the State Jewish Theatre (GOSFT). Assassinated by Stalin's order in 1948.

Molière, or The Cabal of Hypocrites 1936 play (banned until 1966) by Mikhail Bulgakov (1891–1940), of which Efros directed several versions: Lenkom Theatre (1966), Central Television (1973), Guthrie Theatre, Minneapolis (1979) and All-Union Radio (1981).

Moscow Art Theatre II In 1912, Stanislavsky and his creative assistant, Leopold Sulerzhitsky, founded the First Studio of the Moscow Art Theatre to train young actors in the emergent Stanislavsky system. In 1924, the studio was reorganized as the Second Moscow Art Theatre (MAT II), which was led by Michael Chekhov until 1928, Ivan Bersenev until 1931, and Boris Sushkevich until the theatre was closed in 1936. Over time, the confluence of these different leaderships contributed to the development of the Moscow Art Theatre itself.

Moscow Art Theatre School Conservatory affiliated with MAT, founded in 1943 by Vladimir Nemirovich-Danchenko, after whom it was subsequently named

Moscow State Jewish Theatre (GOSET) Yiddish theatre company established Moscow in 1919 and shut down in 1948 by the Soviet authorities.

Mosfilm Film studio that is among the largest and oldest in the Russian Federation and in Europe.

Mossoviet Theatre The Mossoviet Theatre was established in 1923 and located a short distance northeast of Red Square. It was led by Yuri Zavadsky, a direct student of both Stanislavsky and Evgeny Vakhtangov. It was at the Mossoviet Acting Studio that Efros's first direct contact with the Moscow Art Theatre legacy began.

"move to another region" (pyeryeyezd v drugoy region) Phrasing of an official request to move to another city, requiring a change to one's internal passport. An internal passport is still required in Russia to control and monitor the internal movement and residence of its citizens.

My Poor Marat   1964 play by Alexander Volodin, directed by Efros at the Lenkom Theatre in 1966, which tells the story of three Leningrad teenagers who struggle to survive the brutal winter of 1942, when the city is under siege by Nazi forces.

Nemirovich-Danchenko, Vladimir   (1858–1943). Soviet–Russian stage director, playwright, author and teacher, co-founder of the Moscow Art Theatre and founder in 1943 of the Moscow Art Theatre School.

Olesha, Yuri   (1899–1960). Russian–Soviet author said to be one of the greatest Russian novelists of the twentieth century.

Ostrovsky, Alexander   (1823–1886) Nineteenth-century Russian playwright, considered the progenitor of Russian drama, especially its realistic societal aspects. Namesake of the Maly Theatre, where most of his plays premiered.

Pelevin, Alexander   (1914–1970) Soviet–Russian actor. Roles for Efros at the Lenkom: Molière (*Molière*, 1966), Kirill (*Making a Movie* 1973), Dorn (*The Seagull*, 1966).

Plotnikov, Nikolai   (1897–1979) Soviet–Russian actor and director of theatre and film. Prominent actor of the Vakhtangov Theatre, where he often played the role of Lenin.

Plyatskovska, Nellie   Russian theatre historian. Graduated from GITIS Theatre Studies Faculty. Co-transcriber of rehearsal records for *The Seagull*.

Ponomareva, Lyumilla   (1922–2003). Lenkom actress who was cast as the second actress for the role of Arkadina in Efros's production of *The Seagull*.

Popov, Alexei   (1892–1961). Influential Russian–Soviet actor, theatre director, teacher, theorist. Head of Directing Faculty at GITIS (1940–1961).

Radzinsky, Edvard   (b. 1936) Russian playwright, whose works expressed the latent features of animosity, skepticism and incommunicability in everyday life. Plays directed by Efros: *104 Pages about Love* (Lenkom Theatre, 1965), *Making a Movie* (Malaya Bronnaya Theatre, 1973).

Raevsky, Joseph   (1901–1972) Soviet–Russian director and actor, member of the Moscow Art Theatre (1922–1972).

Rozov, Viktor   (1913–2004). Russian playwright whose works depicted the plight of young people in a corrupt world. Plays directed by Efros: *Good Luck!* (CCT 1954), *In Search of Happiness* (CCT 1957), *Unequal Battle* (CCT 1960), *Before Supper* (CCT 1962), *The Wedding Day* (CCT 1964); Brother Alyosha (from The Brothers Karamazov, Malaya Bronnaya Theatre, 1972).

Saifulin, Gennady   (b. 1941). Soviet and Russian film and stage actor and director. Roles with Efros at the Lenkom Theatre: *Judicial Chronicle* (1966), *To Each His Own* (1966). With Efros at CCT (1961–1964), Lenkom Theatre (1964–1967), Malaya Bronnaya Theatre (1967–1984).

Shchukin School Conservatory affiliated with the Vakhtangov Theatre and named after Soviet stage and film actor Boris Shchukin (1894–1939).

Shirvindt, Alexander (b. 1934) Soviet and Russian theatre and film actor, director and scenarist. Roles for Efros at the Lenkom: Fyodor Nechaev (*Making a Movie*, 1965), Guderian (*To Each His Own*, 1965), Boris Alekseevich Trigorin *The Seagull*, 1966). With Efros at the Malaya Bronnaya Theatre (1968–1970).

Sidorina, Inez Co-transcriber of rehearsal records for *The Seagull*.

Skegina, Nonna Literary Manager of Anatoly Efros, theatre theorist, editor–compiler of books about Anatoly Efros: *Chaika* (*The Seagull*, Moscow, 2010) and *Tri Cestri* (*Three Sisters*, Moscow, 2011).

Slaviansky (Slavic) Bazaar, Moscow Restaurant where Stanislavski and Nemirovich-Danchenko discussed the idea of a future Moscow Art Theatre.

Smeliansky, Anatoly (b. 1942) Preeminent Russian theatre writer, scholar, critic and author. Moscow Art Theatre Literary Director (c. 1980), Associate Artistic Director (c. 2000); Moscow Art Theatre School (Academic Program Head (1986–2000), Dean (2000–2014), President (c. 2014). Editor-in-Chief of the new edition of the *Complete Works Konstantin Stanislavsky* and *The Moscow Art Theatre Encyclopedia*.

Smoktunovsky, Innokenty (1925–1994). Legendary stage and film actor, one of the foremost actors in the history of the Moscow Art Theatre

Sofronov, Anatoly (1911–1990). Popular Russian and Soviet author, playwright, poet, journalist, composer and public figure. According to University of Sheffield Russian scholar Evgeny Dobrenko, Sofronov was "the most consistent Stalinist and anti-Semite in Soviet literature" and "one of the most terrible literary hangmen of the Stalin era."

Solovyov, Vladimir (1909–1968). Russian–Soviet theatre and film actor. Roles with Efros at the Lenkom Theatre: Shamraev, *The Seagull* (1966).

Sosunov, Nikolai (1908–1970). Russian technical director, teacher and author of stagecraft books, generally worked in partnership with scenery designer Vladimir Lalevich.

Sovremennik Theatre Founded in 1956 by graduates of the Moscow Art Theatre School (Oleg Yefremov, Galina Volchek, Igor Kvasha, Lilia Tolmacheva, Evgeni Yevstigneev, Oleg Tabakov) in opposition to the fading legacy of the Sovietized Moscow Art Theatre.

Stanitsyn, Viktor (1897–1976) Soviet–Russian actor, member of the Moscow Art Theatre (1918–1976).

Strepetova, Polina (1850–1903). Russian actor said to have led a complicated and mysterious life, known for her natural talent in performing characters from lower- and middle-class society.

Tabakov, Oleg (1935–2018) Distinguished Soviet Russian theatre and film actor and Artistic Director of the Moscow Art Theatre (2000–2018).

Taganka Theatre (est. 1946) Artistic Director Yuri Lyubimov (1964–1984, 1989–2011), Artistic Director Anatoly Efros (1984–1987), committed to the artistic principles of Bertolt Brecht and Evgeny Vakhtangov.

Tairov, Alexander (1985–1950) Soviet–Russian theatre director, founder of the Kamerny Theatre, dedicated to "synthetic theatre," integrating all the performing arts—ballet, opera, music, mime, and drama.

Tarkhanov, Mikhail (1877–1948) Stage name of Soviet–Russian theatre and film actor, director and teacher (real name Moskvin), member of the Moscow Art Theatre (1922–1948).

Teatr (Theatre) *(est. 1937)* Soviet–Russian and Russian magazine of drama, theatre, and theatre criticism.

Theatre of Mood Term coined by Meyerhold to describe the Moscow Art Theatre's production style for Chekhov's plays, for which see Vsevelod Meyerhold, "The Naturalistic Theatre and the Theatre of Mood," *Meyerhold on Theatre*, Trans. Edward Braun (London: Methuen, 1969) 23–53.

Topol, Joseph (1935–2015). Czech playwright and dissident.

Tovstonogov, Georgi (1915–1989) Legendary Russian theatre director, Artistic Director of the Bolshoi Drama Theatre (BDT) in St. Petersburg, which now bears his name.

Truffault, François (1932–1984) French film actor, director, screen writer and one of the founders of the French New Wave, known for shooting films about social-political issues, on location, and using experimental cinematic forms.

Turgenev, Ivan (1818–1883) Russian Novelist and playwright. Author of *Fathers and Sons* (1862) and the play, *A Month in the Country* (1872), which Efros directed at the Malaya Bronnaya in 1977.

Vakhtangov, Yevgeny (1883–1922). Legendary Russian actor, director and Head of the Moscow Art Theatre's Third Studio (est. 1921), which subsequently became the Vakhtangov Theatre. Personal student of Stanislavsky and Nemirovich-Danchenko. Created the style "fantastic realism."

Volodin, Alexander (1919–2001). Russian playwright. Known for characters who overcome custom and prejudice to achieve success. Plays directed by Efros: *Away and at Home* (Yermolova Theatre, 1960).

Vovsi, Arkady (1900–1971). Russian theatre and film actor. Roles for Efros at the Lenkom: Petr Nikolaevich Sorin (*The Seagull*, 1966); Otchim Yevdokimov (*104 Pages about Love*, 1965), Jean-Jacques Buton (*Molière [The Cabal of Hypocrites]* by Mikhail Bulgakov, *1967*).

Waterloo Bridge 1931 film adaptation of Robert E. Sherwood's 1930 play of the same name. In 1940 MGM released a remake also called *Waterloo Bridge*. Directed by Mervyn LeRoy and starring Vivien Leigh and Robert Taylor. Efros probably saw the 1940 film version.

Yakovleva, Olga (b. 1941) Soviet–Russian actor, Lenkom Theatre (1962–1967), Malaya Bronnaya Theatre (1967–1984), Taganka Theatre (1984–1987), Mayakovsky Theatre (1987–2004). Moscow Art Theatre c. 2004). Roles for Efros: Nina in *The Seagull* (1966) and numerous others.

Yefremov, Oleg (1927–2000). Legendary Soviet–Russian stage and film actor and director. Co-founder of the Sovremennik Theatre in 1956 and Artistic Director of the Moscow Art Theatre (1970–2000).

Yermolova, Maria (1852–1928). Legendary Russian actor, said to be the greatest actor in the history of Moscow's historic Maly Theatre.

Zavadsky, Yuri (1894–1977) Influential Soviet–Russian actor, director and teacher; member of the Moscow Art Theatre (1924–1931); Artistic Director (Theatre of the Red Army (1932–1935), Rostov Gorky Theatre (1936–1940), Mossoviet Theatre (1940–1977).

Bibliography

Russian

Alekseev, L. "Pervoe znakomstvo." *Sov. Litva.* Vilnius, 18 Marta 1966.
Brusilovskaya, M. "Chekhovskim klyuchom: 'Chaika' v postanovke Moskovskovo teatra im. Leninskovo komsomola." *Komsomolskoye Znamia.* Kiev, 12 Iulia 1966.
Efros, Anatoly. *Rabota Rezhissera Nad Spektaklem.* Moskva: Tsentral'nyi dom narodnogo tvorchestva (1960).
Efros, Anatoly. "Premera sostoitsya v Vilniuse." *Sov. Litva.* Vilnius, 10 Marta 1966.
Efros, Anatoly. "Kak bystro idet vremja!" *Teatr 2* (1967): 66–70.
Efros, Anatoly. *Repetitsia–Liubov Moìa.* Fond Russki Teatr. Moskva: Panas, 1993 (1975).
Efros, Anatoly. *Professia: Rezhisser.* Fond Russkii Teatr. Moskva: Panac, 1993 (1976).
Efros, Anatoly. *Prodolzhenie Teatralnova Romana.* Fond Russkii Teatr. Moskva: Panas, 1993 (1985).
Efros, Anatoly. *Kniga Chetvertaia.* Fond Russkii Teatr. Moskva: Panas, 1993.
Efros, Anatoly. *Anatoly Efros: Chaika* (Sankt-Peterburg: Baltiiskie Sezon, 2010).
Efros, Anatoly. *Anatoly Efros: Tri sestry* (Sankt-Peterburg: Baltiiskie Sezon, 2012).
Fridshtein, Y. G. *Anatoly Efros–Poet Teatra.* Moskva: Mezhdunarodnyi kommercheskii soiuz, 1993.
Ignatova, N. "Chekhov drugoy, 'Chayka' drugaya." *Ogonek 23* (1966): 23, 26–27.
Kashnitsky, I. "Chaika' prodolzhaet polet." *Sov. Litva.* Vilnius, 22 Marta 1966.
Kochetov, V. P., ed. *Anatoly Efros–Professia: Rezhisser.* Moskva: Vagrius, 2000.
Krymko, F. M. and E. M Tinyanova, eds., *Anatoly Vasilevich Efros: Bibliograficheskii Ukazatel.* Moskva: Tsentralnaya Nauchnaia Biblioteka. 1992.
Kuzicheva, A. P. "Repetiruet A. V. Efros: Tri Sestry." *Chekov: "Tri Sestry"–100 Let.* Eds. M. O. Goriacheva, V. B., and A. P. Chudakov. Moskva: Nauka, 2002: 259–93.
Larionov, V. "Vopreki traditsiyam." *Molodezh Estonii.* Tallin, 27 November 1966.
Lerman, S. "Vchera i sevodnya: 'Chaika' A.P. Chekhova v Teatre im. Leninskovo komsomola." *Сов. Sov. Estonia.* Tallin 11 December 1966.
Markov, Pavel. "Ob Anatoly Efrose." *O Teatr.* Moskva: Isskustvo, 1977, 4: 556–68.
Nikolskaya, Sonya. *Zhivoi Teatr A. Efrosa.* Moskva: Philologicheskii Fakultet MGU, 1995.
Poliakov, M. "Zapiski bez daty." *Nash sovremennik 4* (1967): 101–106.
Poliakova, E. "Geretichesky-genialnaya piesa." *Teatr 8* (1966): 37–43.
Shak-Azizova, T. K. "Anatoly Efros: Linia Zhizni." *Liudi i Sudby Xx Vek.* Moskva: OGI, 2002. 206–16.

Tsitriniak, Grigorii. "Iz-Za Takoi Teatr." *Literaturnaia Gazeta 38.5208* (1988): 8.
Vilenkin, Vitaly. *Vl. I. Nemirovich-Danchenko vedet repetitsiu "Tri sestry"* (Moskva: Iskusstvo, 1965)
Yakovleva, Olga. "Nina Zarechnaya." *Moskovsksia Pravda* 11 May 1966: 11.
Yevseyev, B. "Anatoliy Efros repetiruet... i rasskazyvaet. *Mosk. Komsomolets* 23 January 1966.
Zaionts, M. G., ed. *Teatr Anatolia Efrosa: Vospominania, Ctati*. Moskva. Artist-rezhisser-teatr, 2000.
Zolotukhin, Valeri. *Moi Efros: Dnevniki*. Kiev: KMTIS Poezia, 1997.
Zubkov, Yu. "Razvedka chekhovskoy temy." *Teatralnaia Zhizn 13* (1966): 12–14.

English

Beumers, Birgit. "Performing Culture: Theatre," in Catriona Kelly and David Shepherd, eds. *Russian Cultural Studies*. Oxford: Oxford University Press, 1998, 104.
Dixon, Ros. "Slaughtering Sacred Seagulls: An Analysis of Anatoly Efros's Production of *The Seagull* at the Lenkom Theatre in 1967." *Irish Slavonic Studies* (2001): 49–73.
Efros, Anatoly. "Energy, Enervation, and the Mathematics of Intrigue: Anatoly Efros in Conversation with Spencer Golub." *Theatre Quarterly 7.26* (1977): 28–33.
Efros, Anatoly. "Directing Victor Rozov's Plays: The 'Thaw' and the Young Audience." *Through the Magic Curtain: Theatre for Children, Adolescents and Youth in the U.S.S.R.: 27 Authoritative Essays*. Trans. Miriam Morton. Eds. Miriam Morton, Natalya Sats and N. Krymova, New Orleans, LA: Anchorage, 1979: 137–40.
Efros, Anatoly. "What Is Hecuba to Them? Nikolai Gogol's *Marriage* at the Guthrie Theatre." Trans. James Thomas. *Theatre Topics 3.2* (1993): 177–95.
Efros, Anatoly. *The Joy of Rehearsal*. Trans. James Thomas. New York: Peter Lang, 2006.
Efros, Anatoly. *The Craft of Rehearsal*. Trans. James Thomas. New York: Peter Lang, 2007.
Efros, Anatoly. *Beyond Rehearsal*. Trans. James Thomas. New York: Peter Lang, 2009.
Gershkovich, Aleksandr Abramovich. *The Theatre of Yuri Lyubimov: Art and Politics at the Taganka Theatre in Moscow*. New York: Paragon House, 1989.
Golub, Spencer. "Acting on the Run: Efros and the Contemporary Soviet Theatre." *Theatre Quarterly 7.26* (1977): 18–28.
Lamont, Rosette. "The Taganka of Anatoly Efros." *Performing Arts Journal 10.3* (1977): 96–101.
Leach, Robert, Victor Borovsky and Andy Davies, eds. *A History of Russian Theatre*. Cambridge: Cambridge University, 1999.
Olkhovich, Elena. "Produced Abroad." *Soviet Literature 4.433* (1984): 206–8.
Senelick, Laurence. "Chekhov on Stage." *A Chekhov Companion*. Ed. Toby W. Clyman. Westport, CT: Greenwood, 1985, 209–232.
Senelick, Laurence. "Directors' Chekhov." *The Cambridge Companion to Chekhov*. Eds. Vera Gottlieb and Paul Allain. Cambridge: Cambridge University, 2000: 176–200.
Senelick, Laurence, ed. *The Chekhov Theatre: A Century of the Plays in Performance*. Cambridge: Cambridge University, 1997.
Shevstova, Maria. "Anatolij Efros Directs Chekhov's *The Cherry Orchard* and Gogol's *Marriage*." *Theatre Quarterly 7.26* (1977): 34–46.

Shevstova, Maria. *The Theatre Practice of Anatoly Efros, a Contemporary Soviet Director*. Devon: Department of Theatre Dartington College of Arts, 1978.
Slonim, Marc. *Soviet Russian Literature: Writers and Problems, 1917–1977*. New York: Oxford University, 1977.
Smeliansky, Anatoly and Patrick Miles. *The Russian Theatre after Stalin*. Cambridge: Cambridge University, 1999.
Solovyova, Inna, and Jean Benedetti. "The Theatre and Socialist Realism, 1929–1953." *A History of Russian Theatre*. Eds. Robert Leach, Victor Borovsky and Andy Davies: Cambridge: Cambridge University, 1999: 325–57.
Thomas, James. "Anatoly Efros's Principles of Acting and Directing," Amy Skinner, *Russian Theatre in Practice*. London: Bloomsbury, 2018.
Thomas, James. *A Director's Guide to Stanislavsky's Active Analysis*. London: Bloomsbury, 2016.
Wilson, Kyle. "Splinters of a Shattered Mirror: Experimentation and Innovation in Contemporary Soviet Theatre." *Transformations in Modern European Drama*. Ed. Ian Donaldson. Atlantic Highlands, NJ: Humanities, 1983: 99–118.

Index

Page numbers in **bold** refer to figures

400 Blows, film 82, 165n27

academic tradition xviii
Active Analysis 83, 129, 165n28, 165n30; and Stanislavsky x, xiv, 193
adaptations 102, 193
Adventures of a Dentist, film 73, 193
aggression 7–9, 74
Aksyonov, Vasily 174, 193
Albee, Edward, *Who's Afraid of Virginia Wolf* 95, 166n33
Alexandrinsky Theatre, St Petersburg 1–2, 193
All-Union Radio xi, 193
All-Union Theatre Society 15, 193
Alyoshin, Samuel x, 193
Andreevna, Polina *see* Polina Andreevna (in *The Seagull*)
anti-Semitism x, xi, xii
apartment, communal 48, 165n11, 195
Appointment (Volodin) 73, 194
Arbuzov, Alexei x, xviii, 194
Arkadina, Irina Nikolaevna (in *The Seagull*) xvii, 16, 17, 18, 152, 160–1, 167, 168; Act I 57–8, 61, 67–9, 74, 103–6, 109, 133, 146, 160–1, **179**, **180**, **189**; Act II 39, 75, 110–14, 116, 118–19, 124–5, 128, 134–8, 140, 143, 148, 158, **181**, **182**; Act III 45–8, 50, 51, 52, 80–6, 90–1, 120–1, 159, **183–4**; Act IV 96, 97, 101, **187**; as an actress 45, 111–12; and aging/youth 75, 111–12, 113–14, 118; and art 74, 160; boredom 116, 124, 138, 140, 158; chairs, low 48, 52; and Dorn 128, 135, 137–8; and Masha 118, 124, 134–6, **182**; and Nina 17, 39, 116; and Shakespeare 57–8, 61, 67, 74, 104–5, 119, 133, 143; and Shamraev 125, **187**; and Sorin 52, 84, 90, 101, 120–1, 137–8; spirituality 46, 148; and Treplev xvii; and Treplev Act I 57–8, 67–9, 103–6, 109, 146, 148; and Treplev Act II 119, 148, 158–9, **181**; and Treplev Act III 45–6, 47, 51, 81–2, 84–5, 90–1, 121, **183–4**; and Trigorin Act I 106, **189**; and Trigorin Act II 39, 41, 148; and Trigorin Act III 47, 50, 80–1, 85–6, 90–1, 121, 159; *see also* Fadeeva, Elena; Ponomareva, Lyumilla
art 60–2, 66–7, 69, 72, 74

Babochkin, Boris 4, 194
Bakhrushin Theatre Museum, Moscow xii, xiii, 194
Belgrade International Theatre Festival xii
Belinsky, Vassarion 66, 194
Bersenev, Ivan x, 194, 198
black, wearing (Masha) 20–1, 24, 55, 65, 103, 106, 111, 171
Blok, Alexander 73, 172, 194
Bolshoi Dramatic Theatre, St. Petersburg 4, 194
boredom 8, 138, 158–9, 171; Arkadina 116, 124, 138, 140, 158; Masha 21, 44, 129, 159
Boris Godunov (Pushkin) 41
Braun, Edward 1, 2

Brecht, Bertolt xii, 7; Brechtian approach 5, 14, 19, 143, 171
Brezhnev, Leonid 14, 194
Brook, Peter 7
Bulgakov, Mikhail, *Molière, or The Cabal of Hypocrites* 14, 15, 92, 166n32, 173, 174, 194, 198

Cat on the Rails (Topol) 173
Central Children's Theatre (CCT), Moscow ix–x, 160, 173, 194
Central Television xi
Chadin, Pavel 60, 66, 165n14
Chekhov, Anton 24, 40; *Cherry Orchard* xii, 23, 27n14; decontamination of xvii, 195; and Efros xi, xii, xiv, 13, 15–16; life according to 24, 25, 83–4; objectivity 4–5, 27n19; productions of 4–5, 169–70; psychology 18–19, 40–1; and *The Seagull* 2, 3, 10, 13, 18–19, 37, 168; and Stanislavsky 2, 3; *see also* Seagull (Chekhov); *Three Sisters* (Chekhov)
Chekhov, Michael 195, 198
communication: continuous xviii, 195; direct 39, 42, 88–9, 93, 94, 107, 151; indirect 123; open, free 136; stormy xviii, 16, 38; without contact xviii, 38, 40, 195; without understanding xviii, 8, 16, 38, 70
Communist Party ix, xi
Communist Youth League x
confusion 48
contact without communication xviii, 38, 40, 195
Cook (in *The Seagull*) 34
croquet 123; and Dorn 17, 35, 39, 42, 57; woodenness 38, 48, 170
cruelty 71
Culture Channel xiii

de Filippo, Eduardo 46, 195
departure, sense of 17, 44, 46, 79
despair 162; Shamraev 98, 102; Treplev 29, 31, 76
de Vega, Lope, *Dog in the Manger* ix
Directing Program, GITIS ix
Dixon, Ros xi, 1
Dmitrieva, Antonina 9, 34, 195; *see also* Masha, Marya Ilyinichna (in *The Seagull*)
doctor-patient relationship 9, 17, 39, 42, 100–1, 115, 124, 128, 137

Don Juan (Molière) xi
Don Quixote (Carvantes) 173
Dorn, Evgeny Sergeevich (in *The Seagull*): Act I 35, 36–7, 39, 57, 65, 72–3, 75, 104, 107–8, 109–10, 147, 150, **179**, **180**, **185**; Act II 42, 112, 115, 124, 128, 135, 136, 137–8, 143, 155, 158; Act III 123, 159, **188**; Act IV 96, 98–9, 101, 102, 161; and Arkadina 128, 135, 137–8; and croquet 17, 35, 39, 42, 57; emotional energy 35, 42; and Masha 75, 110, 150, **185**; and the performance 72–3, 123; and Polina 35, 65, 104, 107–8, 122–3, **188**; and Sorin, doctor-patient relationship 9, 17, 39, 42, 96, 115, 124, 128, 137–8; and Sorin, quarrelling 96, 98–9, 101, 102, 112, 128, 153, 157; and Treplev 9, 36–7, 109–10, 158; and youth 35, 75, 104, 107, 124; *see also* Pelevin, Alexander; Smoktunovsky, Innokenty
Dostoevsky, Fyodor 16
Duisburg Theatre Festival xi
Durov, Lev 8, 34, 195; *see also* Medvedenko, Simeon Semyonitch (in *The Seagull*)

Efros, Anatoly Vasilievich (Natan Isayevich) viii–xiii; Brechtian approach 5, 14, 19, 143, 171; and Chekhov xii, xiv, 13, 15–16; intuition xviii–xix, xxn2; and Lenkom viii, x, xiii, xiv, xvii–xviii, xix, 15; Malaya Bronnaya Theatre xiv, 15–16; and MAT viii, xi, xviii, 6–7; and Mossoviet Theatre viii, xi; psychological theatre/acting x, 37–8, 86, 88; and *The Seagull* vii–viii, xi, 4, 5–6, 7–14, 16–26, 34; and Stanislavsky 1, 6–7; and *Three Sisters* xi, xiv, 15, 173; *see also* Seagull (Chekhov)
Efros, Isaac Vasilievich viii
Ehrenberg, Ilya, *The Thaw* viii, 195
emotional energy 35, 42, 98, 102
emotional responses 8, 43
English acting and actors 6, 23, 27n26, 169–70
etudes xiv, 83–4, 88, 91, 193
events 17, 37, 38, 43, 193, 195–6; super-events 97, 101
experience 25, 48

Fadeeva, Elena 9, 33, 43, 196; *see also* Arkadina, Irina Nikolaevna (in *The Seagull*)
Fellini, Federico 7, 196; *La Strada* 64, 70, 197
First and Second Studios, Stanislavsky's x
freedom, artistic 6–7, 14
Fridshtein, Yury 16

Gaft, Valentin 33, 65, 70–1, 76, 107, 196; *see also* Treplev, Konstantin Gavrilovich (in *The Seagull*)
Genoa 53, 94, 97, 99–100, 102–3, 159, 161
Gogol, Nikolai xi, 16, 116, 127, 166n36, 166n40
Goncharov, Ivan, *An Ordinary Story* 154, 193
Gorky, Maxim xii, 196
Gorshkova, Nina 34, 196
Goshev, Dmitry 34, 196
Guthrie Theatre, Minneapolis xi

Hamlet (Shakespeare) 169, 173; Arkadina 57–8, 61, 67, 74, 104–5, 143
happiness 46, 52; Masha 46–7, 111, 124, 145, 153, 156; Nina 111, 126; Trigorin 142, 149
Hemingway 78, 141; and Nina 17, 38, 39, 41, 42, 72, 73
Hermitage Theatre 2
horses 12, 39, 116, 125
"How quickly time passes" (*Teatr 2*) 6, 167–74

Ibsen, Henrik, *Hedda Gabler* xii
Ignatova, N. 8, 12–13
Impressionism 38, 41, 48
incompatibility 16, 54, 170
Irish Slavonic Studies 1
Ivanov (Babochkin) 4

Jacob (in *The Seagull*) 34, 105, 107, 132–3; *see also* Kashirin, Nikolai

Kamerny Theatre, Moscow 4, 196, 201
Kanevsky, Leonid 129, 196
Kashirin, Nikolai 34, 196
Khmelev, Nikolai 173, 196
Kholodova, G. 10

Khrushchev, Nikita viii, 196
Knebel, Maria ix, x, xiv, 13, 194, 196
Kolevatov, Anatoly 114–15, 153, 196
Kozakov, Mikhail 154, 193, 197
Krejča, Otomar 173, 197
Kuchelbecker, Wilhelm 174, 197
Kuznetsova, Zoya 34, 197; *see also* Polina Andreevna (in *The Seagull*)
Kvasha, Igor 54–5, 197

Lalevich, Vladimir 11, 34, 197
Lamont, Rose 15
Larionov, Vsevelod 34; *see also* Trigorin, Boris Arkadevich (in *The Seagull*)
La Strada (Fellini) 64, 70, 197
Lenin Komsomol Theatre (Lenkom), Moscow viii, x–xi, xiii, xiv, xvii–xviii, xix, 5, 13, 15
Lermontov, Mikhail 16
life: according to Chekhov 24, 25, 83–4; horror of 99–100, 102; of the human spirit x, 197; rhythms of xviii, 52, 89–90
Look Back in Anger (Osborne) 51, 54–5, 197
lotto 10, 95, 129, 130, 131, 160, 161
love 23; Arkadina and Trigorin 81, 121; Masha and Medvedenko 20, 56, 82, 86–7, 122, 132, 145; Masha and Treplev 9, 34–5, 37, 59, 94, 119; Nina and Treplev 35, 54, 65, 73, 77, 104, 132; Polina and Dorn 35, 64, 104, 107–8, 122–3, 150, 155, 158; Treplev, need for 18, 32–3, 50; Treplev and Arkadina 18, 20, 45–6, 47, 74, 80, 170; Trigorin and Nina 36, 41, 86, 163; *see also* individual characters; parent-child relationships
Lunacharsky State Institute for Theatre Arts (GITIS) ix, 6, 197
lyricism 8, 14, 98, 109
Lyubimov, Yuri xii, 197

madness 129
Maid (in *The Seagull*) 34
Making a Film (Radzinsky) 14, 119, 121, 125, 164, 172–3, 197
Malaya Bronnaya Theatre (Moscow Drama Theatre) xi, xiv, 15–16, 197
Maly Theatre, Moscow 4, 197–8, 199

Maretskaya, Vera 51, 198
Markov, Pavel 13, 198
Marriage (Gogol) xi
martyrdom 11, 14, 128
Masha, Marya Ilyinichna (in *The Seagull*) 17, 34, 42; Act I 7, 34–5, 37, 39, 47, 55–6, 59, 65, 73, 75, 103, 106, 121–2, 132, 133, 145, 156, 162, 170–1, **179**, **180**, **185**; Act II 9, 111, 118, 124–5, 129, 136–7, 148, 150, 153, 154, 155, 159, 163, **182**; Act III 44, 46–7, 51, 52, 81, 82–3, 86–9, 119–20, 159, 160–1, **186**; Act IV 53, 93–4, 95–7, 100, 101, 145, **188**, **190**; and Arkadina 118, 124, 134–6, **182**; black clothing 20–1, 24, 55, 65, 103, 106, 111, 171; boredom 21, 44, 129, 159; and Dorn 110, 124–5, 150, 153, **185**; happiness/unhappiness 46–7, 111, 124, 145, 153, 156; and Medvedenko 7, 20, 55–6, 82, 93, 95–7, 100, 101, 121–2, 132, 134, 145, 152, 170–1; spirituality 20, 132; suffering 20, 37, 47, 51; and Treplev 9, 34–5, 37, 39, 55–6, 59, 94, 96, 103, 119; and Trigorin 44, 46–7, 52, 82–3, 86–9, 103, 119–20, 160, 161; "youth, youth" 75, 160–1, 162; *see also* Dmitrieva, Antonina
materialism, dialectical ix, 195
Mayakovsky, Vladimir 198
Medvedenko, Simeon Semyonitch (in *The Seagull*) 34; Act I 36, 65, 72, 73, 103, 132, 134, 150, 170–1, **179**, **180**; Act II 129; Act III 82, 121–2, 160, 161; Act IV 93–6, 97, 99–100, 101, **190**; and Masha 65, 82, 93, 95–6, 97, 99–100, 101, 121–2, 132, 134, 170–1; and Masha wearing black 7–8, 20, 56; spirituality 8, 132, 171; *see also* Durov, Lev
Meiningen Theatre 26n5
Meyerhold, Vsevelod xiv, 7, 24, 198, 201
Mikhoels, Solomon xi, 197, 198
Ministry of Culture xiv, 15
Misanthrope (Molière) xii
misunderstanding 48, 126; of artists 10, 14; communication without understanding xviii, 8, 16, 38, 70
Molière xi, xii

Molière, or The Cabal of Hypocrites (Bulgakov) 14, 15, 92, 166n32, 173, 174, 198
Moscow Art Theatre (MAT) 174; and Efros viii, xi, xviii, 6–7; MAT II x, 198; and Nemirovich-Danchenko, Vladimir 198, 199; and *The Seagull* 1, 3, 4, 13, 23–4, 30; Socialist Realism 3, 26n11; and Stanislavsky 1, 198; and *Three Sisters* 5, 43
Moscow State Jewish Theatre (GOSET) xi, 198
Mosfilm xi, 198
Mossoviet Theatre, Moscow viii, xi, 44, 198
movement, expressive x, 51, 133
movement, sense of 42, 44, 48
"move to another region" 153, 198–9
multi-tasking 90–1
music, use of 2–3, 4
My Poor Marat (Volodin) 93, 199

Nemirovich-Danchenko, Vladimir ix; and communication xviii, 16, 38, 195; and MAT 1, 5, 198, 199; and *Seagull* 26n4, 167; second plan/"seed" 71, 72, 165n20, 165n21
Nina: happiness 111, 126
Nina Mikhailovna Zarechnaya (in *The Seagull*) 25, 29–31, 34; Act I 22–3, 30, 31, 35, 36, 57, 58–9, 60, 61, 62–3, 65, 71–2, 73, 74, 104, 105, 108, 109, 123, 133–4, 146, 150, **176**, **178**, **179**, **180**; Act II 31, 38, 39, 40, 41, 42, 43, 63, 76–7, 78–9, 112, 116–17, 126, 127–8, 139–42, 143, 144–5, 148–50, 154, 155–6, 161, 163, **191**, **192**; Act III 48, 50, 83, 86, 89, 120; Act IV 53, 54, 102–3, 144–5, **191**, **192**; and Arkadina 17, 39, 116; and Hemingway 17, 38, 39, 41, 42, 73; monologue Act I 22–3, 30, 36, 58, 60, 61, 62–3, 74, 105, 108, 150; monologue Act II 117; monologue Act IV 144–5; and Sorin 139–40, **180**; and Treplev 10; and Treplev Act I 31, 35, 57, 65, 71, 73, 74, 104, 133–4, 146, **178**; and Treplev Act II 31, 76–7, 78–9, 116–17, 127–8, 138–9, 140–1, 144–5, 148–50, 154, 155, 157,

171–2, **191**; and Treplev Act III 48; and Treplev Act IV 53, 54, 102–3, 144; and Trigorin Act I 31, 36, 58–9, 63, 71–2, 109, 123, 146; and Trigorin Act II 31, 38, 40, 41, 43, 78–9, 112, 125–7, 140–2, 149–50, 155–6, 161, 163, **192**; and Trigorin Act III 50, 83, 86, 89, 120; truthfulness 40, 71, 139; *see also* Yakovleva, Olga
Novokuznetsk Cemetery xii

objectivity, complete 4–5, 27n19
Olesha, Yuri 77, 78, 199
Ordinary Story (Goncharov) 154, 193
Ostrovsky, Alexander ix, 198, 199
Ostrovsky Drama Theatre, Mikhailov ix
Othello (Shakespeare) xi

parent-child relationships (Arkadina and Treplev): Act I 20, 36, 57–8, 67–9, 74, 103–5, 109, 146, 170; Act II 119; Act III 18, 45–6, 47, 49–50, 80, 81–2, 84–5, 90, 121
Pelevin, Alexander 9, 34, 143, 199; *see also* Dorn, Evgeny Sergeevich (in *The Seagull*)
People's Artist of the USSR xi
petit bourgeoisie 169
Petrov, Nikolai ix
Picasso, Pablo 99, 102
plasticity/bodily mobility 37–8
Plotnikov, Nikolai 6, 170, 199
Plyatskovska, Gnessa (Nellie) xviii, 33, 199
poetry 38, 41, 61, 68, 159, 172
Poliakova, Yelena 4, 9
Polina Andreevna (in *The Seagull*): Act I 35, 61, 64, 71, 104, 107–8, 150; Act II 155, 158; Act III 122–3, **188**; Act IV 93–4, 96, 100; and Dorn Act I 35, 64, 104, 107–8, 150; and Dorn Act II 155, 158; and Dorn Act III 122–3; *see also* Kuznetsova, Zoya
Polyakov, Mark 13–14
"polyphonic" multiplicity 11
Ponomareva, Lyumilla 119, 166n37, 199
Popov, Alexei ix, 48, 199
Poprishchin (in *Diary of a Madman*) 127, 166n40

Prague Spring xiv
prayer, Nina's monologue 19, 36, 58, 61, 62, 64, 68, 70, 74
Prodolzheniye teatralnovo romana (Theatre Novel Continued) xi
Professia: Rezhisser (Occupation: Director) xi, xii–xiii
propaganda, Soviet 3
psychology 195; Chekhov's 18–19, 40–1; psychological theatre/acting x, 37–8, 86, 88
Pushkin, Alexander 16, 41, 77

quarrelling, Sorin and Dorn 96, 98–9, 101, 102, 112, 128, 153, 157

Radzinsky, Edvard x, xviii, 6, 174, 199; *Making a Film* 14, 119, 121, 125, 164, 172–3, 197
Raevsky, Joseph 4, 199
Rasplyuev (from Sukhovo-Kobylin's plays) 66, 165n17
reality, illusion of 2
rehearsal transcripts xiv–xv
repetition xiv
Repetitsiya-lyubov moia (Rehearsal is My Love) xi
reviews 13, 15, 23, 28n65, 28n72
Rhinoceros (Ionesco) 72, 73
Romeo and Juliet (Shakespeare) xi, 173
Rozov, Viktor x, xviii, 6, 193, 199
RSFSR Writers' Union 15
Rudnitsky, Konstantin 4, 8, 9, 11, 12
Russian Revolution, anniversary of 15
Russian Theatre Agency xii
Russian Theatre Fund xii
Russian Theatre in Practice, exhibition xiii
Rutkovskaya, M. F. 34

Sadovsky, Mikhailovich 66, 165n18
Saifullin, Gennadi 37, 142, 164n4, 199
Seagull (Chekhov): Act I 30–1, 34–7, 55–75, 103–10, 121–3, 131–4, 145–7, 150, 164n5, 170–1, **176–80**; Act II 12, 31, 37–43, 48, 75–9, 110–19, 124, 134–43, 147–8, 150–4, 157–9, 163, 164n5, **181–4**; Act III 12, 17, 44–52, 79–93, 119–21, 163, 164n5; Act IV 52–5, 93–103, 129–31, 143–5, 163, 164n5; reviews 13, 15, 23,

28n65, 28n72; run-through of entire performance 151–64; and Stanislavsky 1–3, 4, 9–10, 24, 63, 167
Seagull, film of xiii, xvii
seagull, killing of 31, 53, 76, 78, 126
"*Seagull* is very difficult to produce" speech (Efros) 25–6
second plan 71, 154, 165n20, 165n21
"seed" 72, 165n21
Senelick, Laurence 2, 9, 14
set design 11–12, 34, 129, **175**, **187**; woodenness 38, 48, 170
Shakespeare, William 108, 163, 173; and Arkadina 57–8, 61, 67, 74, 104–5, 119, 133, 143; English attitude to 6, 27n26, 169–70; *Hamlet* 57–8, 61, 67, 74, 104–5, 143, 169, 173; *Othello* xi; *Romeo and Juliet* xi, 173
Shakh-Azizova, Tatiana 4–5, 8, 11
Shamraev, Ilya Afanasyevich (in *The Seagull*): Act I 67, 74, 104, 118, 147, **179**, **180**; Act II 12, 39, 116, 118, 125; Act IV 98, 102, **187**; despair 98, 102; horses scene 12, 39, 116, 125; *see also* Kanevsky, Leonid; Solovyov, Vladimir
Shchukin School xii, 200
Shirvindt, Alexander 10, 34, 200; *see also* Trigorin, Boris Arkadevich (in *The Seagull*)
Sidorina, Inez xviii, 32, 200
Simov, Viktor 2
Skegina, Nonna Mikhailovna viii, xvii, 200
"Slaughtering Sacred Seagulls: Anatoly Efros's Production of *The Seagull*" 1–16
Slaviansky Bazaar, Moscow 1, 200
Smeliansky, Anatoly x, 6, 9, 14, 200
Smirnitsky, Valentin 10, 33; *see also* Treplev, Konstantin Gavrilovich (in *The Seagull*)
Smoktunovsky, Innokenty 23, 200
Socialist Realism ix, x, 3, 26n11, 196
Sofronov, Anatoly 40, 42, 200
Solovyov, Vladimir 34, 98, 200; *see also* Shamraev, Ilya Afanasyevich (in *The Seagull*)
Sorin, Peter Nikolaevich (in *The Seagull*) 160; Act I 65, 73–4, 102, 103, 107, 132, 150, **177**, **179**; Act II 112, 114, 115, 137–8, 139–40, 157, 158; Act III 45, 49, 79–80, 84, 120–1, 122; Act IV 96, 98–9, 102, **190**; and Arkadina 79–80, 84, 120–1; and Dorn, doctor-patient relationship 9, 17–18, 39, 42, 96, 100–1, 115, 124, 137; and Dorn, quarrelling 96, 98–9, 101, 102, 112, 128, 153, 157; fainting 49, 80, 121; and Nina 114, 139–40; suffering 103, 107; and Treplev 35, 45, 73–4, 103, 122, 160; *see also* Vovsi, Arkady
Sosunov, Nikolai 11, 34, 200
Sovetskaya Litva journal 5
Soviet Union, fall of xii
Sovremennik Theatre, Moscow 193, 194, 197, 200
spirituality 8, 20, 46, 132, 148, 171; *see also* prayer, Nina's monologue
Stalin, Joseph viii
Stanislavsky, Konstantin ix–x; Active Analysis x, xiv, 193; communication, continuous xviii, 195; and Efros 1, 6–7; and MAT 1, 198; and *The Seagull* 1–3, 4, 9–10, 24, 63, 167
Stanitsyn, Viktor 4, 200
State Dramatic Theatre, Ryazan ix
stereotyping viii, 33, 118, 170, 171
Strepetova, Polina 61, 200
Stroeva, Marianna 10, 13, 14
suffering: Masha 20, 37, 47, 51; Sorin 103, 107; Trigorin 79, 127, 145, 161, 169
Svobodin, A. 10

Tabakov, Oleg 154, 193, 201
Taganka Theatre, Moscow xi, xii, 201
Tairov, Aleksander 4, 201
Tarkhanov, Mikhail ix, 201
Tchaikovsky, Pyotr 4
Teatralnaya zhizn journal 15
Teatr Anatolia Efrosa: vospominania i stati (The Theatre of Anatoly Efros: Recollections and Articles) xii–xiii
Teatr magazine 6, 11, 14, 15, 201; *see also* "How quickly time passes" (*Teatr 2*)
Thaw era viii, x, 173
"Theatre of Mood" xiv, xviii, 3, 201

Three Sisters (Chekhov) 27n14; and communication 16, 40; and Efros xi, xiv, 15, 173–4; Malaya Bronnaya Theatre xiv, 15; MAT 5, 43; Tovstonogov's production 4, 5
time, passage of 52–3
Toen Theatre, Tokyo xi
Tolstoy, Alexei 26n5; *Tsar Fyodor* 2
Tolstoy, Lev (Leo) 16
Topol, Joseph 173, 201
Tovstonogov, Georgi 4, 5, 201
Treplev, Konstantin Gavrilovich (in *The Seagull*) xvii, 10–11, 14, 24, 25, 29–31, 160, 167–9; Act I 30–1, 35, 37, 39, 55–8, 59–60, 64–74, 103–10, 122, 132–4, 145–6, 150, **176–9**; Act II 31–2, 40, 76–9, 116–17, 119, 127–8, 138–41, 144–5, 148–50, 153–5, 157–9, 171–2, **181**; Act III 45–51, 80–2, 84–5, 90–2, 121–2, **183–4**; Act IV 53–4, 94–7, 102–3, 144, **190–1**; and Arkadina xvii, 16, 29; and Arkadina Act I 57–8, 67–71, 74, 103–6, 109, 146; and Arkadina Act II 119, 148, 158–9, **181**; and Arkadina Act III 45–7, 49–51, 80–2, 84–5, 90–2, 121–2, **183–4**; despair 29, 31, 76; and Dorn 9, 37, 158; and Masha 9, 37, 39, 55–6, 59, 94, 96, 103, 119; monologues 48, 60, 64, 95, 122, 152, 158; and Nina 10, 29–30, 31; and Nina Act I 30–1, 35, 57, 65, 71, 74, 103–4, 109, 132–4, 146, **178**; and Nina Act II 31, 76–9, 116–17, 127–8, 138–41, 144–5, 148–50, 154–5, 157, 171–2; and Nina Act IV 53–4, 102–3, 144, **191**; and Sorin 152, 160; and Sorin Act I 35, 59–60, 65, 68–9, 70–1, 73–4, 103, 109, **176**; and Sorin Act III 45, 122; suicide/attempted suicide 18, 31–2, 53–4, 74, 76–7; truthfulness 40, 71, 139; *see also* Gaft, Valentin; Smirnitsky, Valentin
Trigorin, Boris Arkadevich (in *The Seagull*) xvii, 10, 25, 172–3; Act I 31, 36, 58–9, 63, 65, 71–3, 103, 106, 109, 123, 146, **179–90**; Act II 31, 38–41, 43, 78–9, 112, 125–7, 136–7, 140–2, 147, 149–51, 155–6, 158, 163, **192**; Act III 44, 46–50, 52, 80–3, 85–9, 119–21, 123, 159, 161; Act IV 95, 131, **189**; and Arkadina 16, 18, 46; and Arkadina Act I 106, **189**; and Arkadina Act II 39, 41; and Arkadina Act III 47, 50, 80–1, 85–6, 121, 159; and Arkadina Act IV 131; and art 72, 172; cane scene 46, 50, 86, 93; happiness/unhappiness 142, 149; and Masha 17, 160; and Masha Act I 103; and Masha Act III 44, 46–7, 52, 82–3, 86–8, 89, 119–20, 161; monologue Act II 147; and Nina 17, 18, 65, 161; and Nina Act I 31, 36, 58–9, 63, 71–2, 109, 123, 146; and Nina Act II 31, 38, 40, 41, 43, 78–9, 112, 125–7, 136–7, 140–2, 149–51, 155–6, 163, **192**; and Nina Act III 50, 83, 86, 89, 120, 123; and Stanislavsky 10, 24; suffering 79, 127, 145, 161, 169; and Treplev xvii, 95; truthfulness 83, 89; as a writer 40, 42, 126, 127, 129; *see also* Larionov, Vsevelod; Shirvindt, Alexander
Truffault, François 165, 201
truthfulness x, 27, 71, 156; super-psychological 83, 88; and Treplev and Nina 40, 71, 139; and Trigorin and Nina 83, 89
Tsar Fyodor (Tolstoy) 2
Turgenev, Ivan xi, 16, 126, 142, 144, 201
Turovskaya, Maya 4
Tuzenbach (in *Three Sisters*) 173–4, 196

understanding 73, 88–9; *see also* misunderstanding

Vagrius Publishers xii–xiii
Vakhtangov, Yevgeny ix, xi, 7, 201; Vakhtangov Theatre xii, 199, 200
Volodin, Alexander 40, 77, 201; *The Appointment* 73, 194; *My Poor Marat* 93, 199
Vovsi, Arkady 9, 201; *see also* Sorin, Peter Nikolaevich (in *The Seagull*)

Waterloo Bridge (Sherwood) 37, 201
Wedding Day (Rozov) 65
Williams, Tennessee, *A Lovely Sunday for a Picnic* xii

wind, puff of/breeze xix, 44, 49
wire, bent xix, xxn3, 194
Woe from Wit (Griboyedov) 65, 165n15

Yakovleva, Olga 9–10, 34, 201;
  see also Nina Mikhailovna Zarechnaya
  (in *The Seagull*)
Yefremov, Oleg 23, 73, 202
Yermolova, Maria 61, 67, 201
Yevseev, B. 8, 9

youth/aging 6; and Arkadina 75, 112,
  113–14, 118; and Dorn 35, 75, 104,
  107, 124; and Masha 75, 160–1, 162

Zarechnaya, Nina Mikhailovna *see*
  Nina Mikhailovna Zarechnaya (in
  The Seagull)
Zavadsky, Yuri viii, ix, 198, 201
Zingerman, Boris xviii
Zubkov, Yuri 9, 11, 12, 15, 28n72

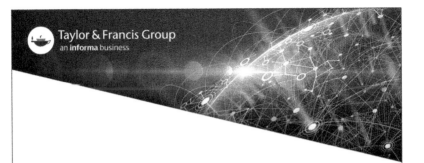